MASTERS

GUSTAVE DORÉ

COLLECTION

A CURATED ARCHIVE OF 154 DOWNLOADABLE MASTERPIECES

SERIES

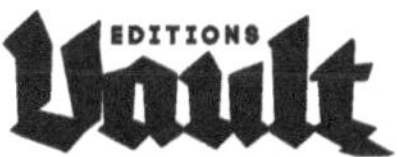

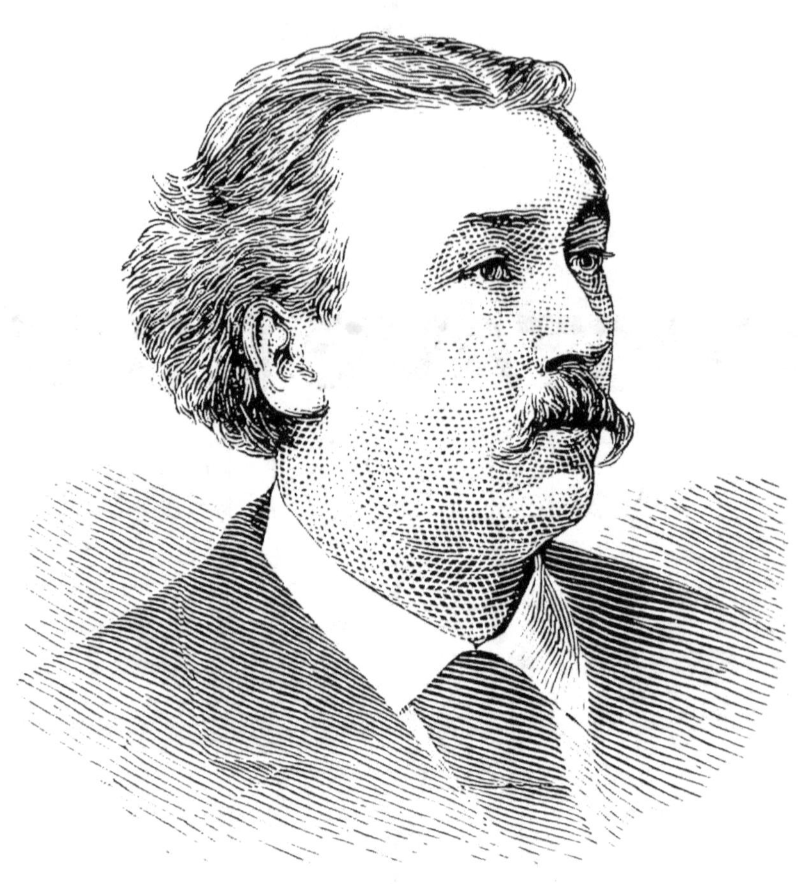

GUSTAVE DORÉ

6 JANUARY 1832 – 23 JANUARY 1883

ISBN: 978-1-922966-45-2

TABLE OF CONTENTS

INTRODUCTION

"They who dream by day are cognizant of many things which escape those who dream only by night"
-Edgar Allan Poe

THE GUSTAVE DORÉ COLLECTION

Gustave Doré's artistic influence continues to inspire artists and designers today. *The Gustave Doré Collection* from Vault Editions celebrates the artist's most dramatic, dark and fantastical literary illustrations. It contains 154 images carefully restored and curated to ignite your imagination and inspire your creativity. Each image in this collection is also available as a downloadable high-resolution digital file. You'll find details of how to access these files on the final page of this book.

THE LIFE AND WORK OF GUSTAVE DORÉ

Paul Gustave Louis Christophe Doré, better known as Gustave Doré, was one of the most prolific and influential illustrators of the 19th century. Born in Strasbourg, France, on January 6, 1832, Doré exhibited a remarkable talent for drawing from a young age. His artistic journey began with caricatures, but over time, his work evolved, and he became best known for illustrating many of the most significant literary works of his time and leaving an indelible mark on the world.

Doré's illustrations were not just mere visual accompaniments to texts, but transformative interpretations that brought stories to life in ways that words alone could not. His ability to capture the emotional depth of a narrative, his technical precision, and his remarkable imagination set him apart from his contemporaries. His innovative use of light and shadow, dynamic compositions, and ability to convey emotion through imagery remain benchmarks in visual storytelling.

His body of work, estimated to contain over 10,000 illustrations, continues to exert a profound influence today. His impact is not limited to book illustration but extends to painting, sculpture, and modern media like film and animation. Though most famous for his illustrations, Doré's influence is felt in all his artistic endeavours, from painting to sculpture. His sculptures often shared the same expressive quality as his illustrations, bringing characters and stories to life in three dimensions.

Doré's talent was especially suited to grand, epic narratives. He excelled in visualising stories that required a balance between intense drama and intricate details. His illustrations for works like Dante's *The Divine Comedy*, Milton's *Paradise Lost*, and Cervantes' *Don Quixote* remain iconic, shaping the visual imagination of readers for generations. His illustrations for these classic works were not just literal representations of the texts but imaginative interpretations that enriched the reading experience.

In his illustrations for Dante's *Inferno*, Doré captured the terrifying vastness of Hell and the emotional weight of the sinner's suffering, using his characteristic mastery of contrast, shading, and composition. His portrayal of the various circles of Hell is one of the most enduring visual interpretations of Dante's work, fusing a gothic sensibility with dramatic realism.

Similarly, his illustrations for *Don Quixote*, published in 1863, transformed Cervantes' satirical adventure into a visual feast. Doré imbued the noble yet delusional knight and his faithful squire, Sancho Panza, with a perfect blend of whimsy and tragedy. These images have become synonymous with the characters, and it's almost impossible to imagine the story without Doré's depictions.

Gustave Doré's artistic legacy is unparalleled. From his iconic literary illustrations to his work as a painter and sculptor, Doré left behind a body of work showcasing his technical brilliance and expanding visual storytelling possibilities. His influence resonates in modern art and media, ensuring his imaginative vision endures well beyond his lifetime. Doré didn't just illustrate stories—he reimagined them, transforming texts into immersive visual experiences that captivated generations.

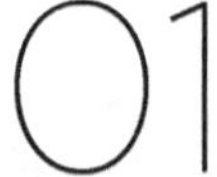

01

THE RIME OF THE ANCIENT MARINER

GUSTAVE DORÉ

Samuel Taylor Coleridge's poem, *The Rime of the Ancient Mariner*, is one of the most iconic poems in English literature. This haunting narrative poem blends elements of the supernatural with profound moral and spiritual themes. The mariner's tale of sin, punishment, and redemption, told through the killing of an albatross and the subsequent curse it brings upon the crew, explores profound philosophical questions about humanity's relationship with nature, guilt, and the possibility of salvation. The poem's vivid, lyrical language has captivated readers since it was first published in 1798.

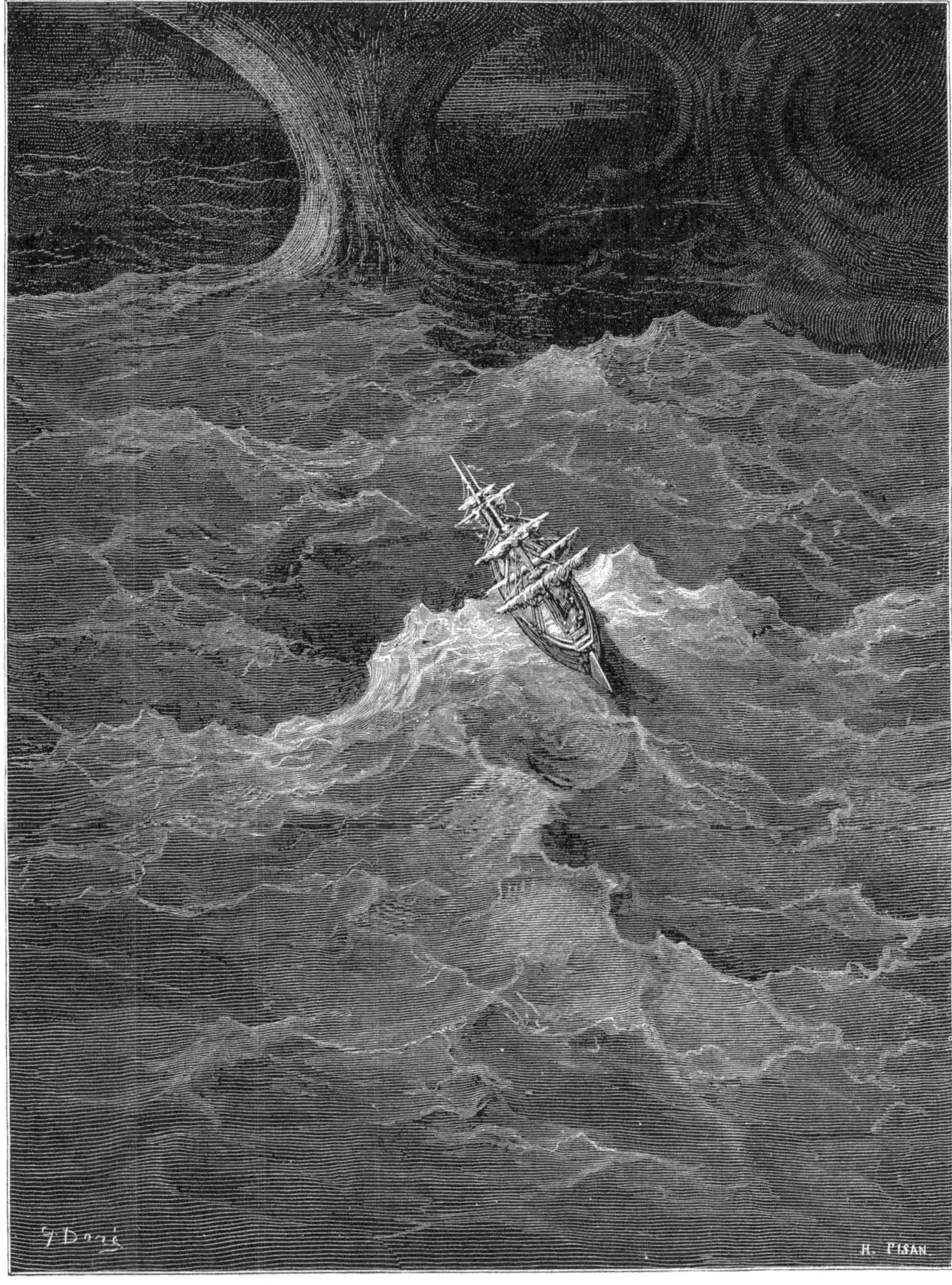

GUSTAVE DORÉ

01. The ship drove fast, loud roared the blast,
And southward aye we fled. Gustave Doré, 1875

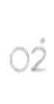

02

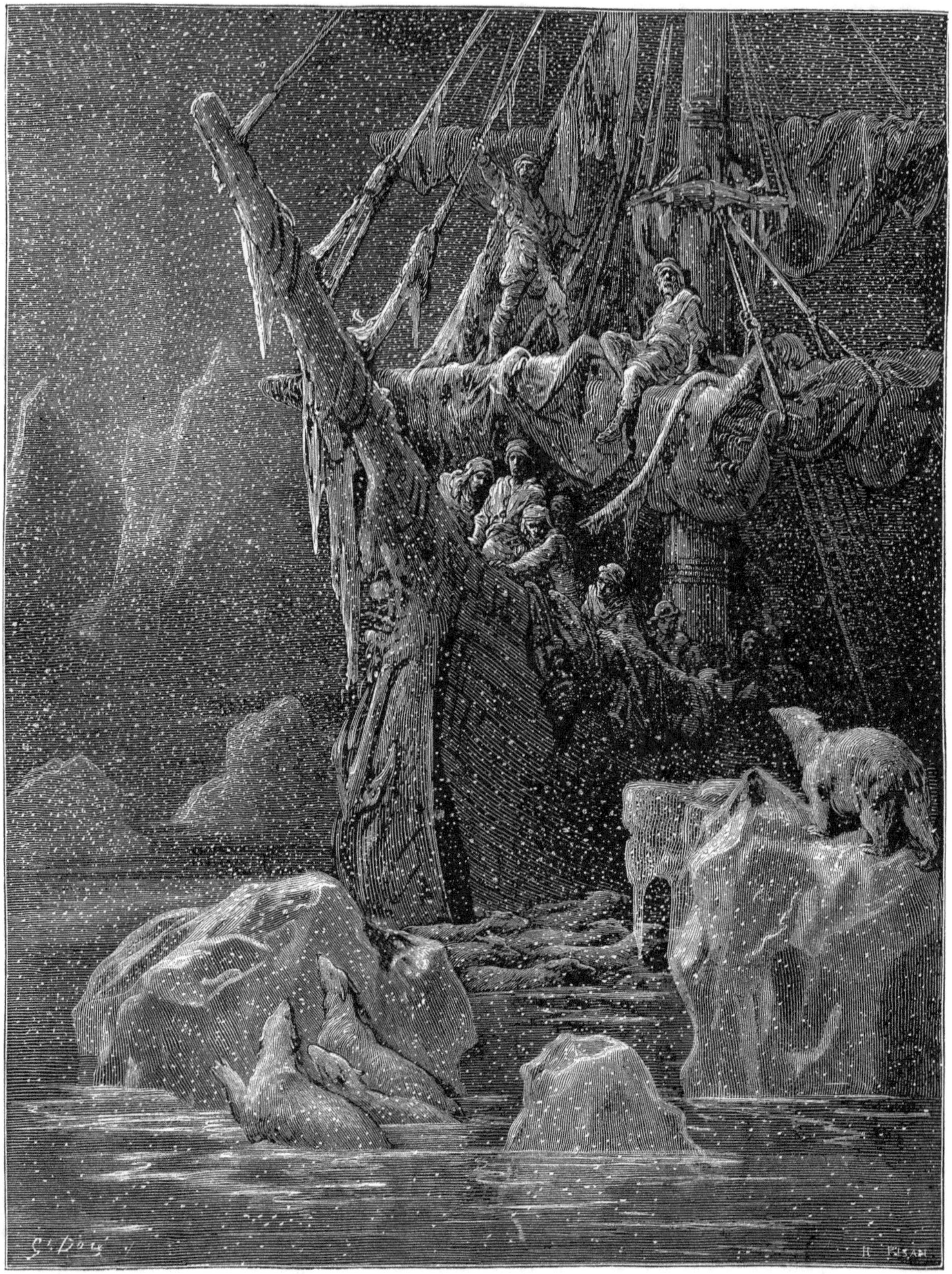

*02. And now there came both mist and snow.
And it grew wondrous cold. Gustave Doré, 1875*

03

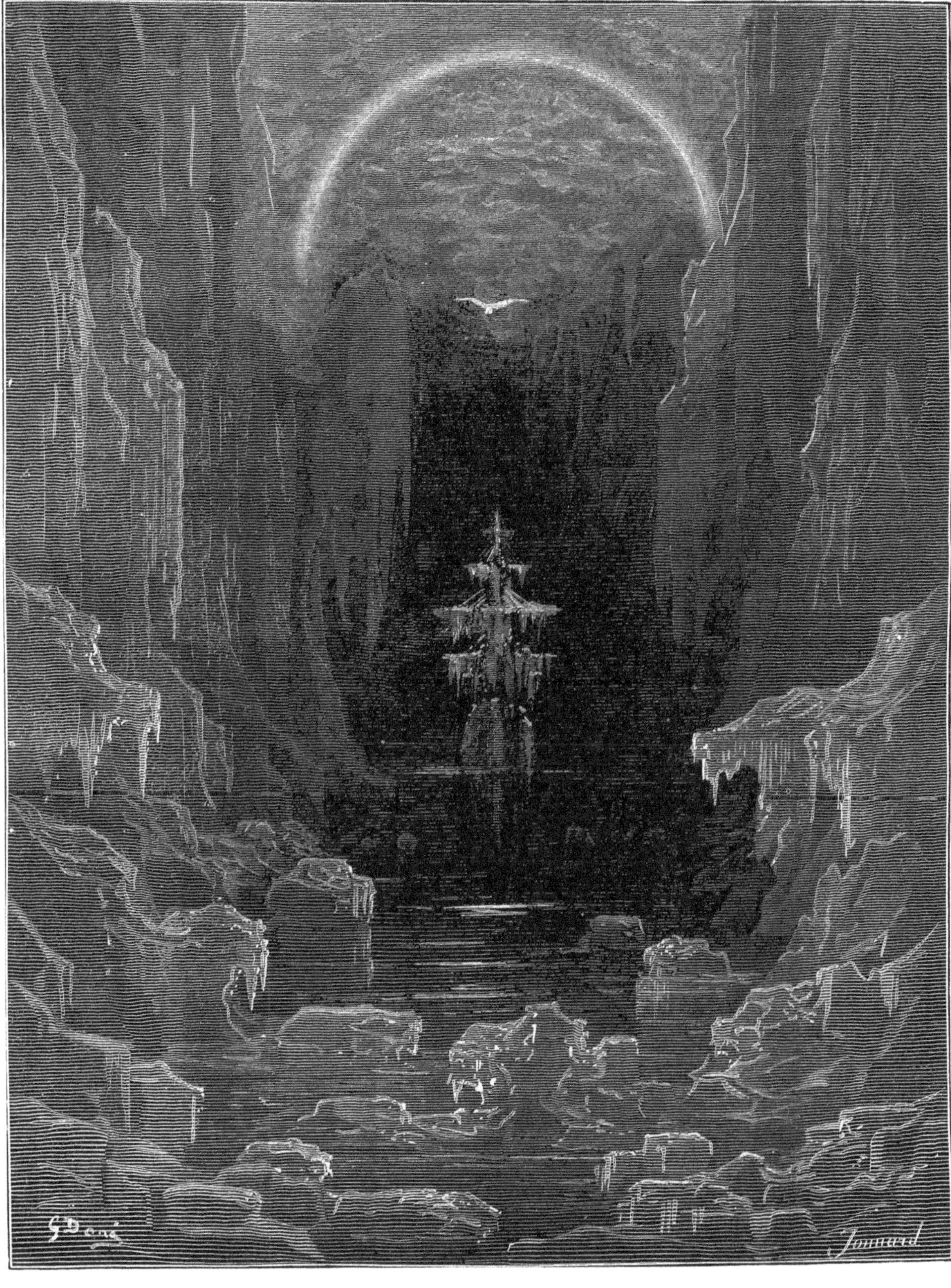

03. The ice was here, the ice was there. The ice
was all around. Gustave Doré. 1875

04

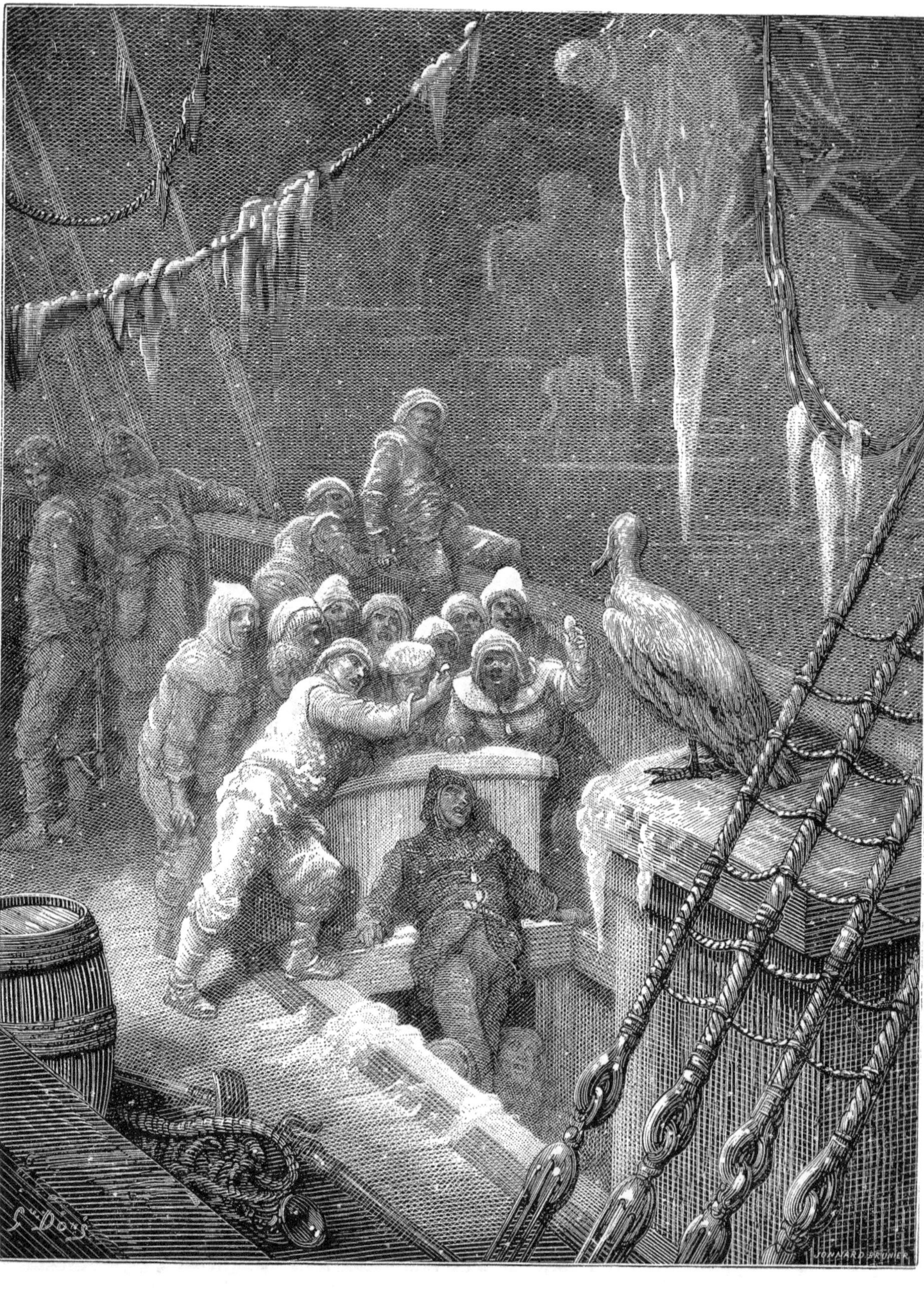

04. *It ate the food it ne'er had eat, Gustave Doré, 1875*

05

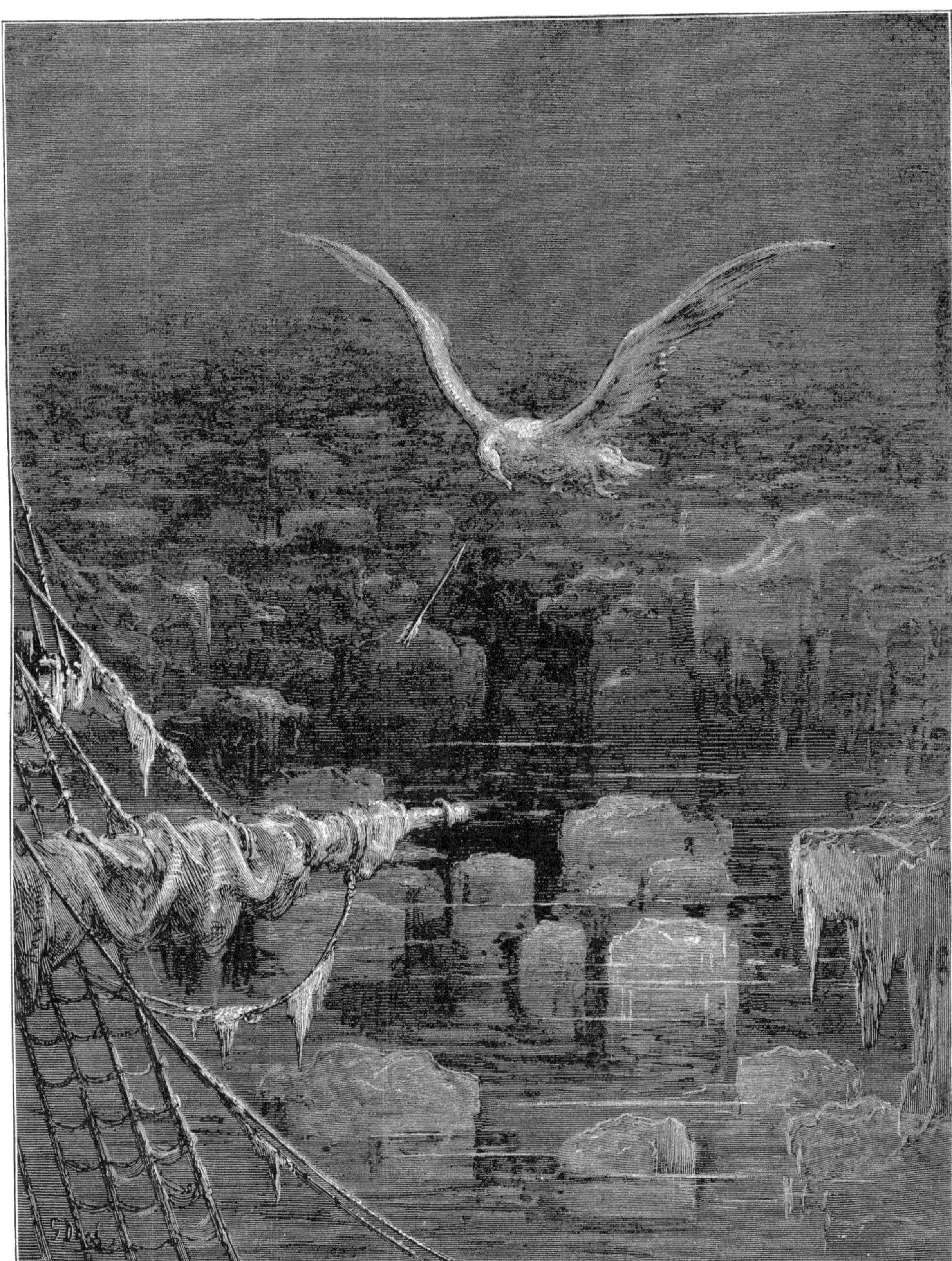

GUSTAVE DORÉ

05. With my cross-bow I shot the ALBATROSS.
Gustave Doré, 1875

06

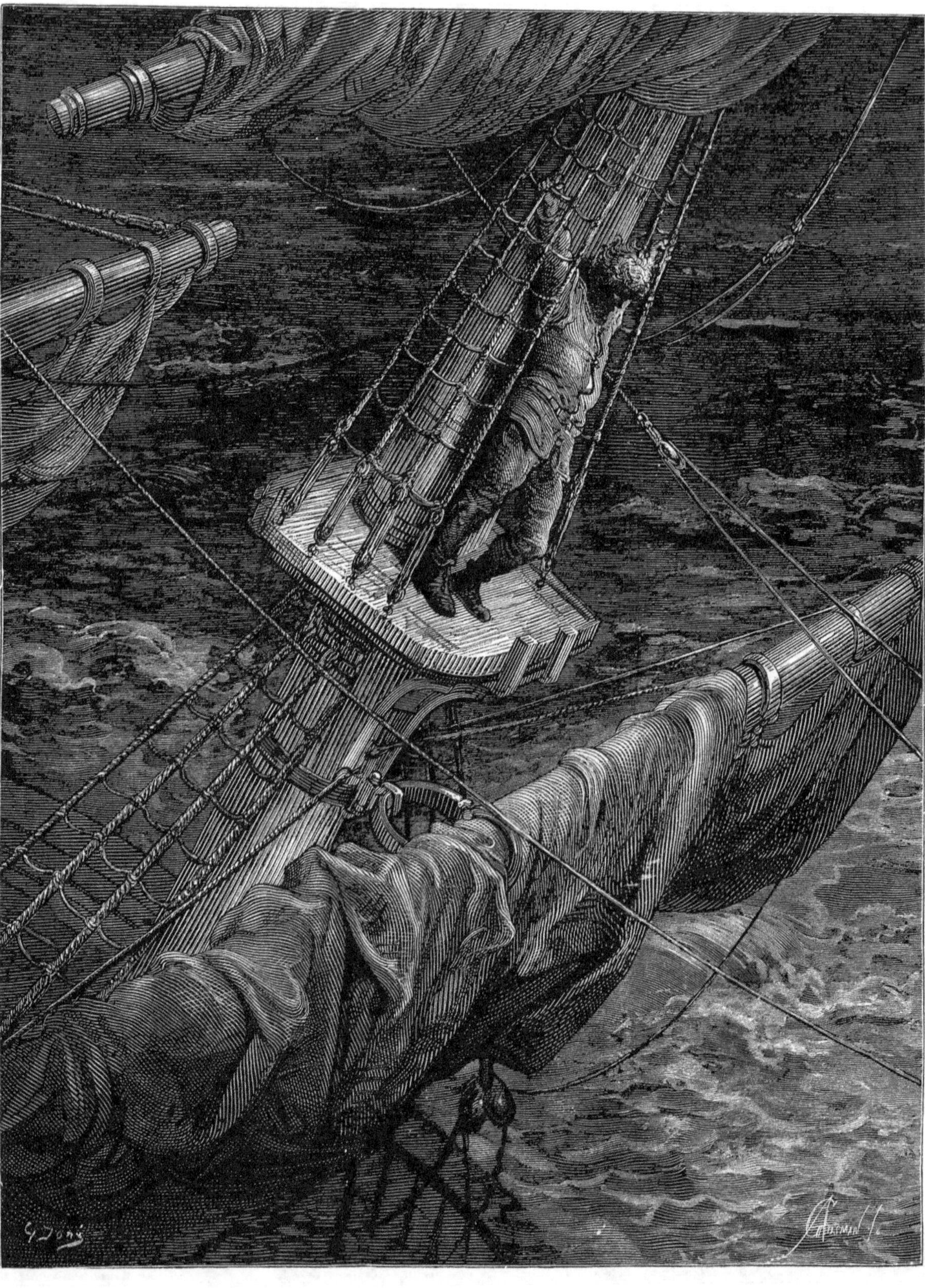

06. And I had done a hellish thing, And it would
work 'em woe, Gustave Doré, 1875

07

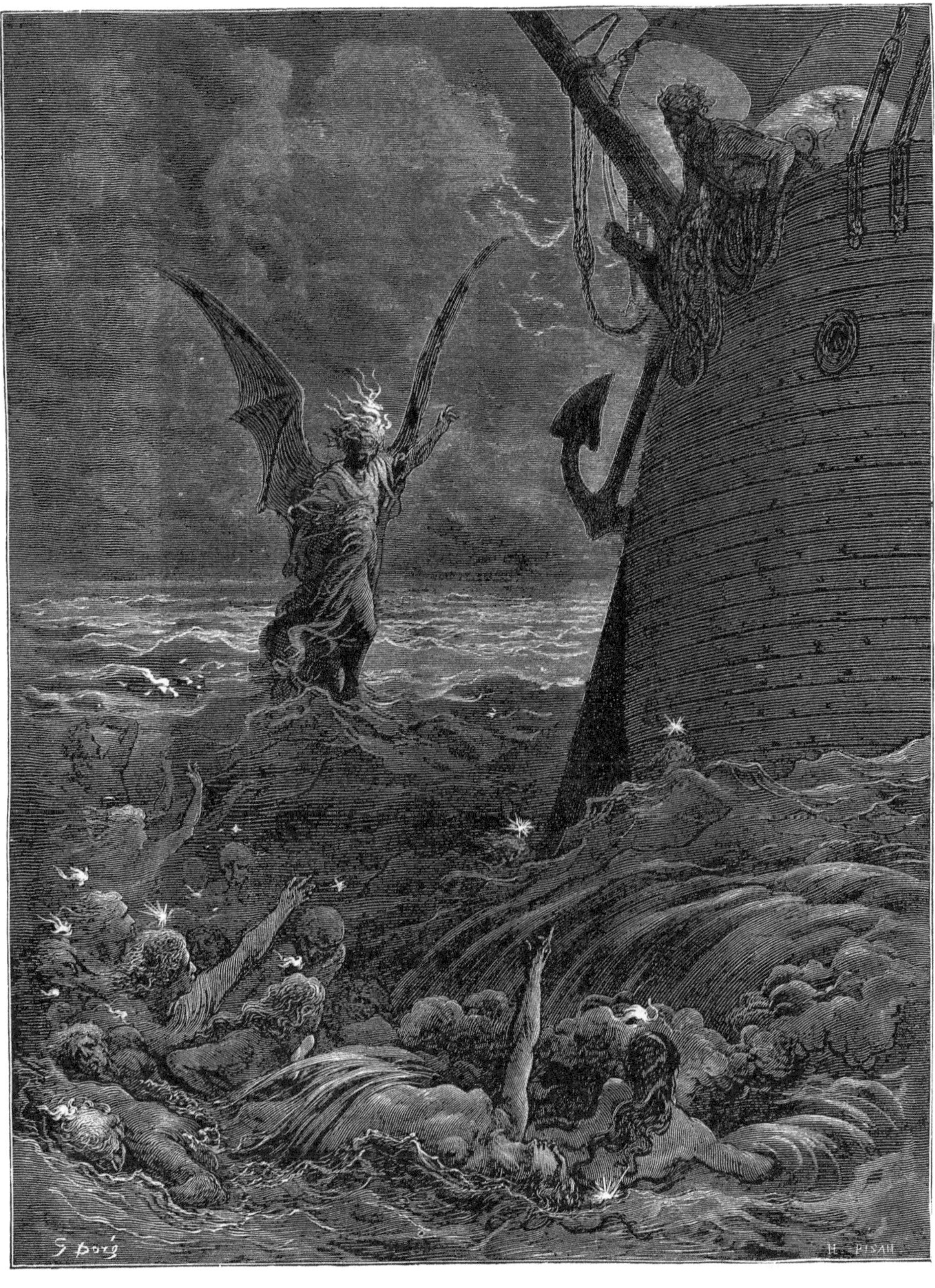

GUSTAVE DORÉ

07. About, about, in reel and rout The death-
fires danced at night. Gustave Doré, 1875

08

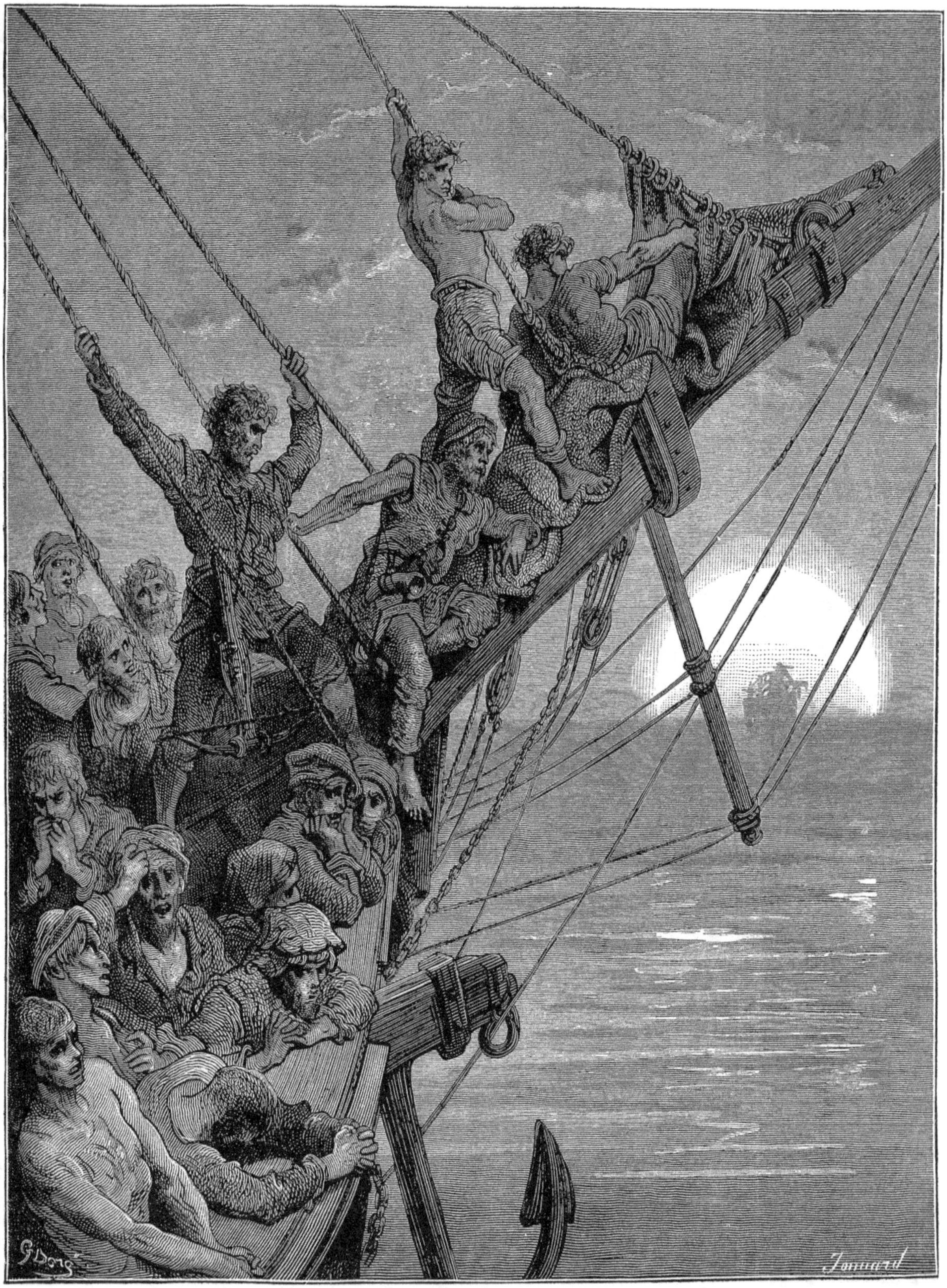

08. A speck, a mist, a shape, I wist! And still it
neared and neared. Gustave Doré, 1875

09

GUSTAVE DORÉ

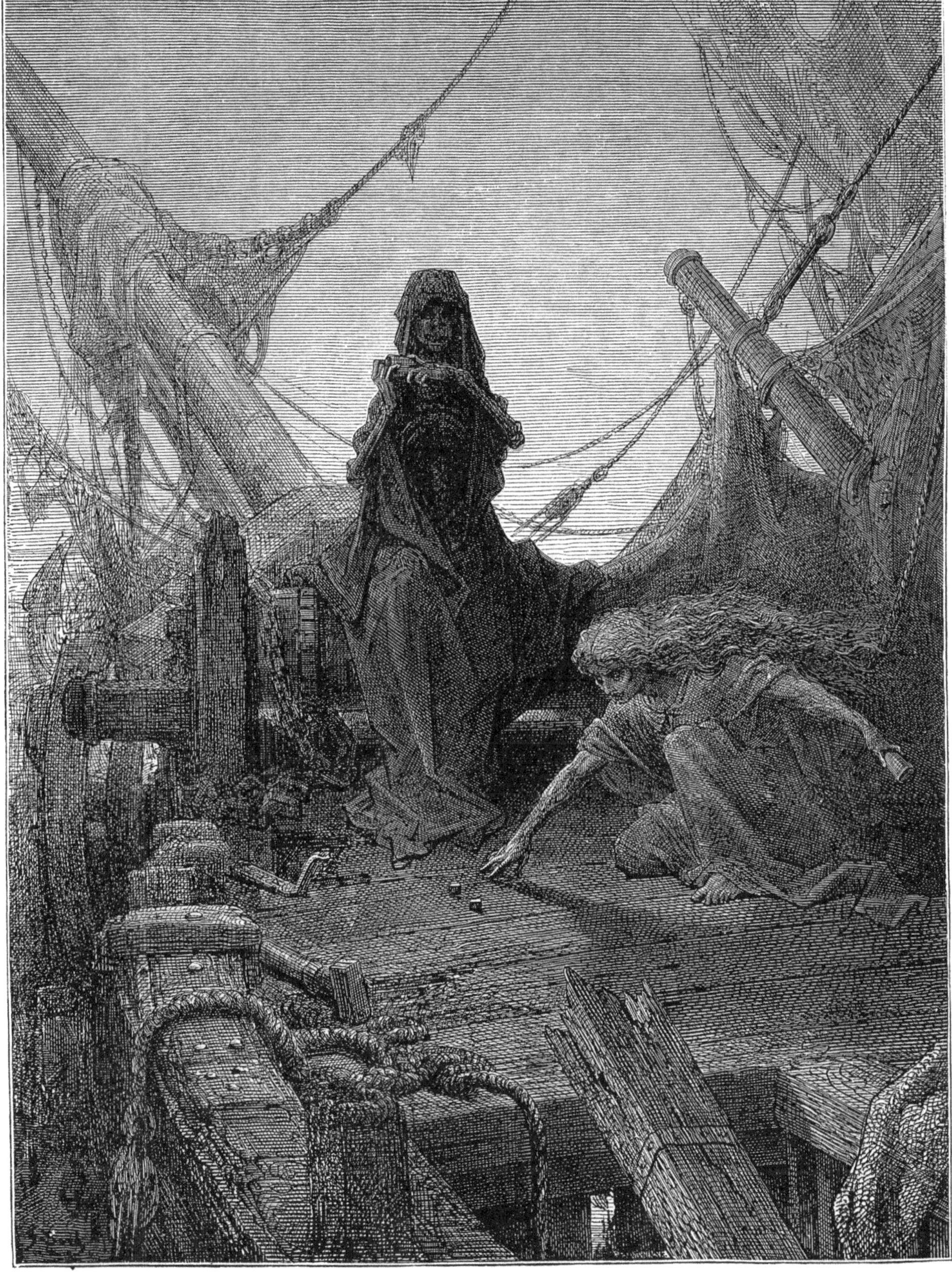

09. The game is done! I've won! I've won! Quoth
she, and whistles thrice. Gustave Doré, 1875

10

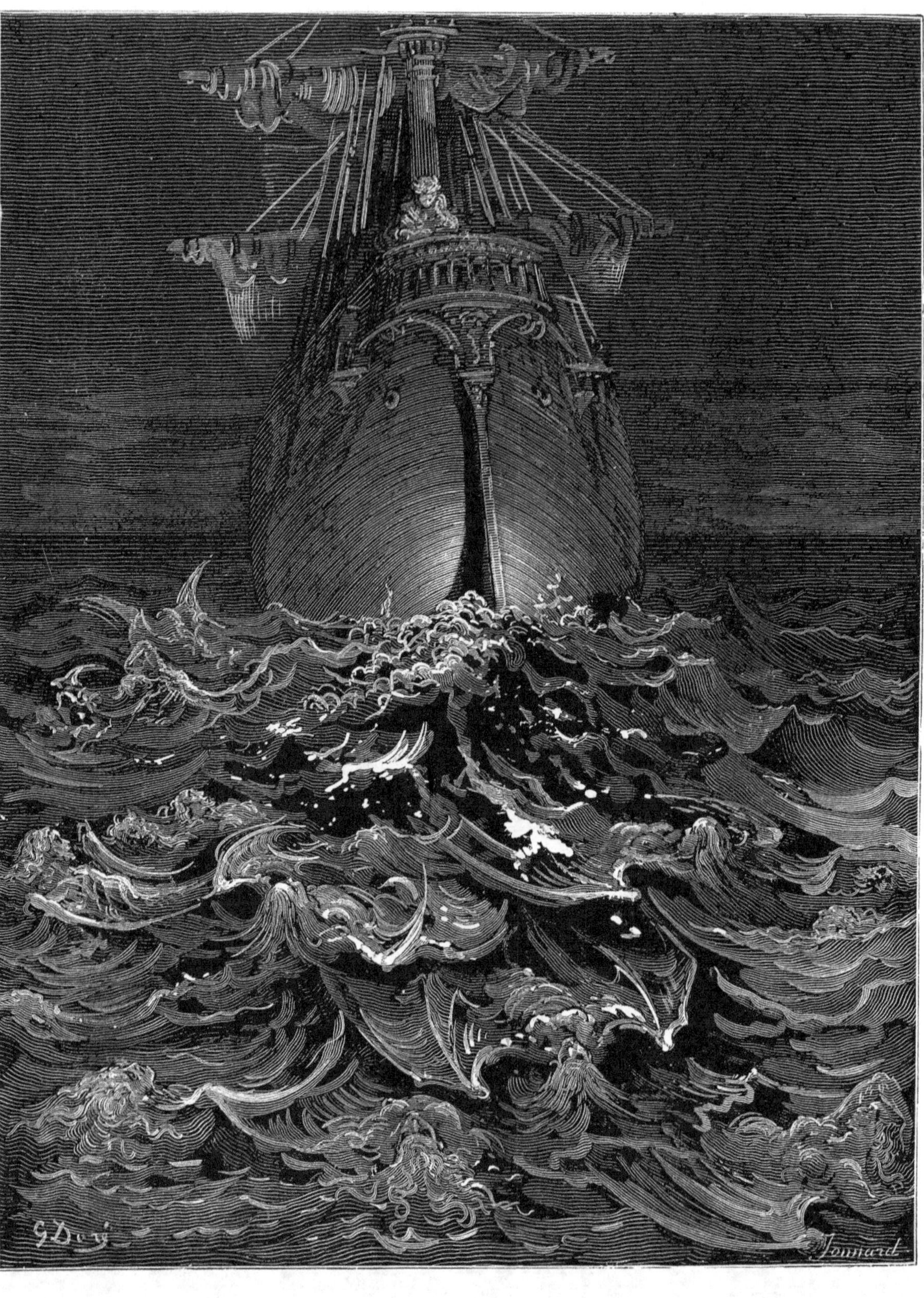

10. I looked upon the rotting sea, And drew my
eyes away, Gustave Doré, 1875

11

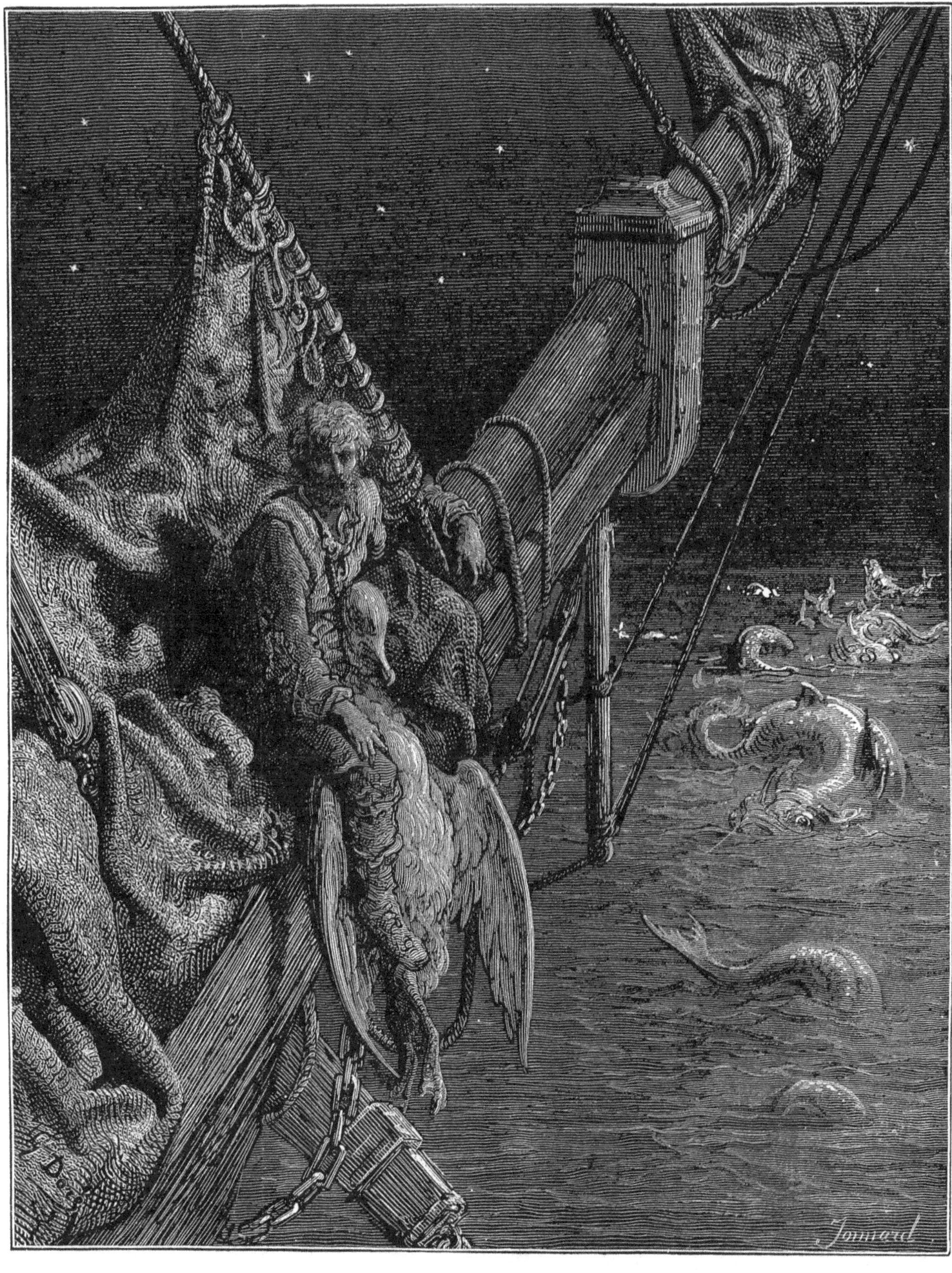

GUSTAVE DORÉ

11. Beyond the shadow of the ship, I watched
the water-snakes. Gustave Doré. 1875

GUSTAVE DORÉ

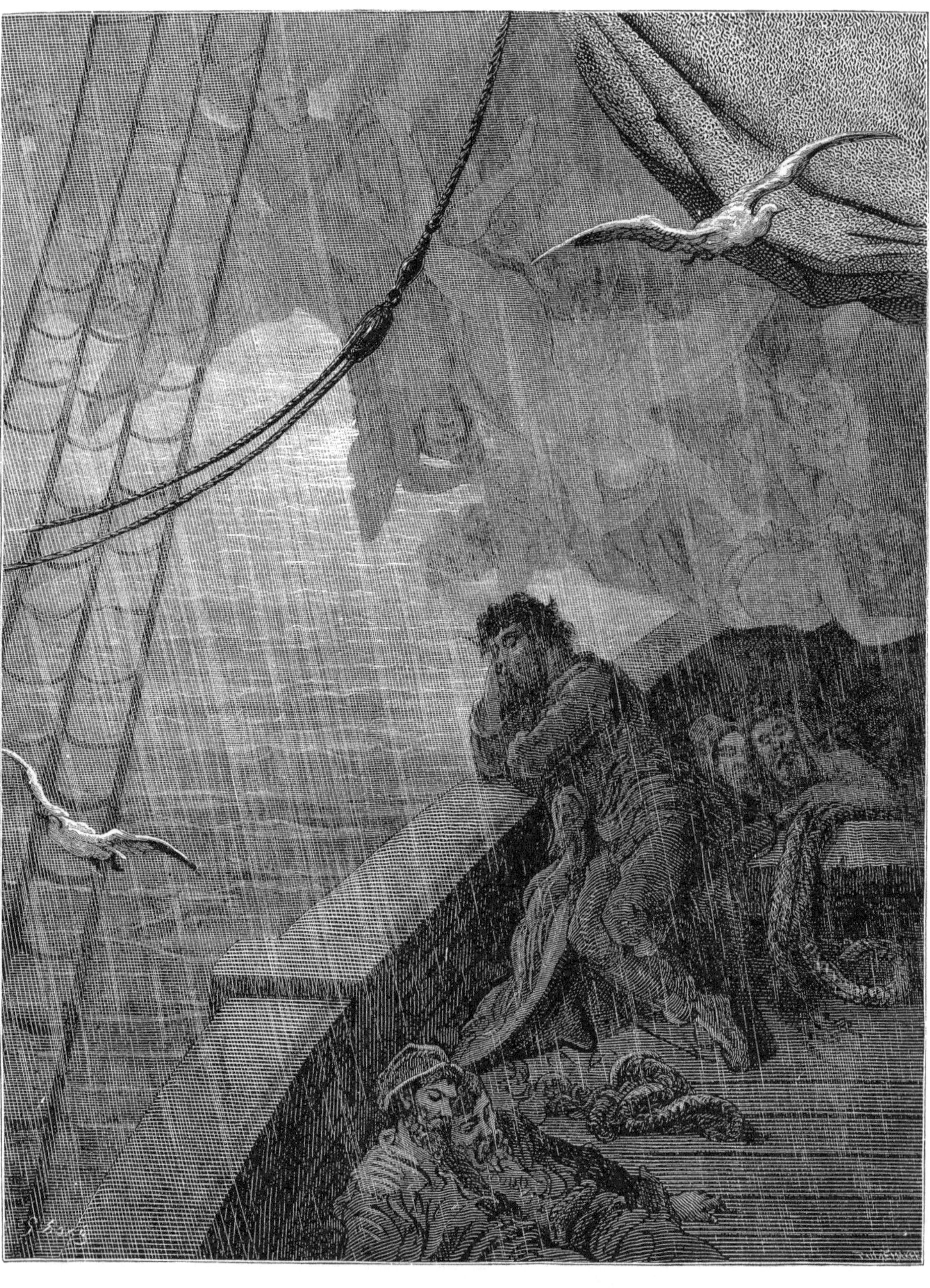

12. And the rain poured down from one black
cloud, Gustave Doré, 1875

13

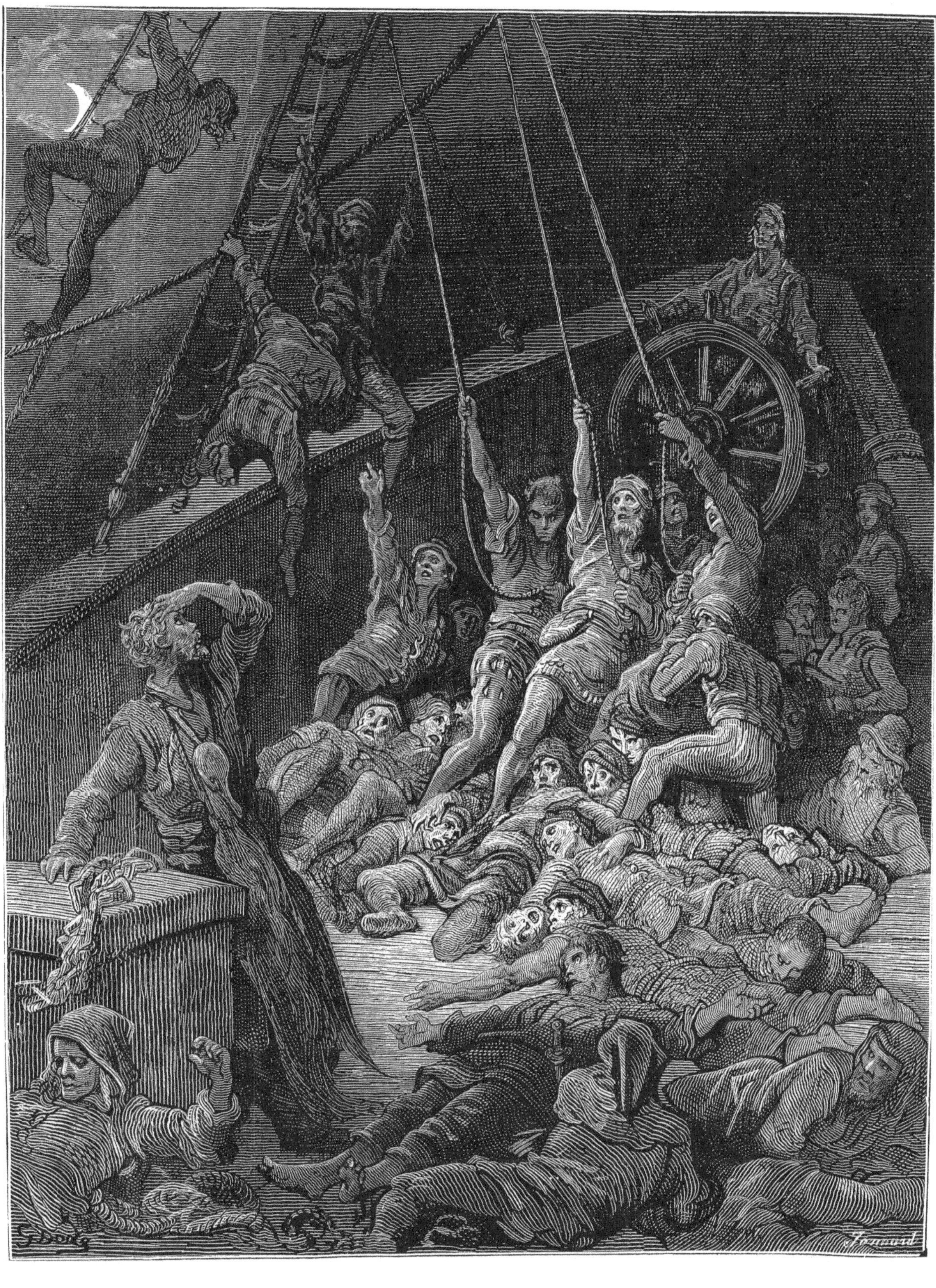

GUSTAVE DORÉ

13. They groaned, they stirred, they all uprose,
Nor spake, nor moved their eyes. Gustave
Doré. 1875

14

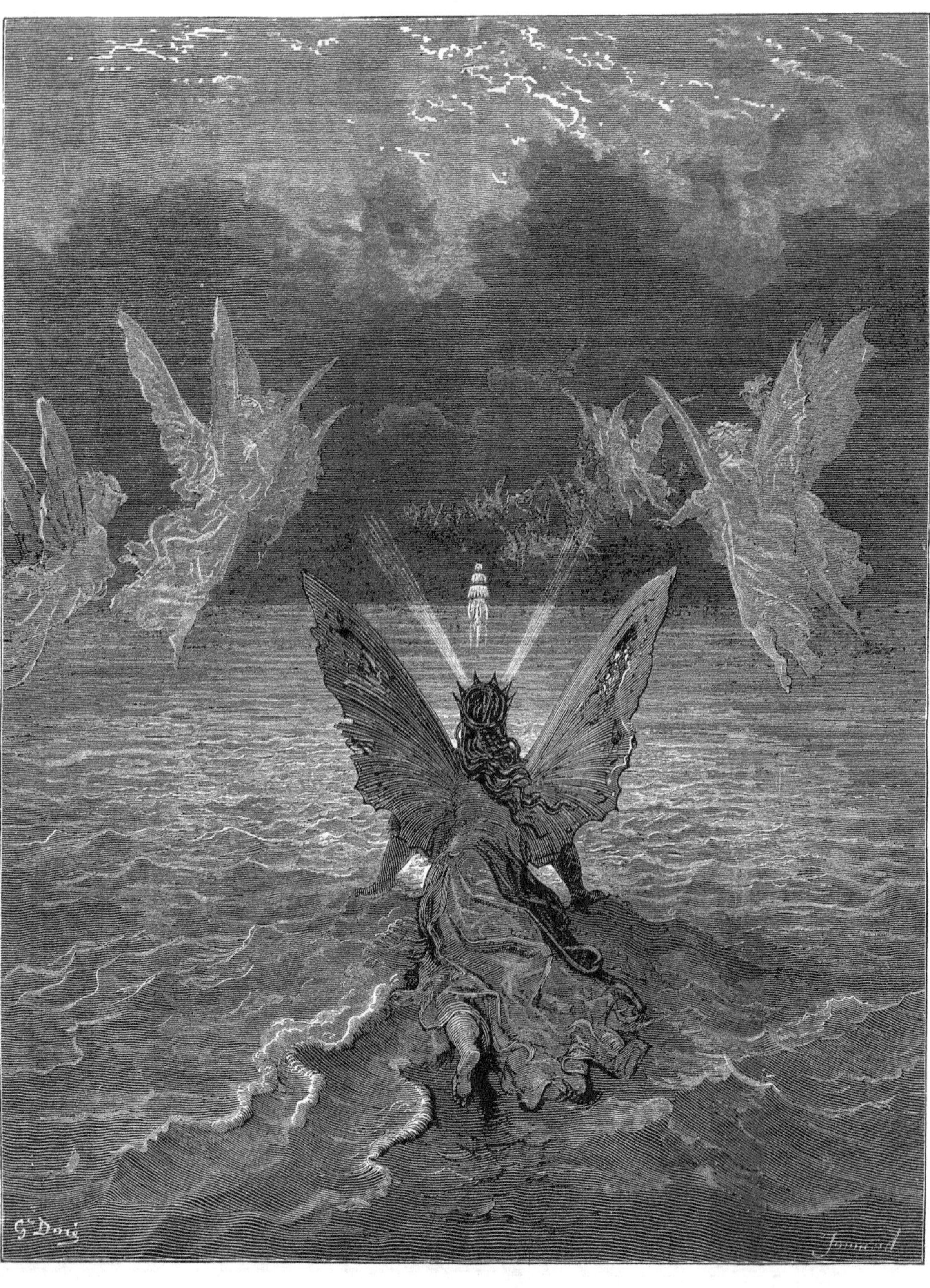

GUSTAVE DORÉ

14. It ceased; yet still the sails made on, A
pleasant noise till noon. Gustave Doré, 1875

15

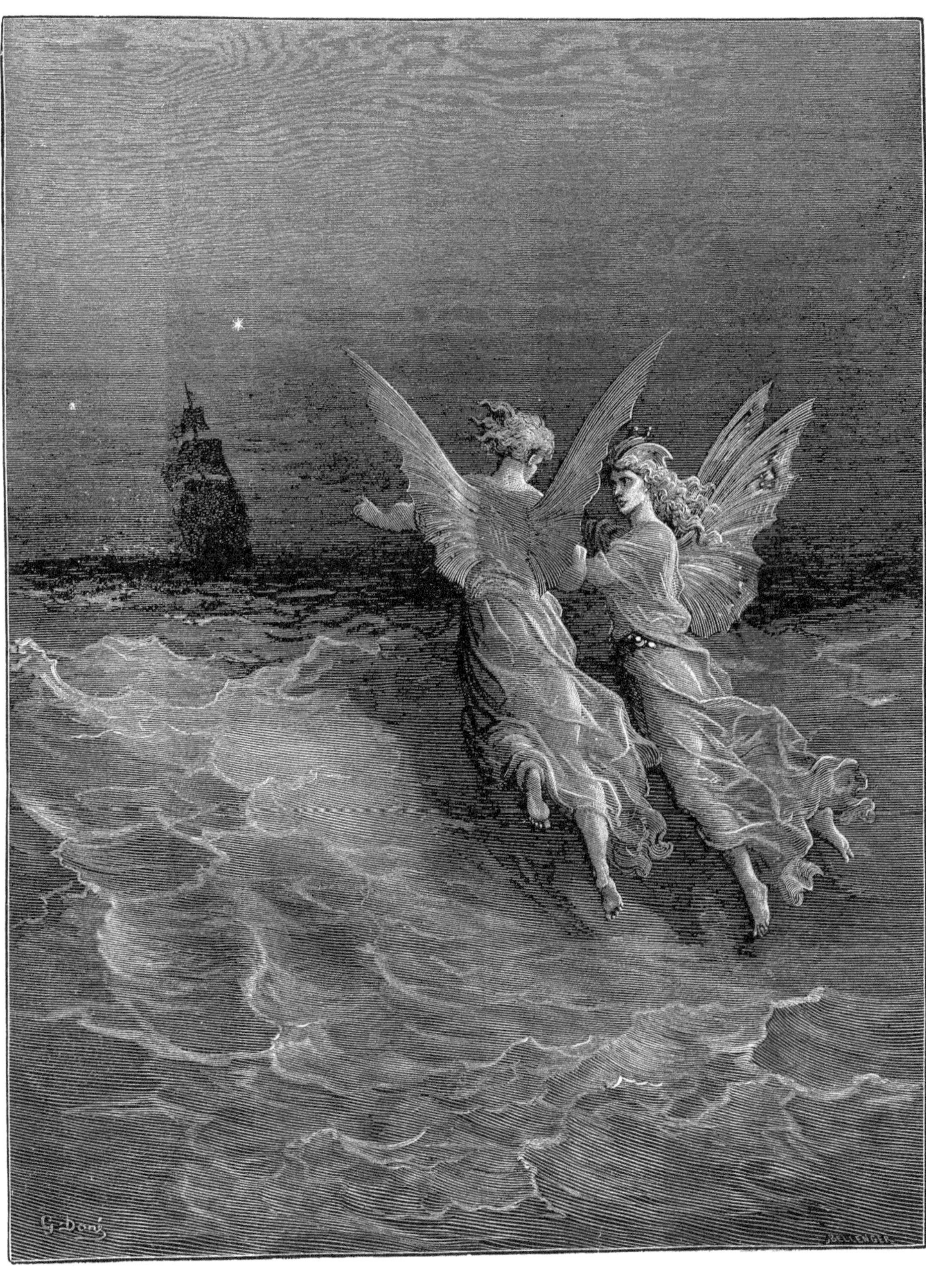

GUSTAVE DORÉ

15. 'But why drives on that ship so fast. Without
or wave or wind?'. Gustave Doré. 1875

16

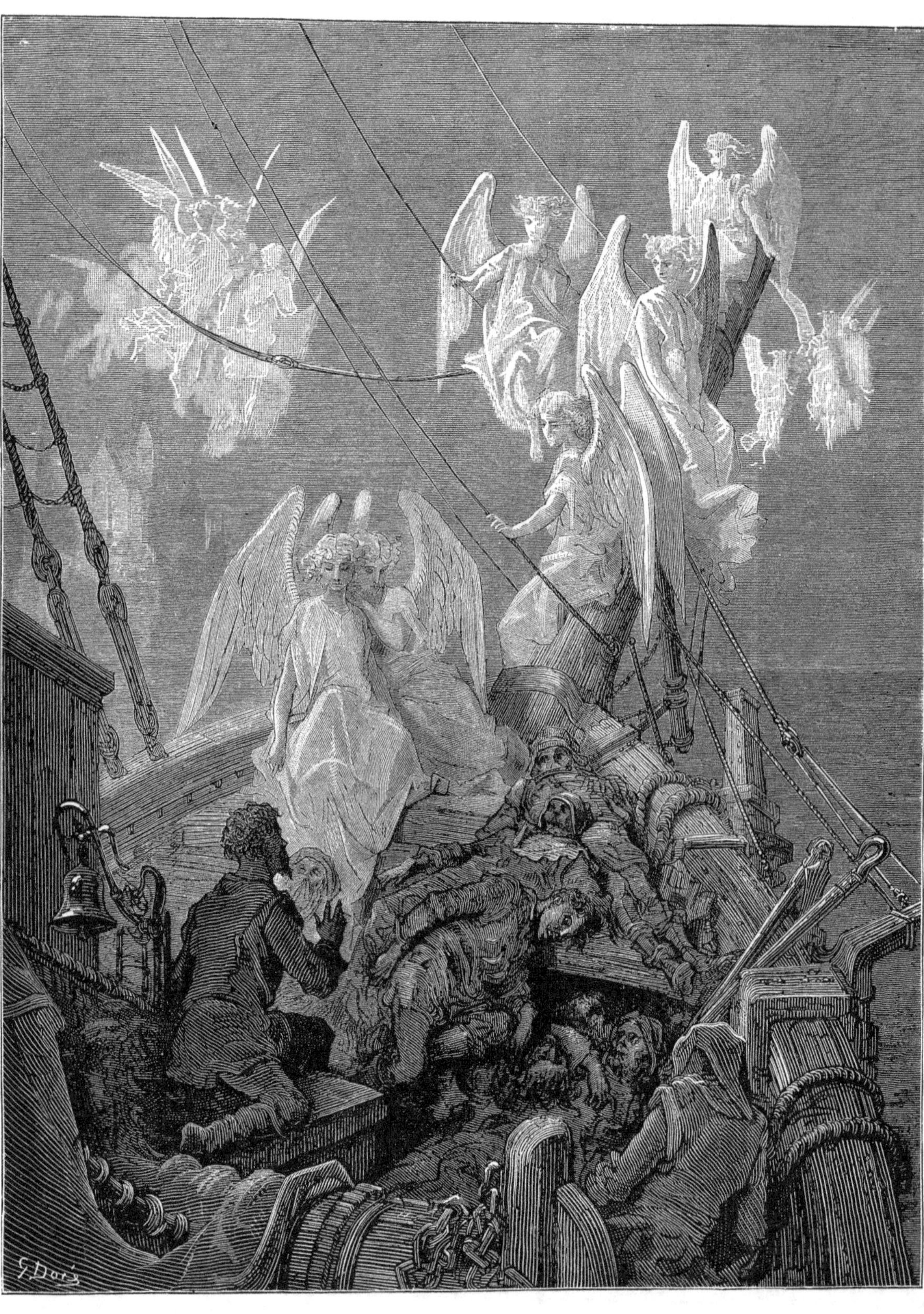

16. This seraph-band, each waved his hand- It
was a heavenly sight! Gustave Doré. 1875

17

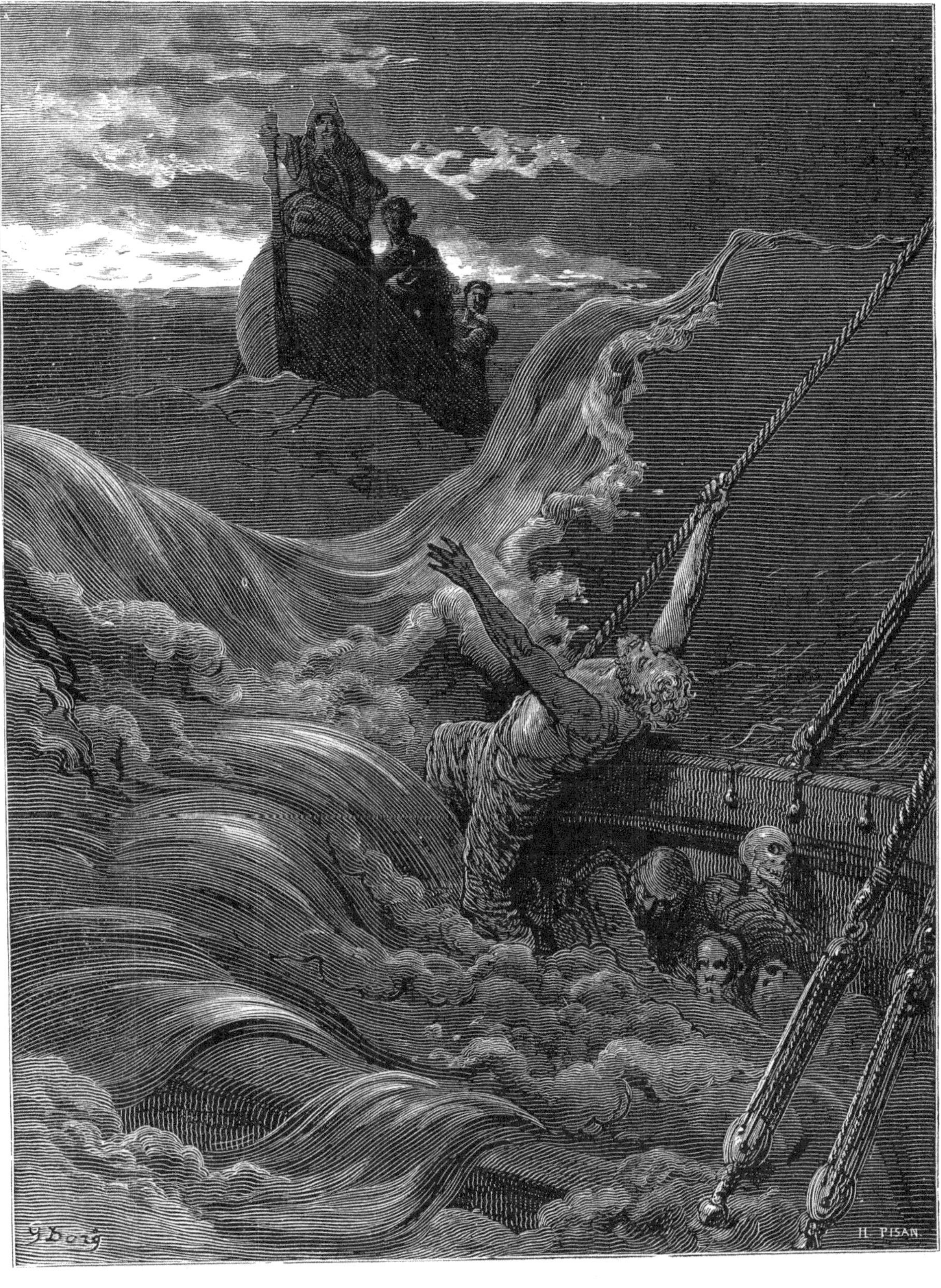

GUSTAVE DORÉ

17. Under the water it rumbled on, Still louder
and more dread., Gustave Doré, 1875

18

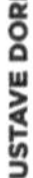

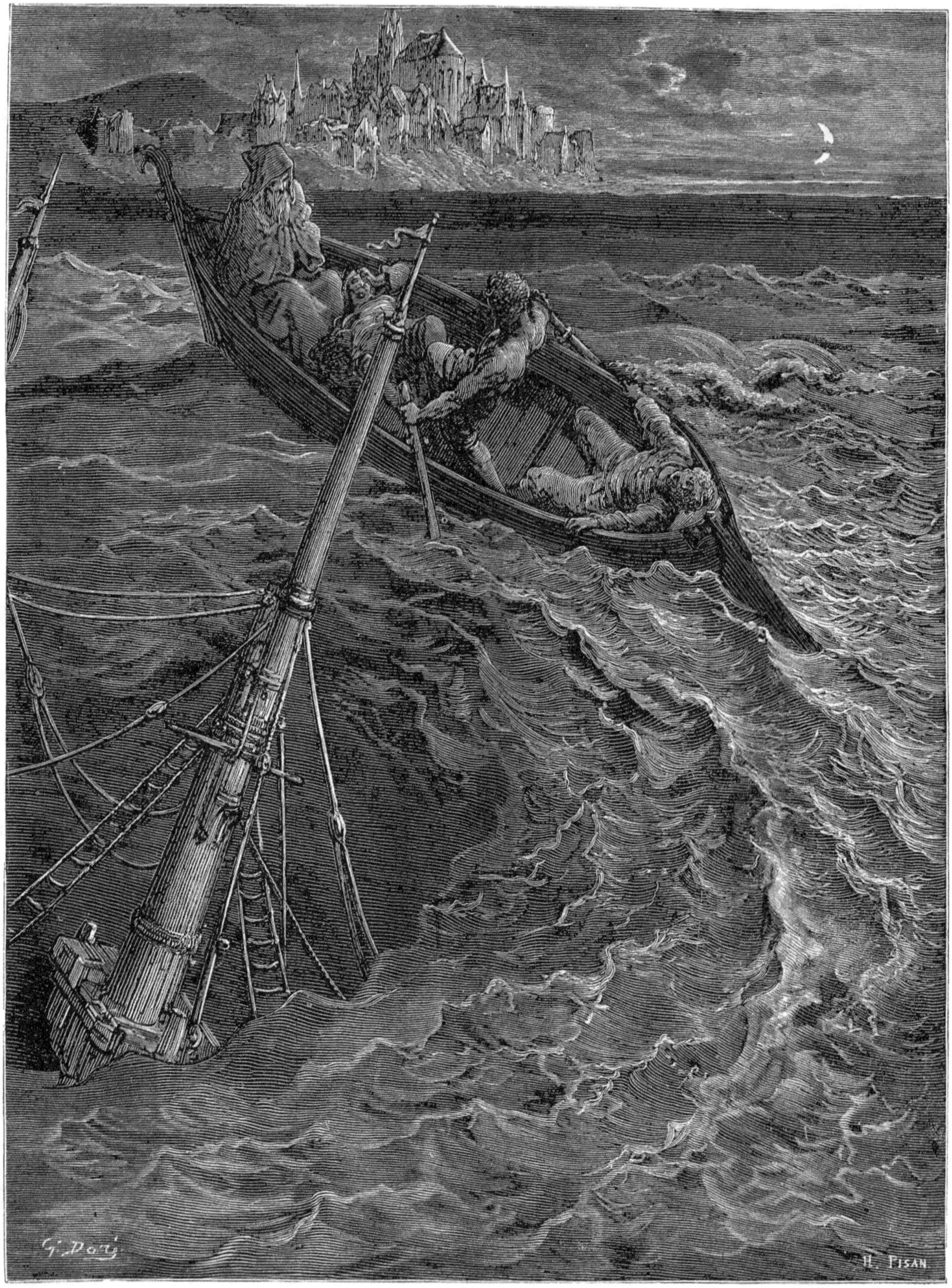

18. Upon the whirl, where sank the ship, The
boat spun round and round. Gustave Doré, 1875

19

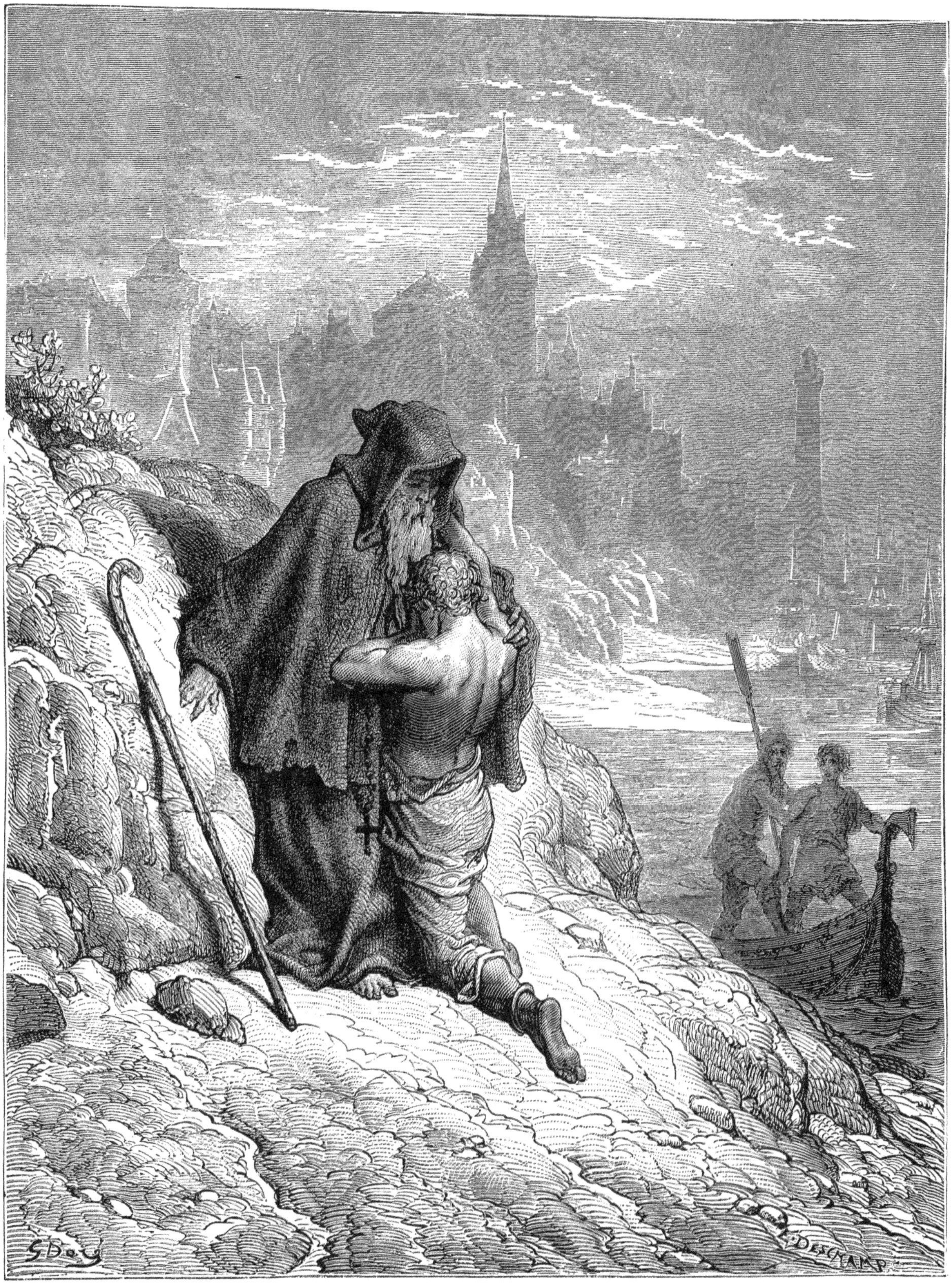

GUSTAVE DORÉ

02

THE DIVINE COMEDY: INFERNO

The Divine Comedy by Dante Alighieri is an epic poem written in the early 14th century, regarded as one of the greatest works of world literature. It chronicles the spiritual journey of the poet, Dante, as he travels through the three realms of the afterlife: Hell (*Inferno*), *Purgatory*, and Heaven (*Paradise*). These three books represent the soul's progression towards God, with each realm symbolising different aspects of sin, redemption, and divine grace.

Gustave Doré's illustration of *The Divine Comedy* originated from an idea he had to create illustrated works to accompany what he defined as 'masterpieces of literature'. He could not find a publisher to fund the lavish folio edition required for his artistic vision, so he decided to fund the costs of a limited edition of the first book, *Inferno*, in 1861. Fortunately, this release garnered immediate success, inspiring Hachette to fund a reprint and publish the second and third parts of the poem, *Purgatory* and *Paradise*, as a single volume in 1868.

Inferno: The story begins with Dante, who is guided by the Roman poet Virgil through the nine circles of Hell. Each circle represents a different sin, with souls suffering punishments that correspond to the nature of their transgressions. The nine circles of Hell in *Inferno* represent increasing levels of sin and punishment. The journey begins in Limbo and moves through Lust, Gluttony, Greed, and Wrath. Each circle punishes souls based on their sins, with more severe transgressions descending deeper: Heresy, Violence, Fraud, and Treachery. The ninth circle holds traitors, where Satan resides, frozen in a lake of ice. Dante witnesses the various torments during his travels and meets historical and mythological figures, ultimately gaining a deeper understanding of sin, justice, and divine retribution.

20

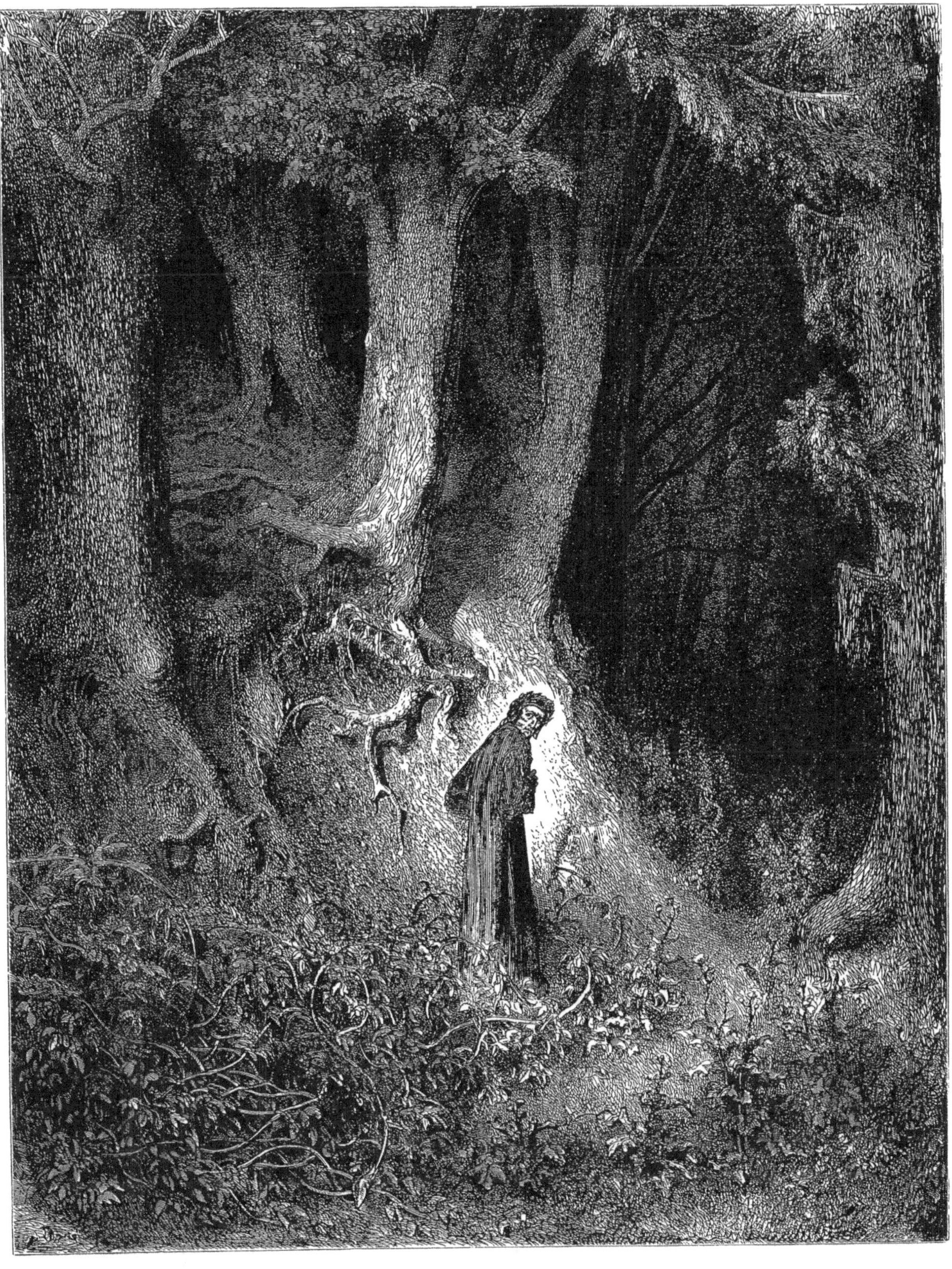

GUSTAVE DORÉ

20 In the midway of this our mortal life, I
found me in a gloomy wood, astray. Gustave
Doré, 1861

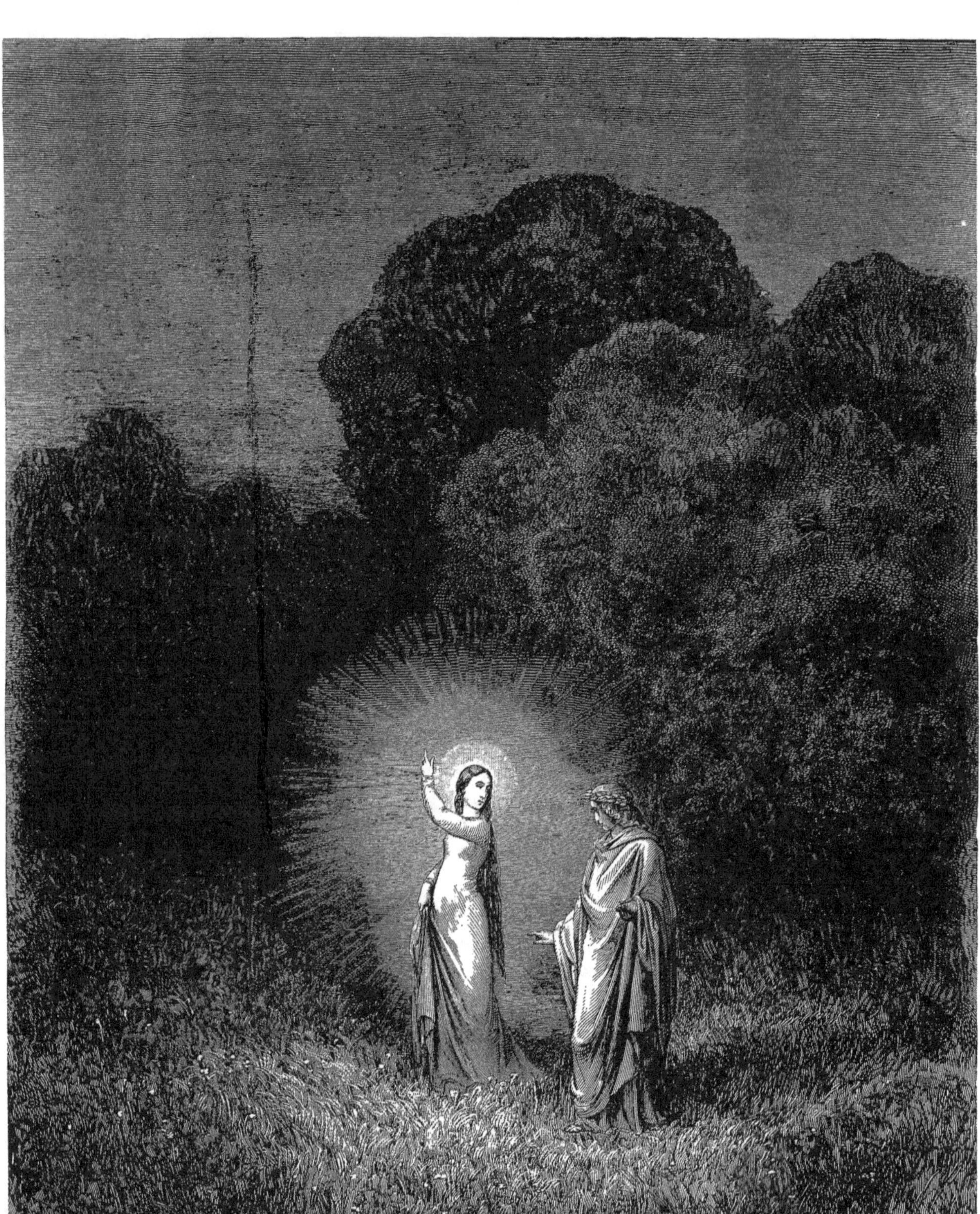

21. Beatrice am I, who do bid thee go. Gustave
Doré, 1861

22

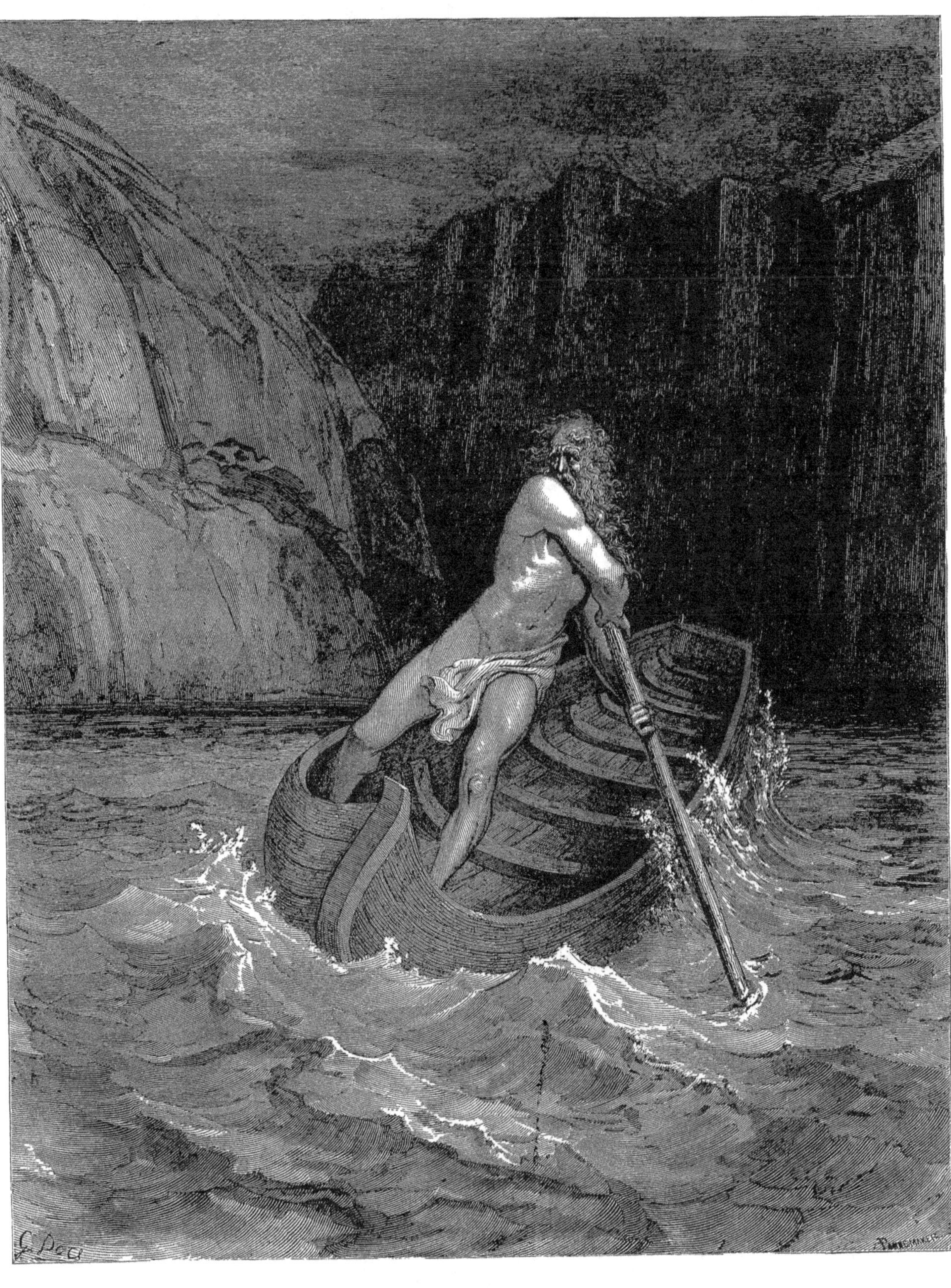

GUSTAVE DORÉ

22. And, lo towards us in a bark. Comes an old man, hoary white with eld, Crying, 'Woe to you, wicked spirits!', Gustave Doré, 1861

23

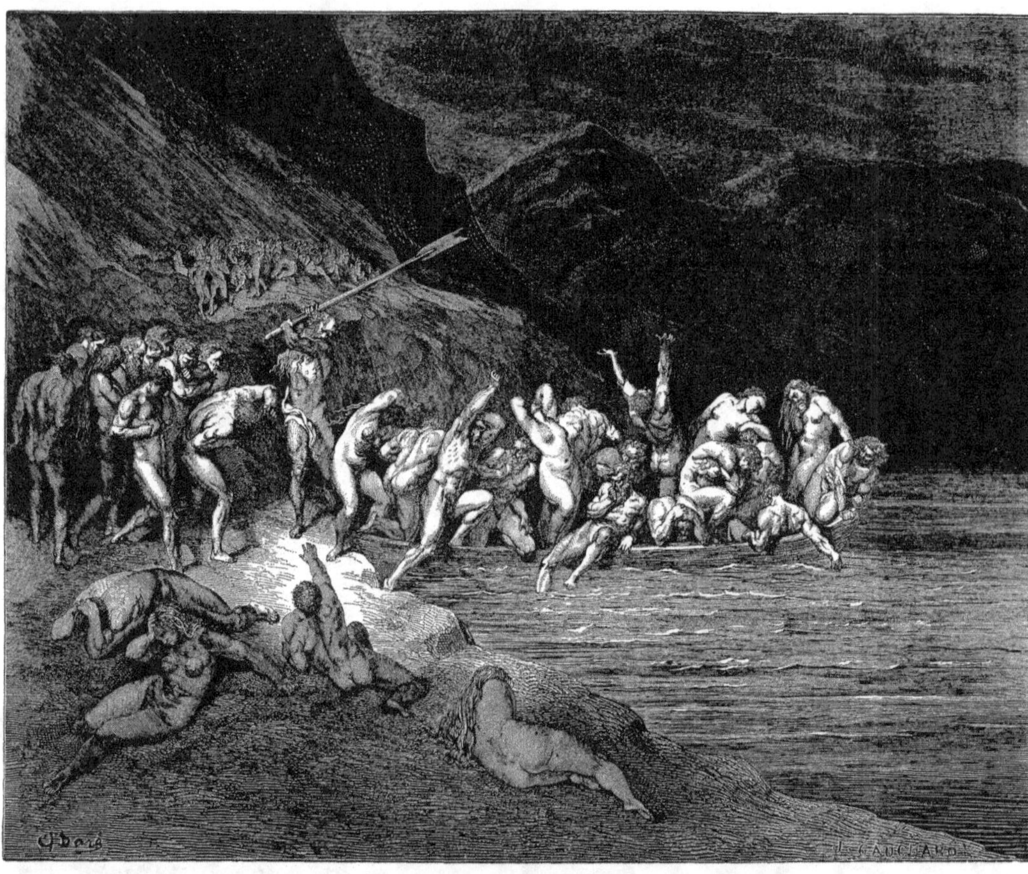

24

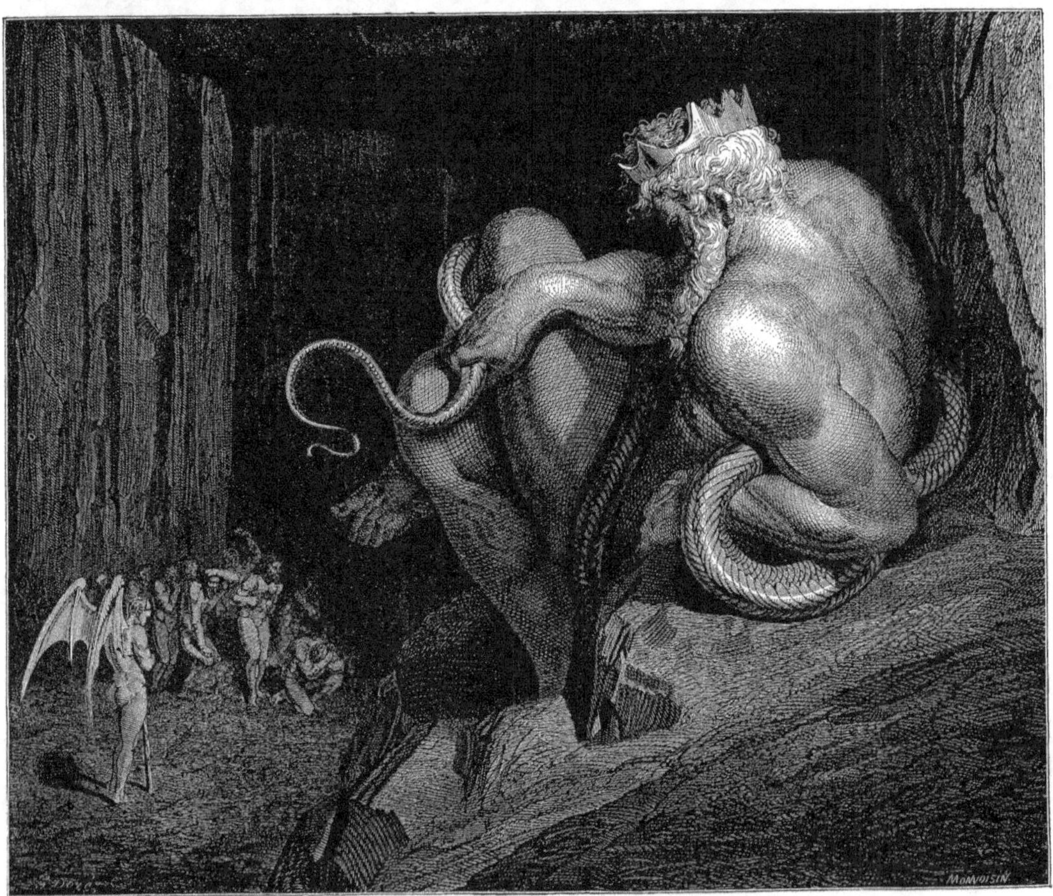

23. Charon herds the sinners onto his boat.
Gustave Doré, 1861

24. Minos judges the transgressions and
dispatches the souls. Gustave Doré, 1861

25

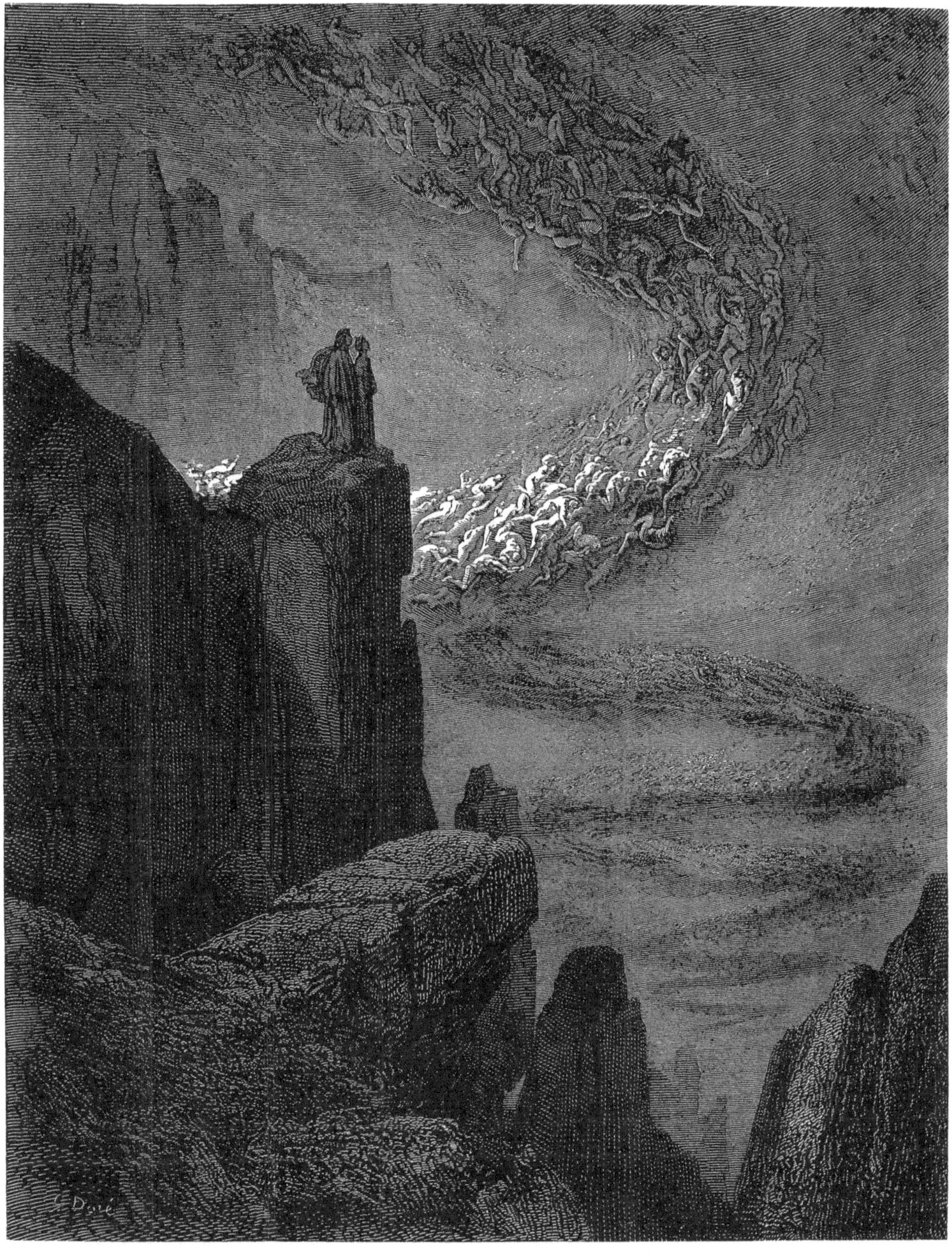

GUSTAVE DORÉ

25. The hurricane of souls. Gustave Doré, 1861

26

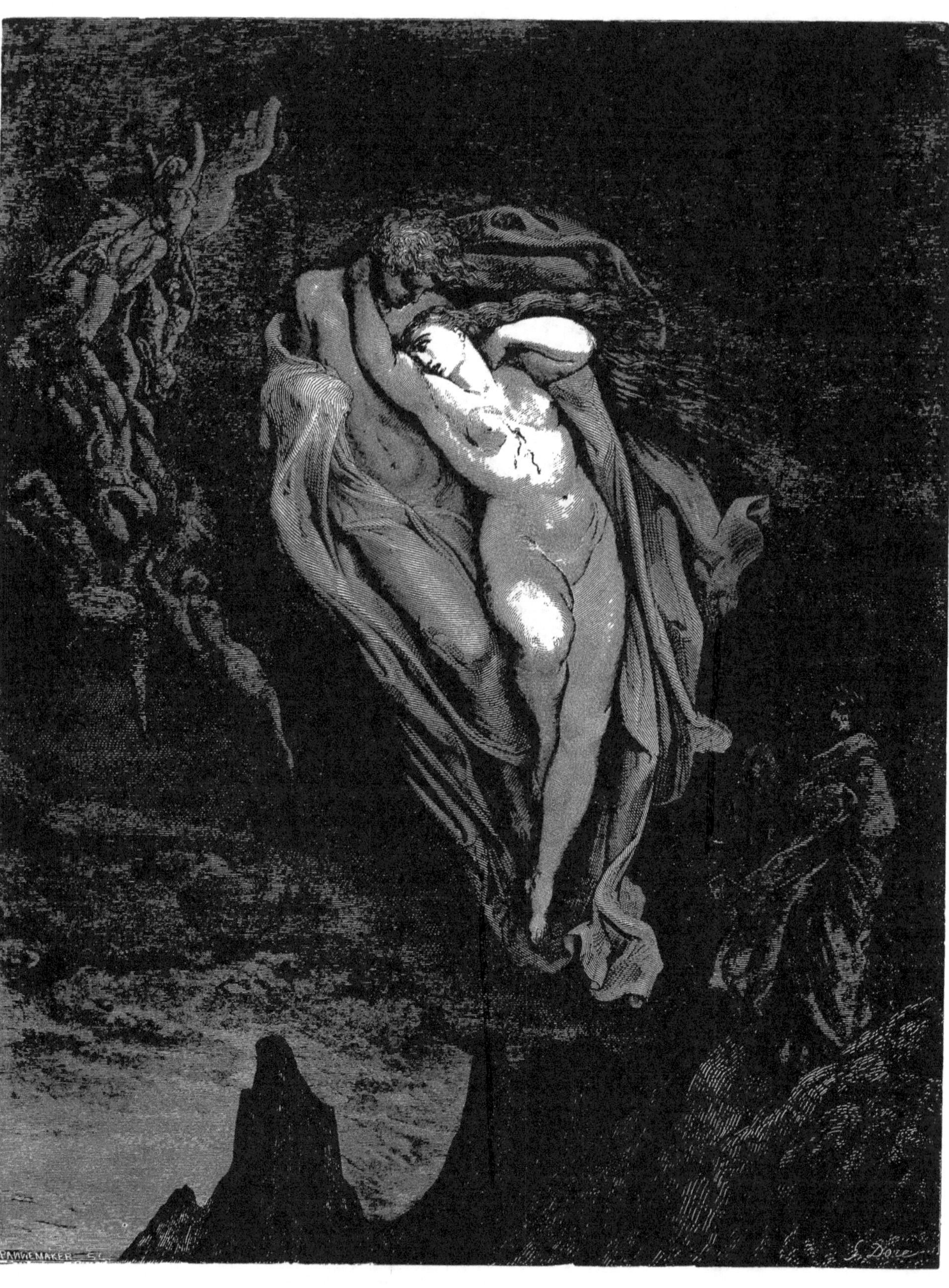

*26. Bard I Willingly I would address those two
together coming. Gustave Doré 1861*

27

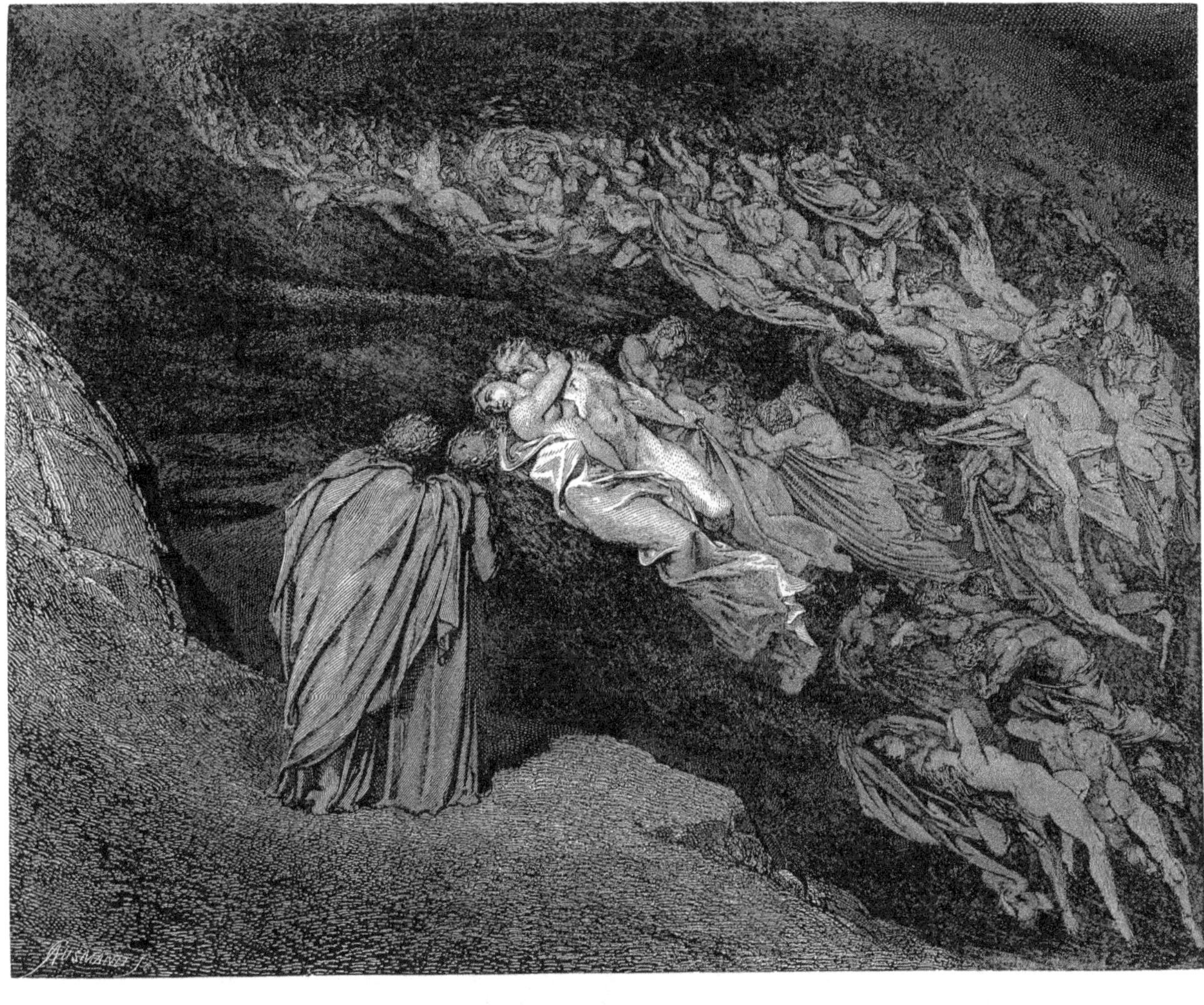

27. Love brought us to one death Caina waits,
The soul who split our life. Gustave Doré, 1861

28

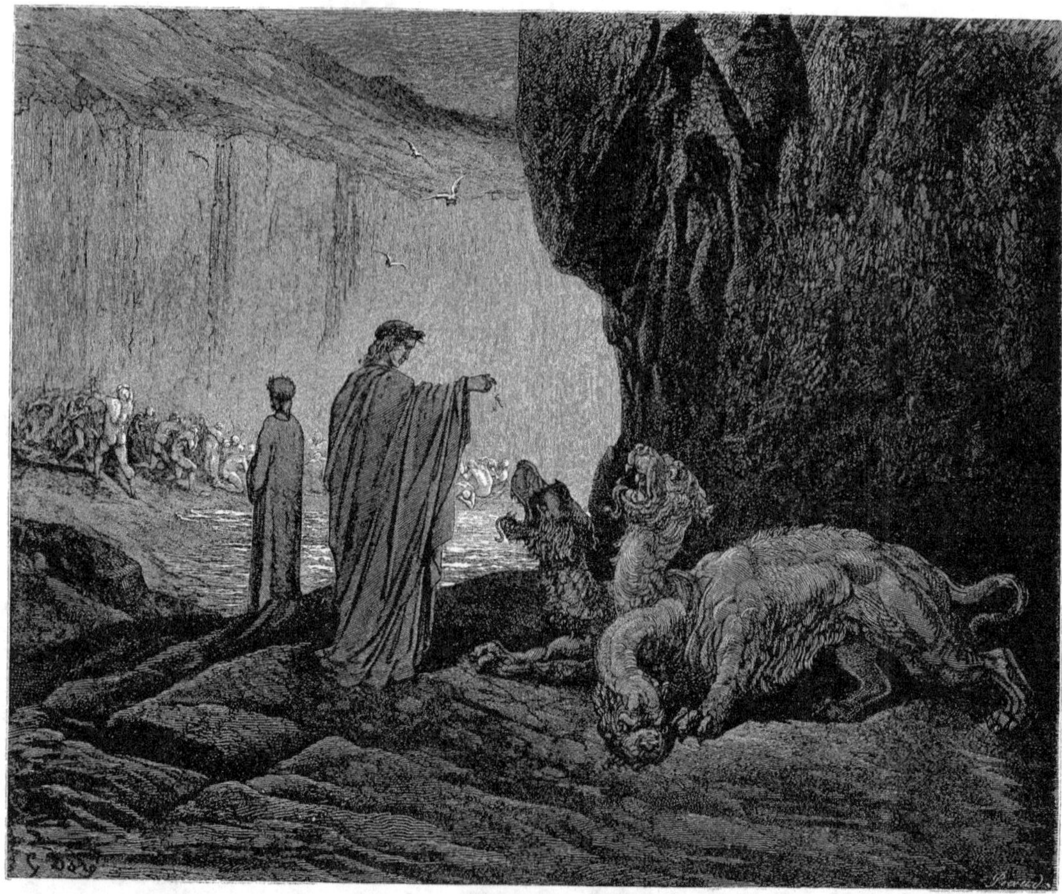

29

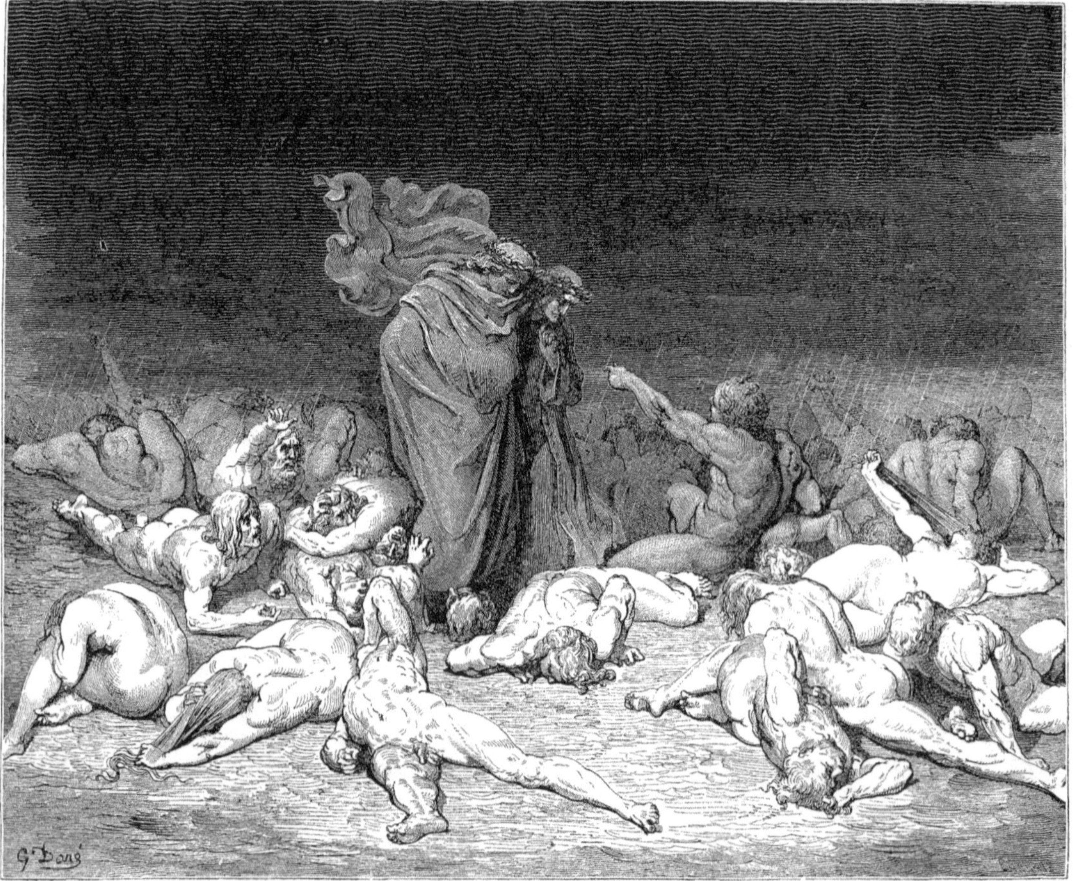

28. My Conductor, with his spans extended,
Took of the earth, and with his fists weel filled,
He threw it into those rapacious gullets.

29. For the pernicious sin of gluttony, I as
thou seest, am battered by this rain, Gustave
Doré, 1861

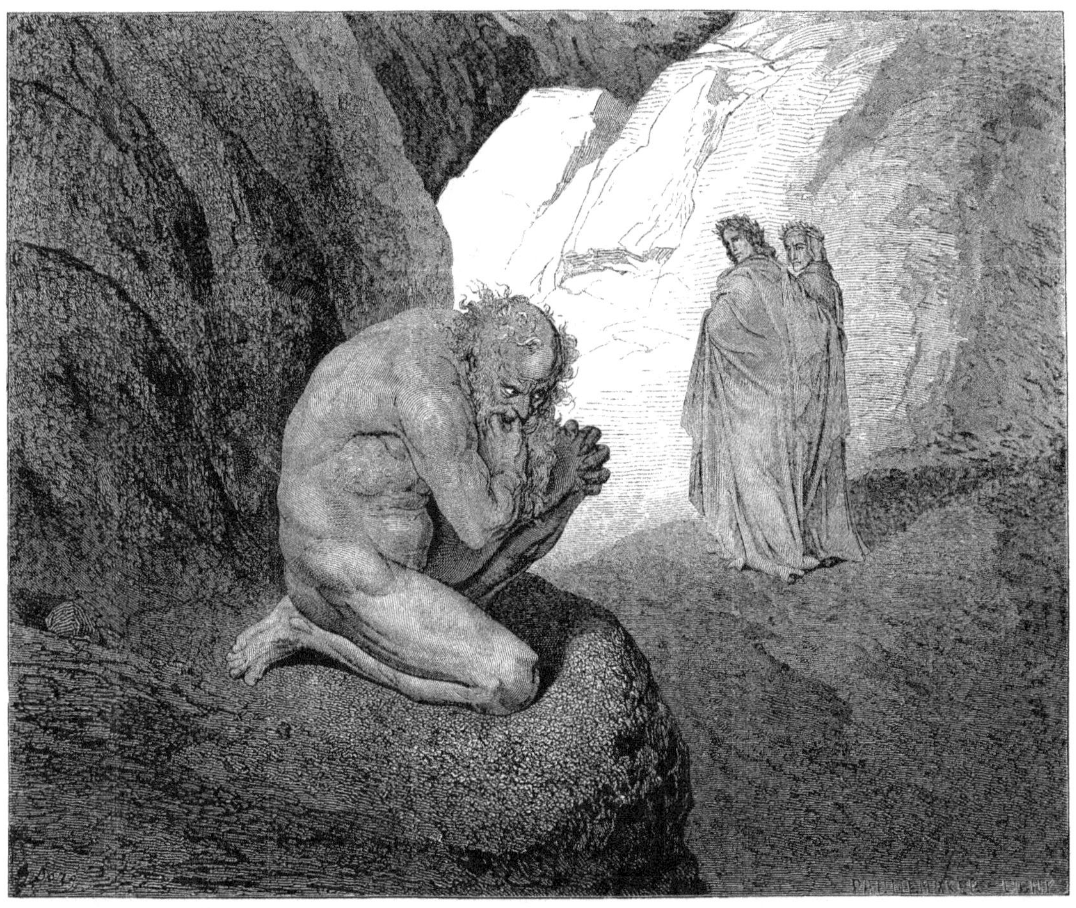

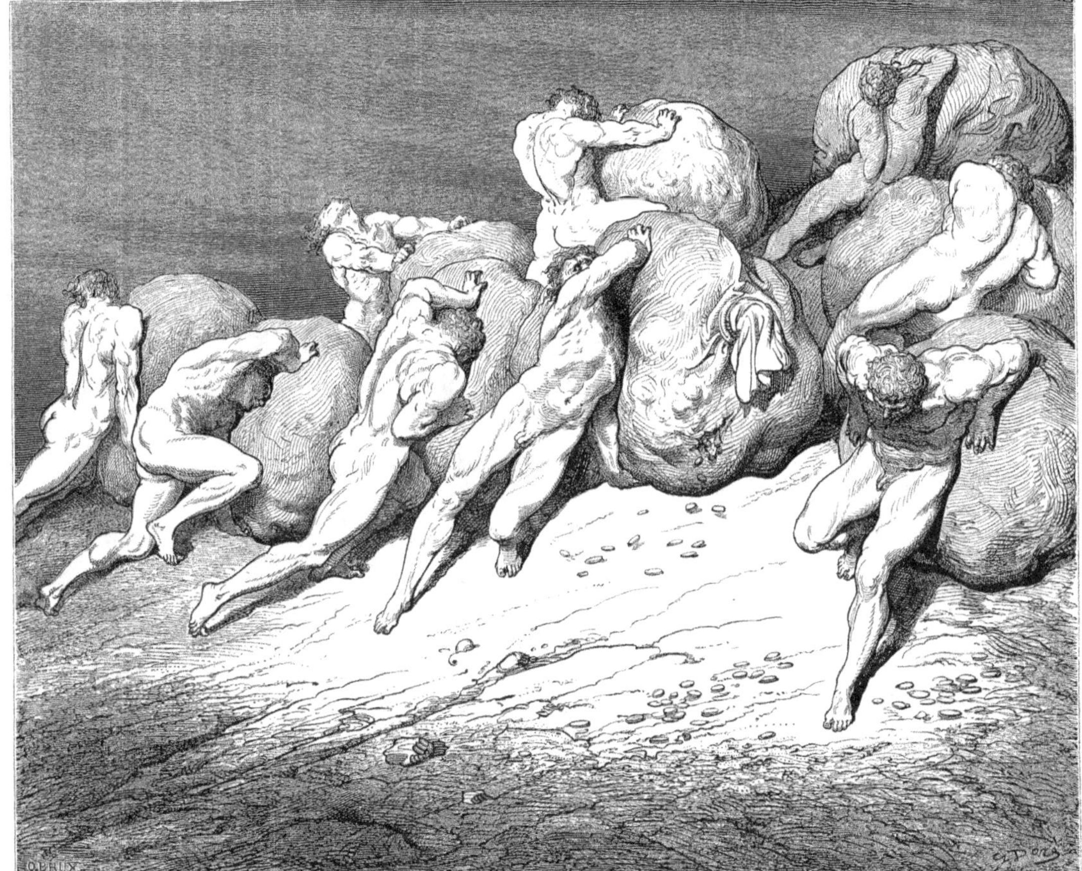

30. Be silent thou accused wolf. Consume within thyself with thine own rage. Gustave Doré, 1861

31. For all the gold that is beneath the moon, Or ever has been, of these weary souls, Could never make a single one repose. G. Doré, 1861

32

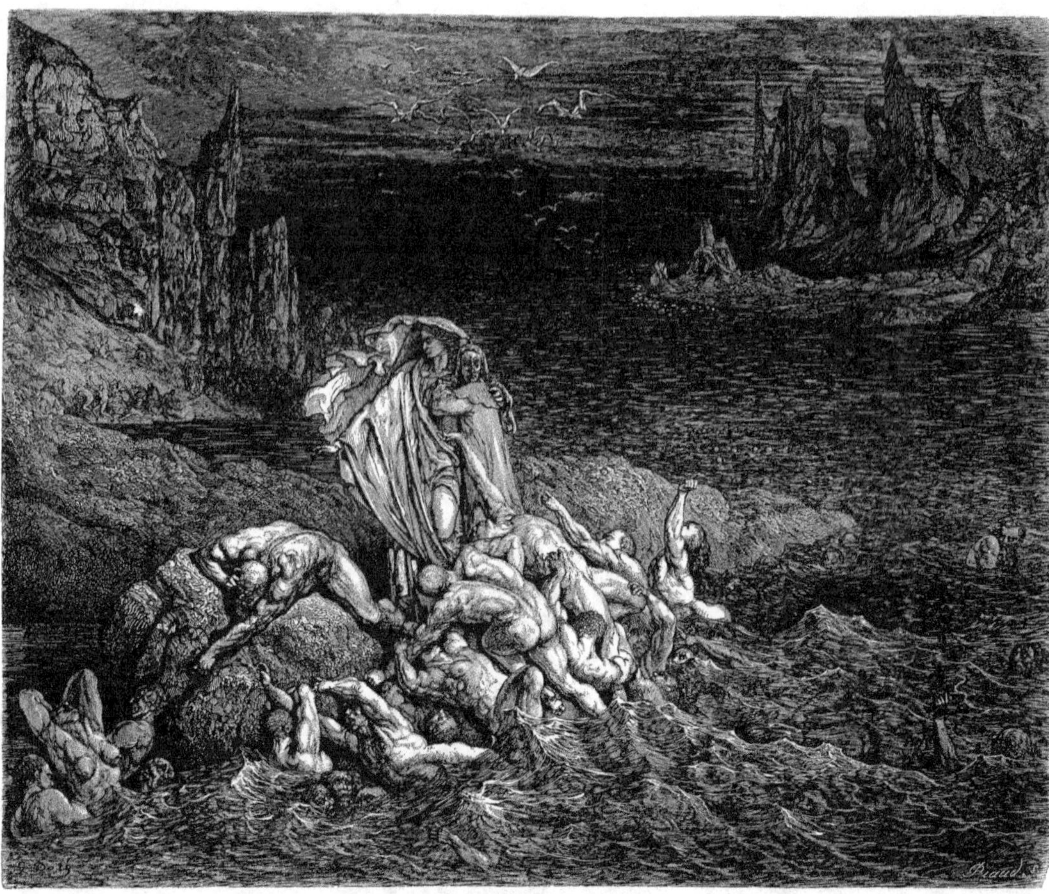

33

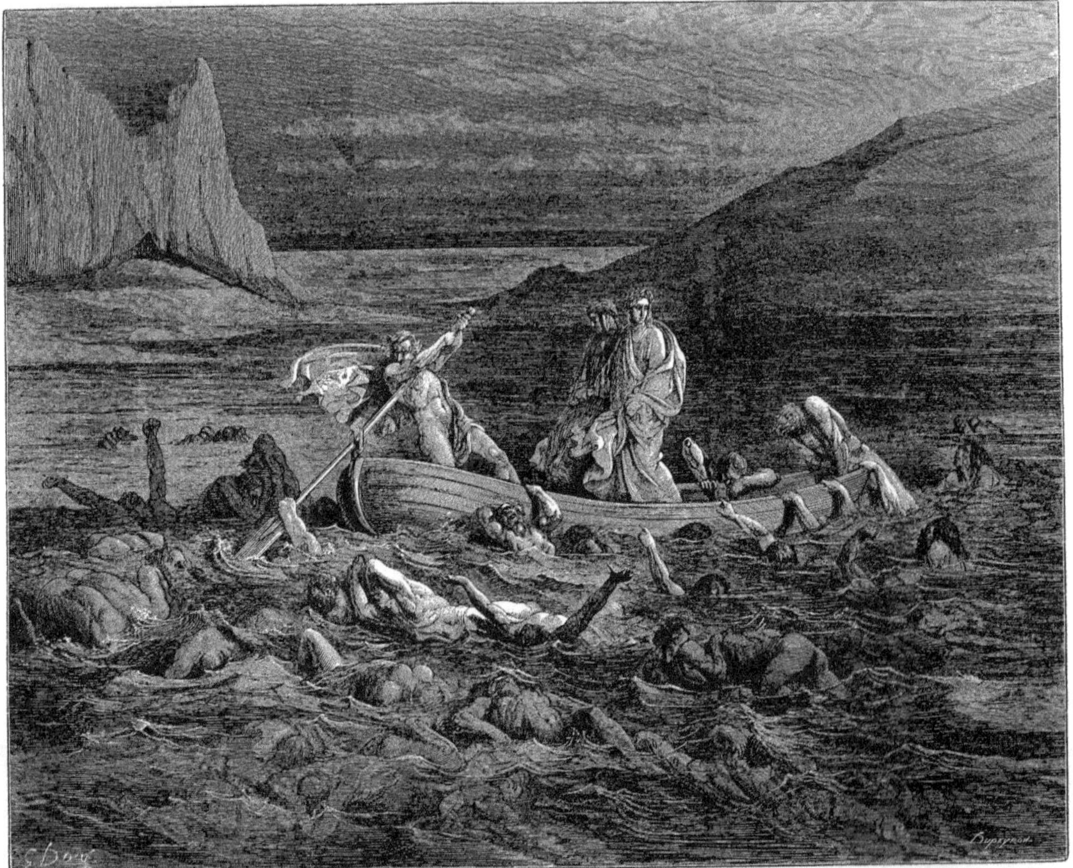

32. Son, thou now beholdest, The souls of those
whom anger overcame, Gustave Doré, 1861

33. The antique prow goes on its way, dividing,
More of the water than it is wont with others,
Gustave Doré, 1861

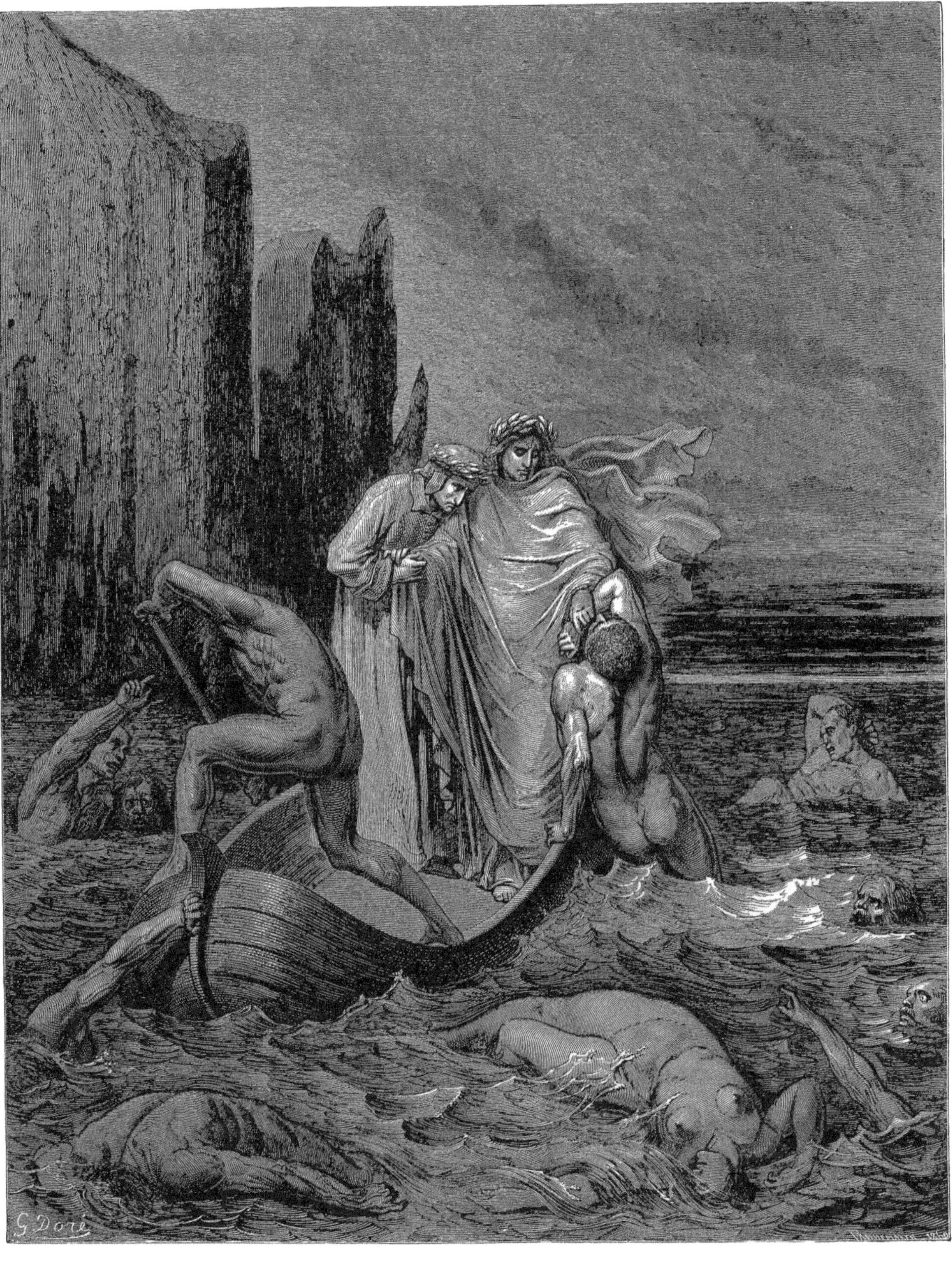

GUSTAVE DORÉ

34 My teacher sage. Aware, thrusting him
back- "Away! down there; To the other dogs.
Gustave Doré, 1861

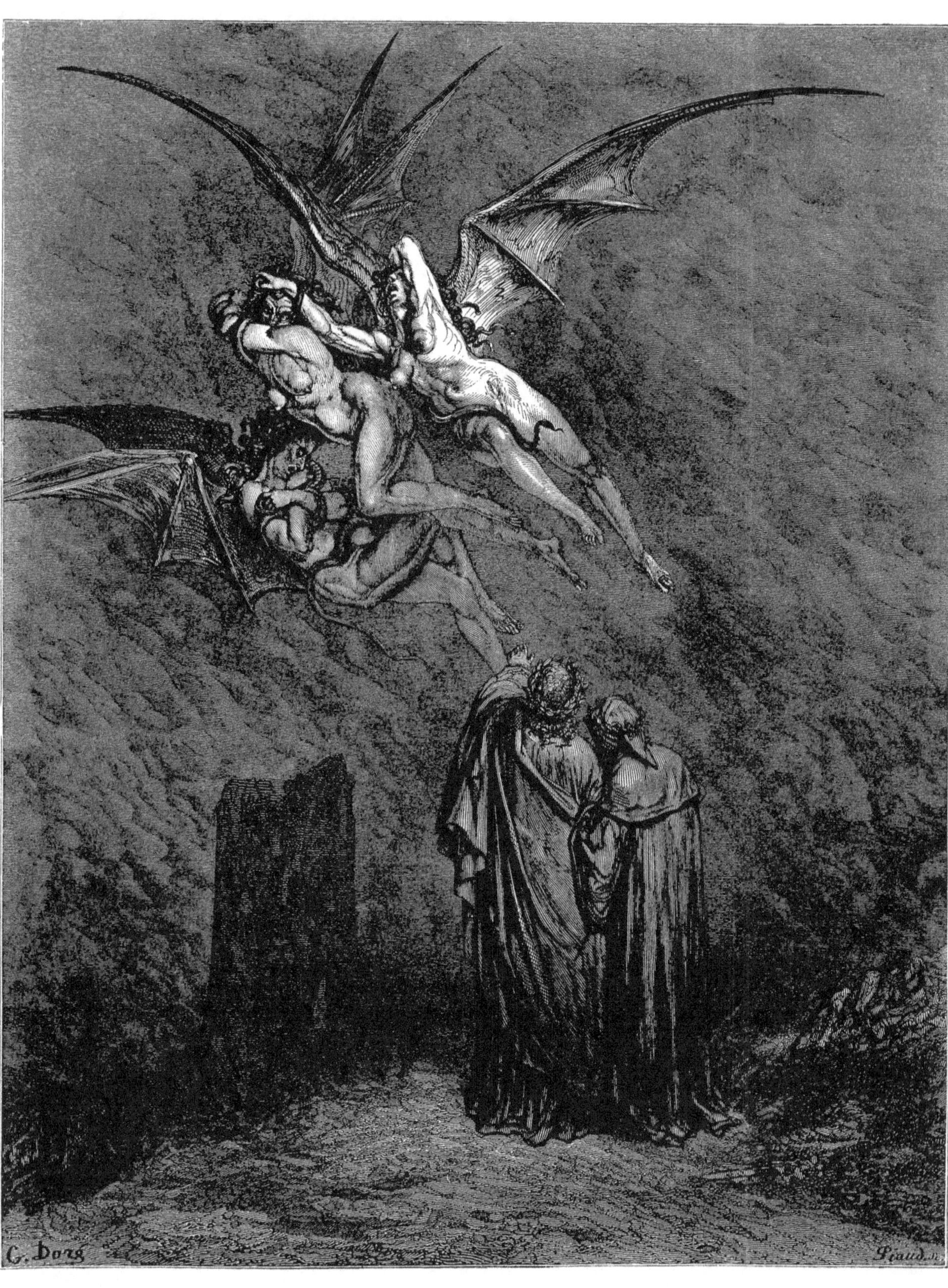

35. *This is Megaera, on the left-hand side;*
She who is weeping on the right; Tisiphone is
between, Gustave Doré, 1861

36

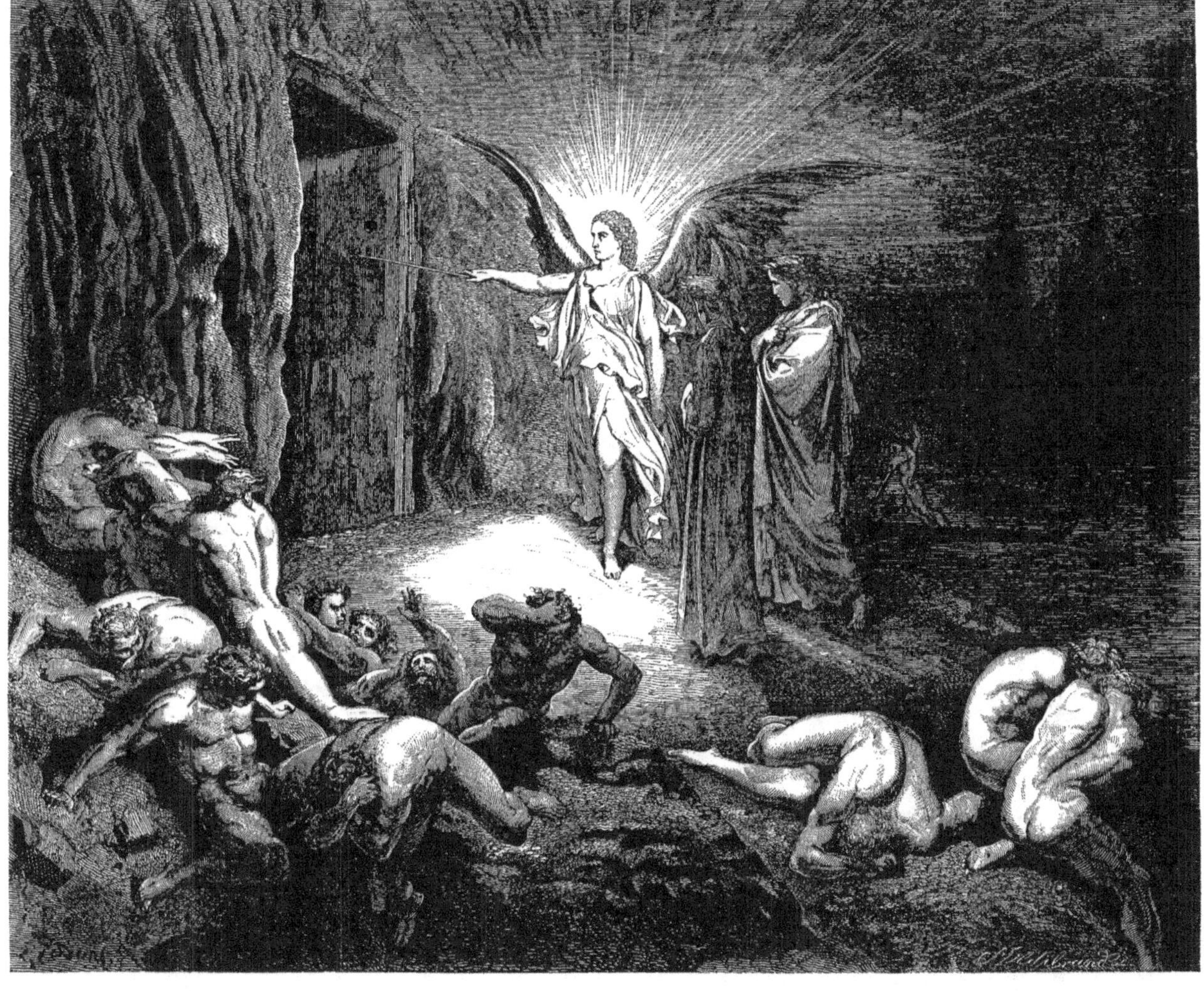

GUSTAVE DORÉ

36. He reached the gate, and with a little rod,
He opened it, for there was no resistance.
Gustave Doré, 1861.

37

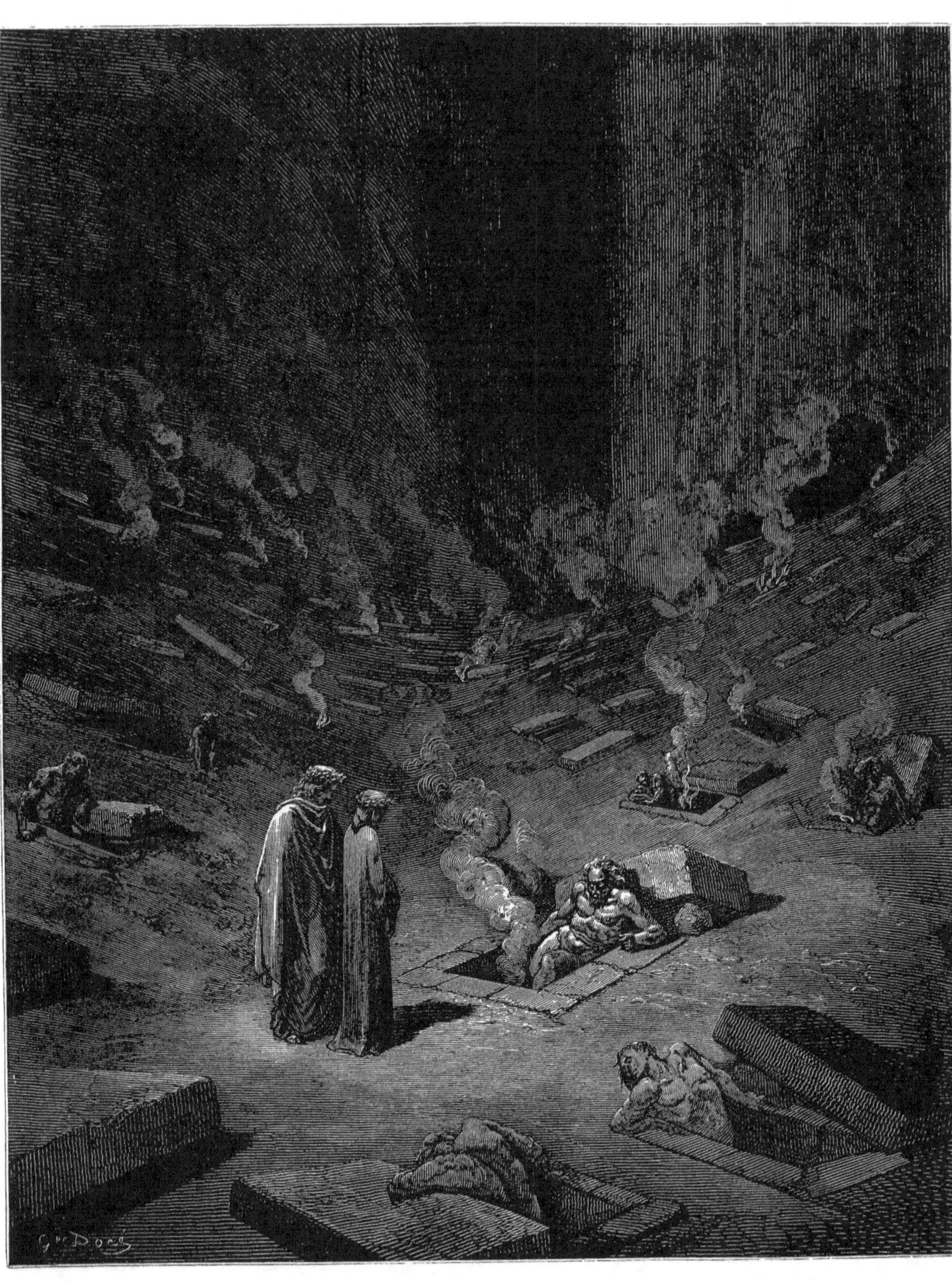

37. My Master, what are all those people Who, having sepulture within those tombs, Make themselves audible by doleful sighs?

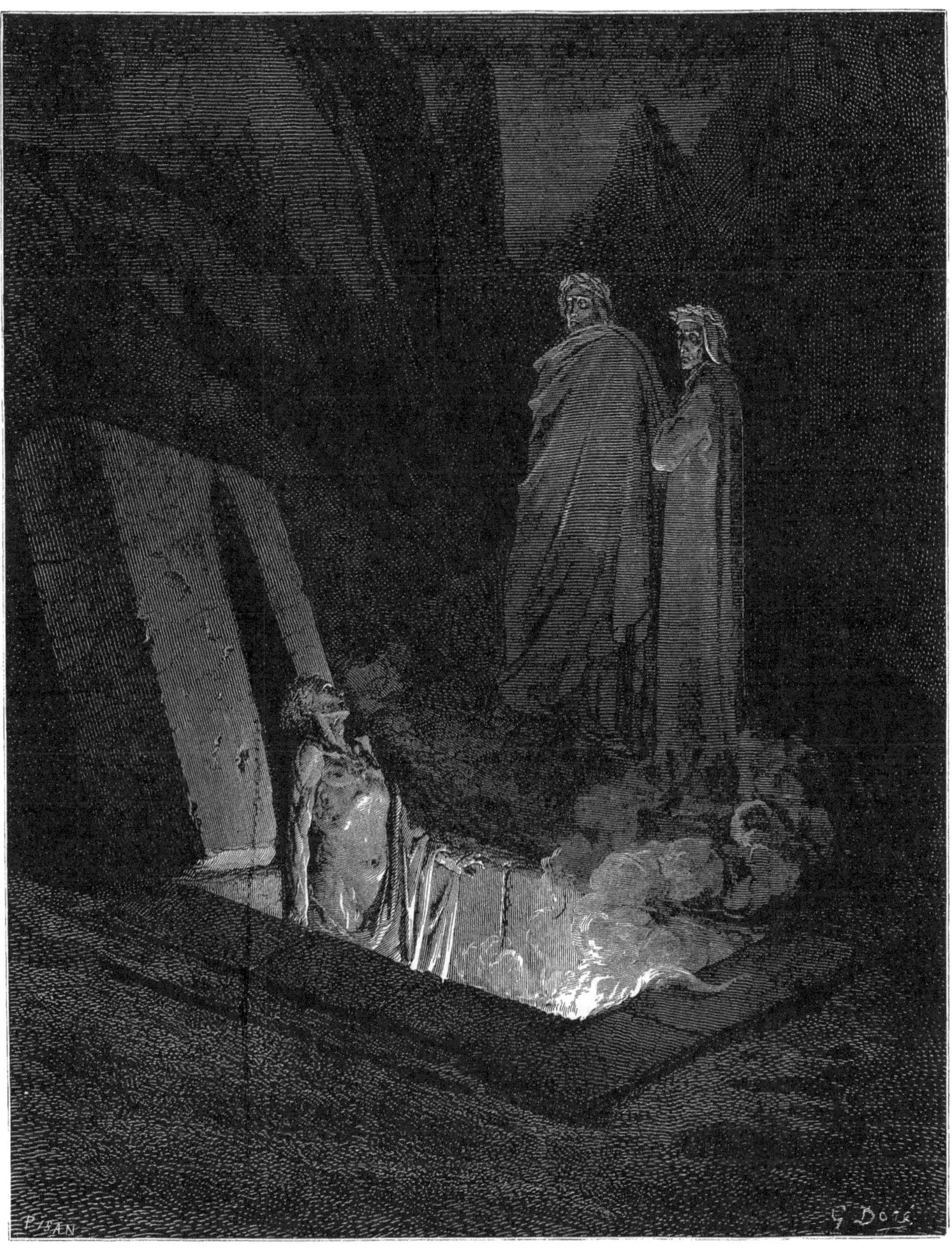

38. As soon as I was at the foot of his tomb,
Somewhat he eyed me, and as if disdainful, Then he
asked of me, "Who were thine ancestors?"

39

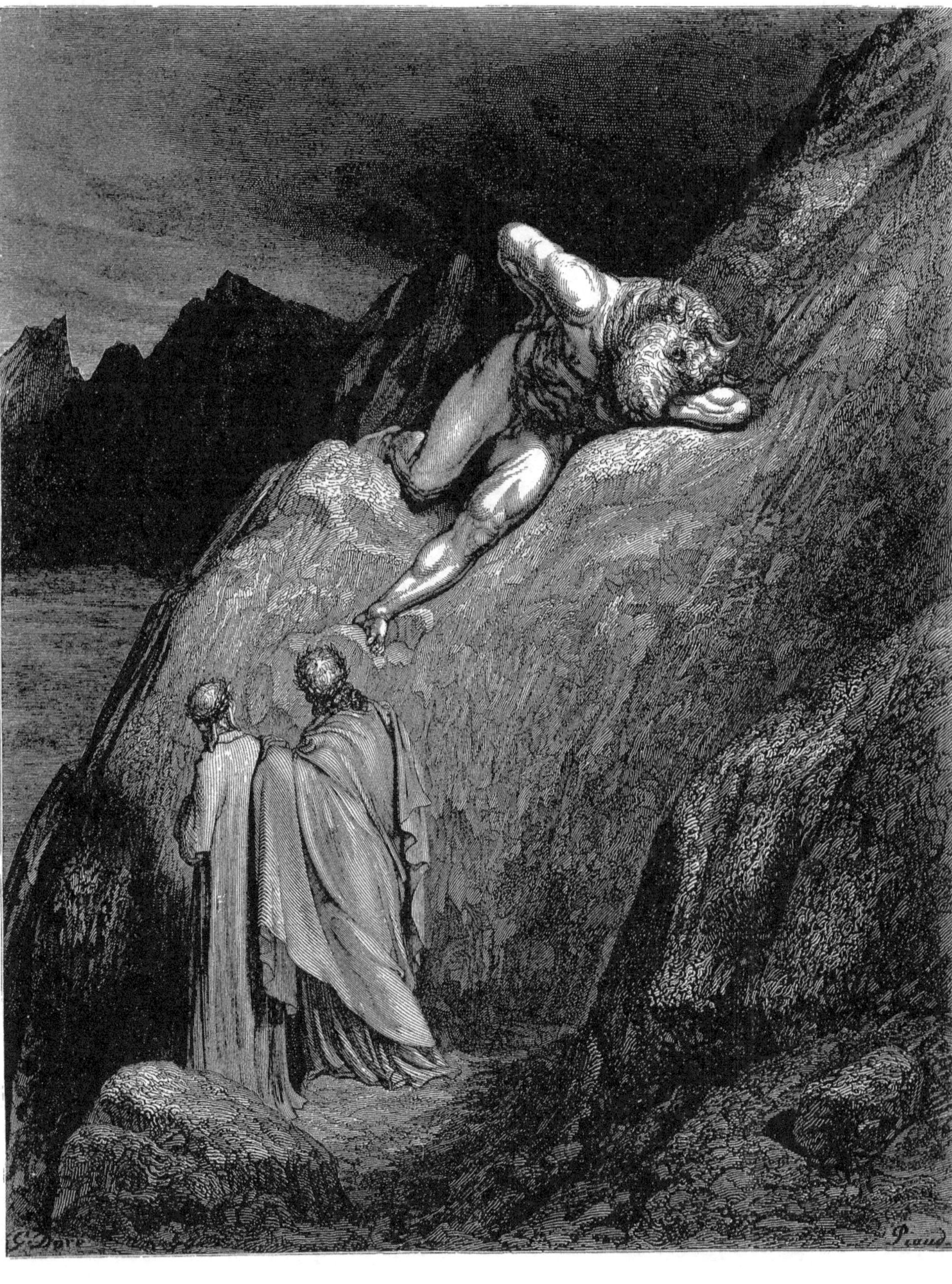

39. And on the border of the broken chasm, The infamy of Create was stretched along, Who was conceived in the ficticious cow. Gustave Doré. 1861

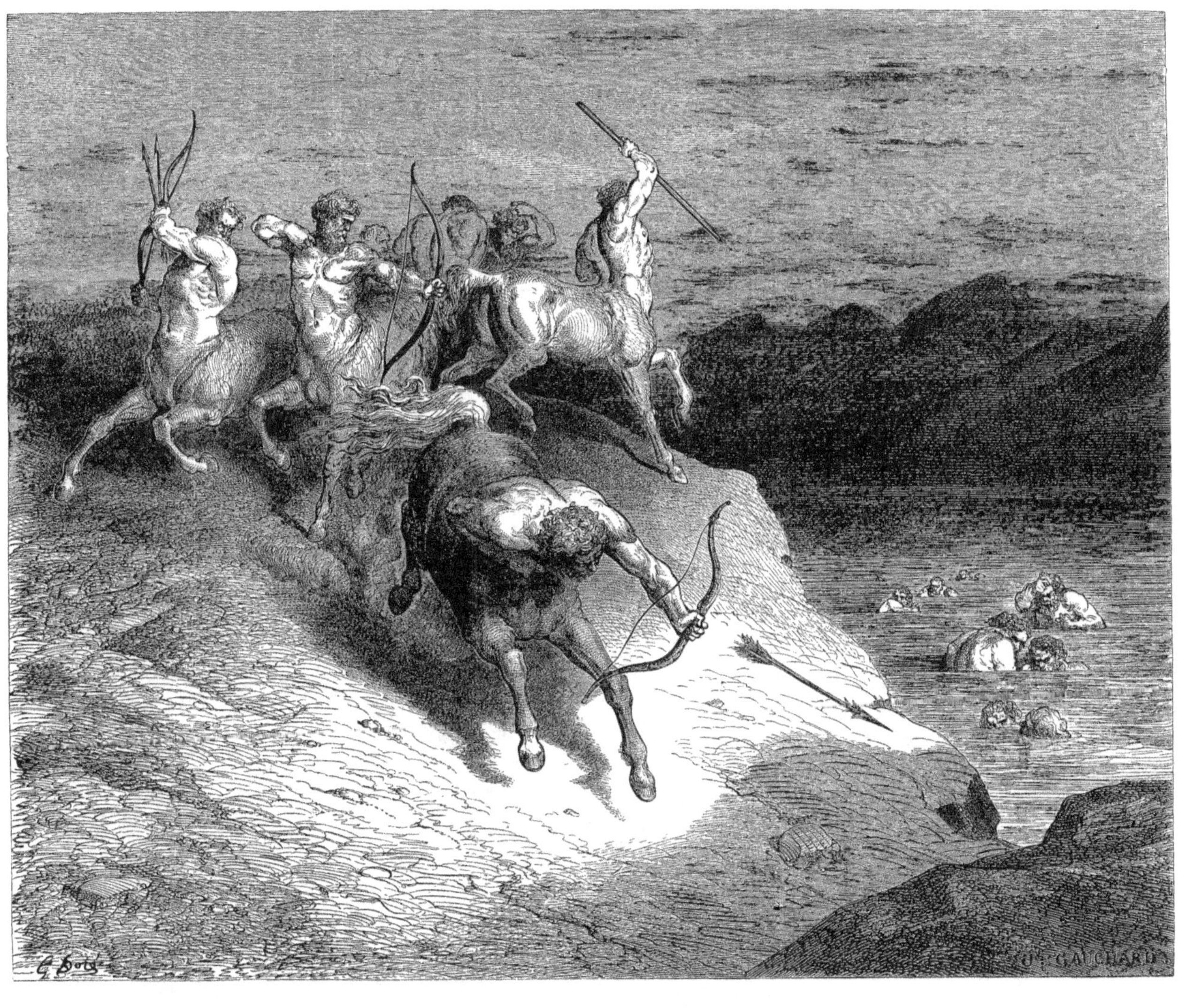

GUSTAVE DORÉ

40. Chiron an arrow took, and with the notch
Backward upon his jaws he put his beard.
Gustave Doré, 1861

41

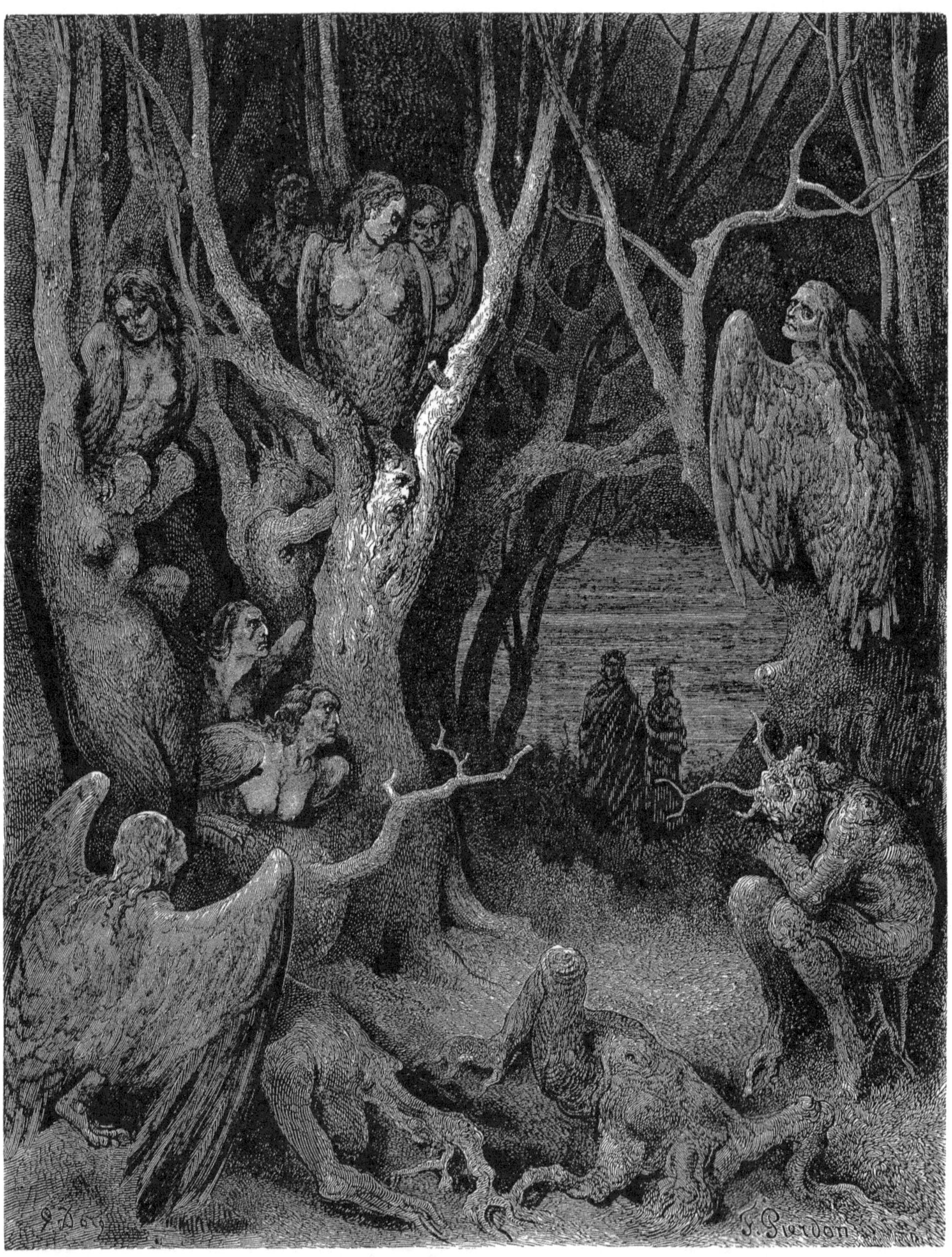

41. They make laments upon the wondrous
trees. Gustave Doré, 1861

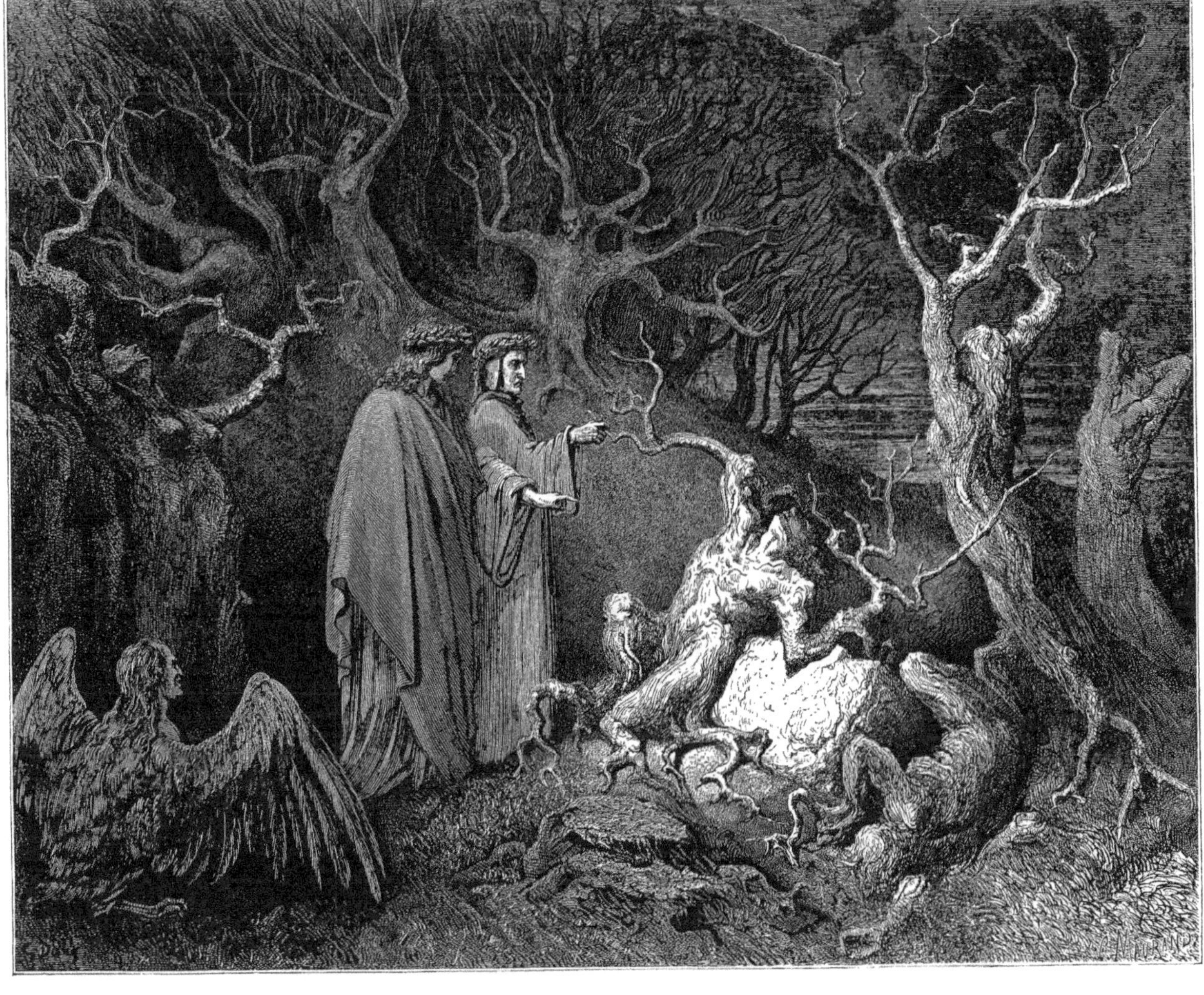

GUSTAVE DORÉ

42. Then stretched I forth my hand a little forward, And plucked a branchlet off from a great thron, And the trunk cried, "Why dost thou mangle me?", Gustave Doré, 1861.

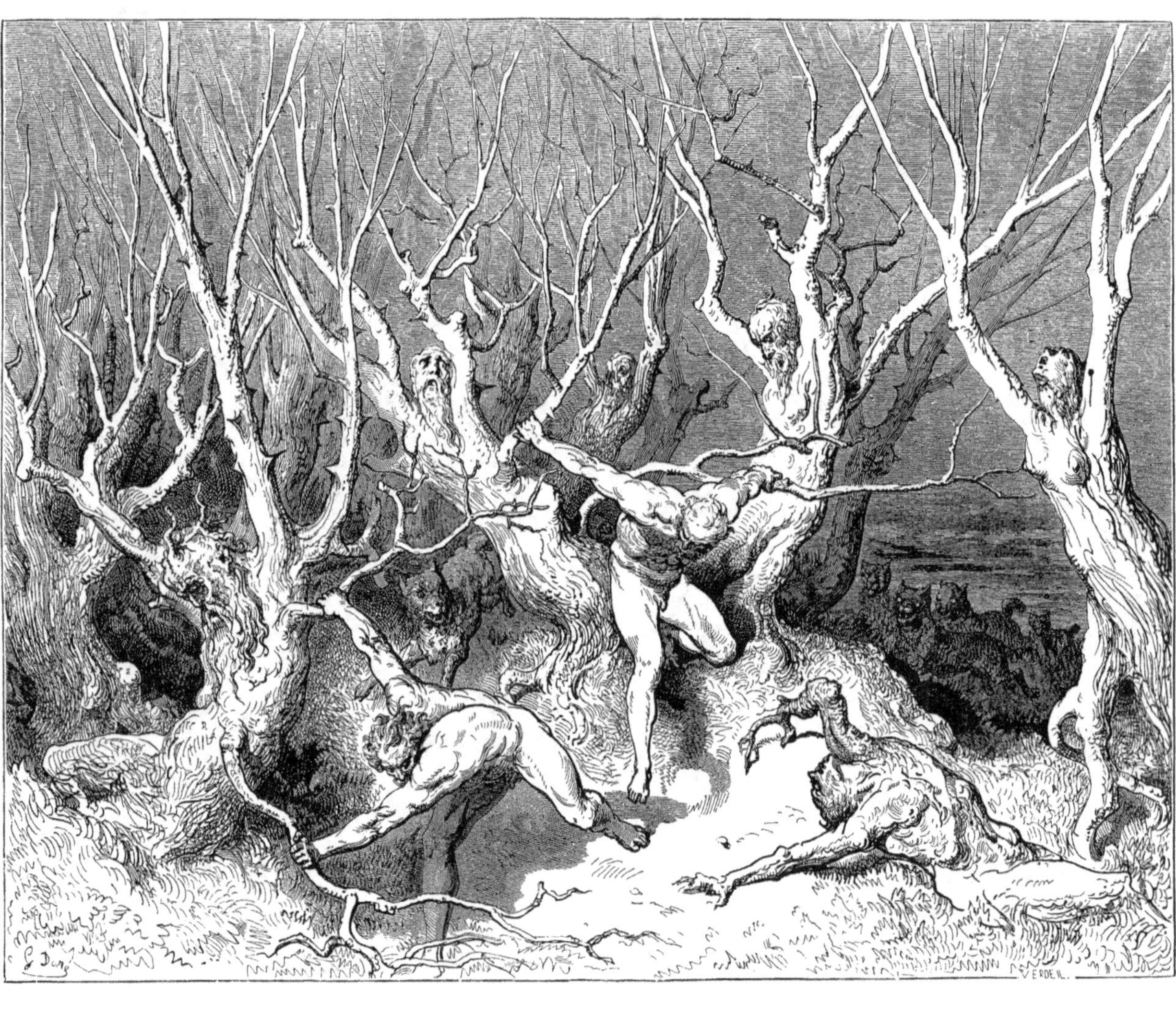

43. And two behold! Upon our left-hand side, Naked
and scratched, fleeing so furiously, That of the forest
every fan they broke, Gustave Doré, 1861

44

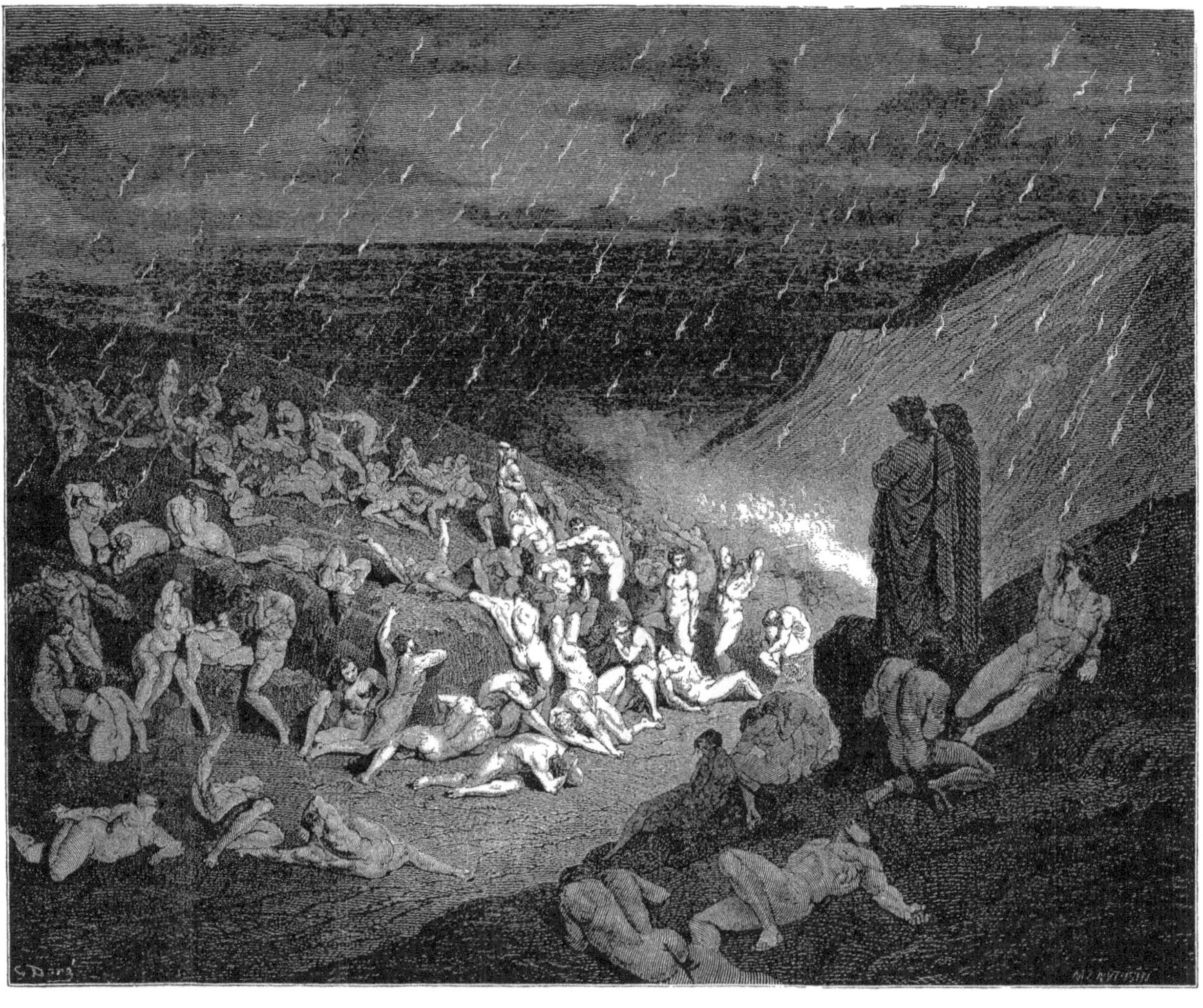

GUSTAVE DORÉ

45

GUSTAVE DORÉ

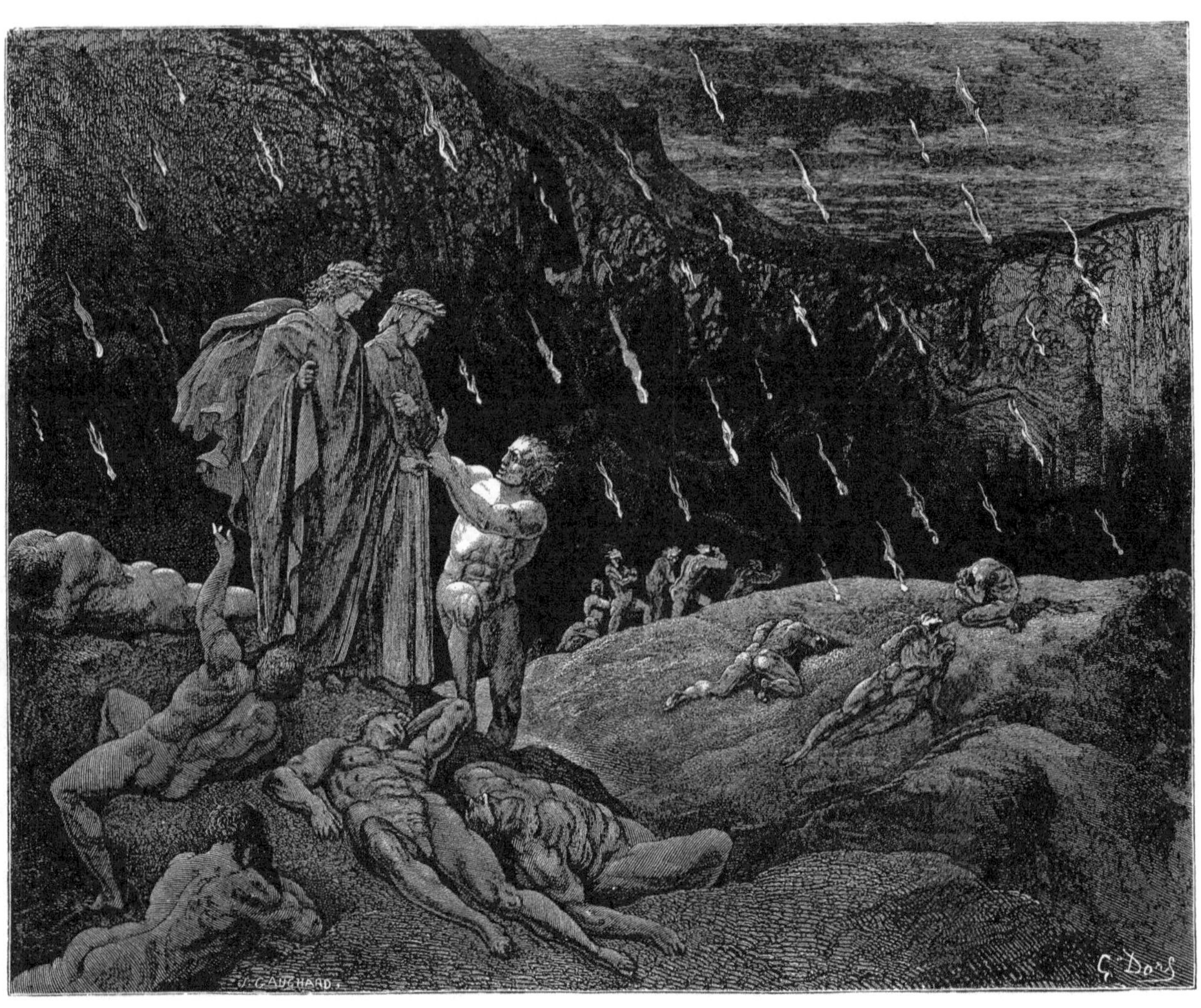

45. Oer all the sand-waste, with a gradual fall,
raining down dialated flakes of fire. Gustave
Doré, 1861

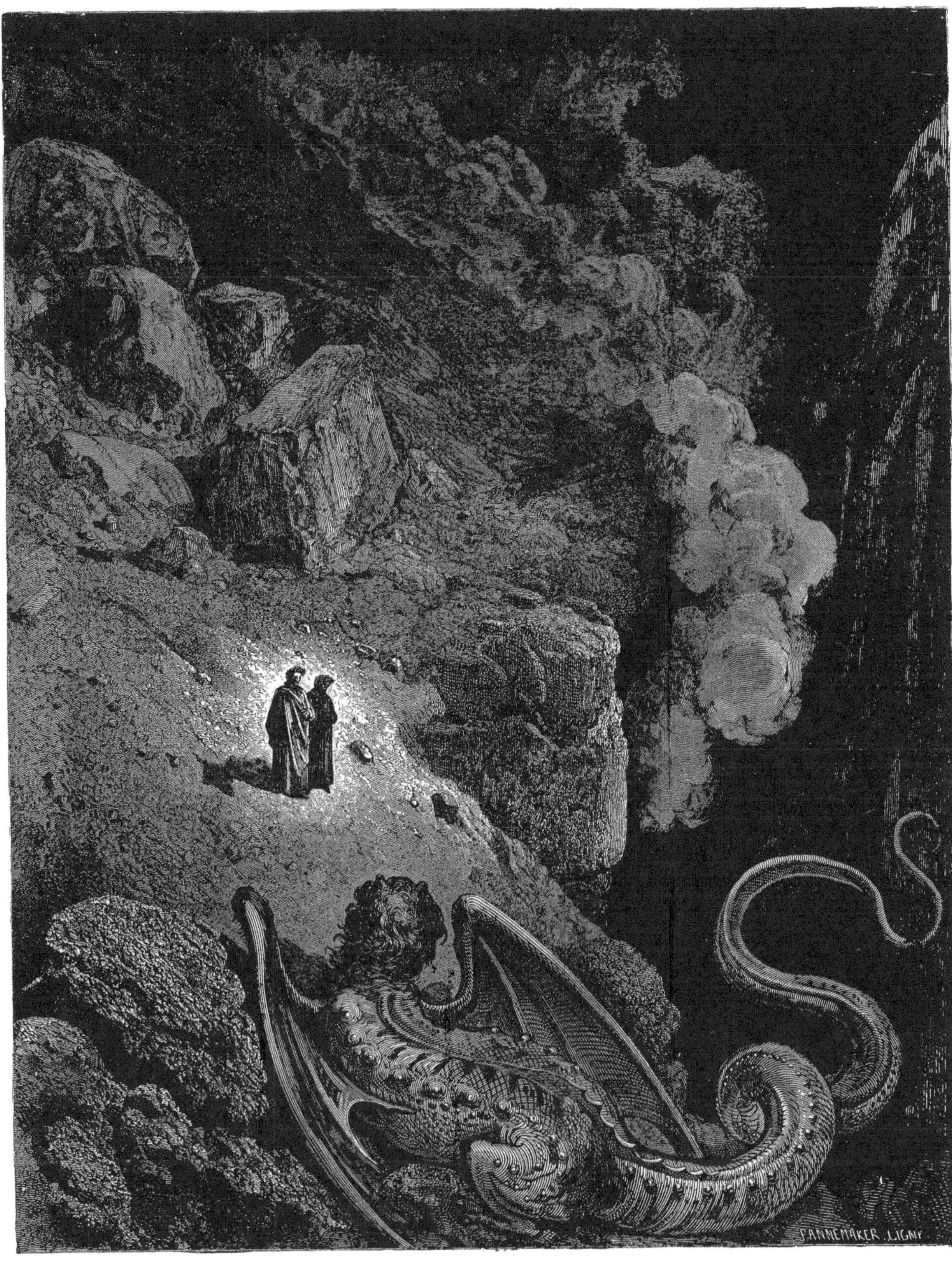

GUSTAVE DORÉ

46. "Are you here Ser Brunetto?", Gustave
Doré, 1861

GUSTAVE DORÉ

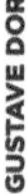

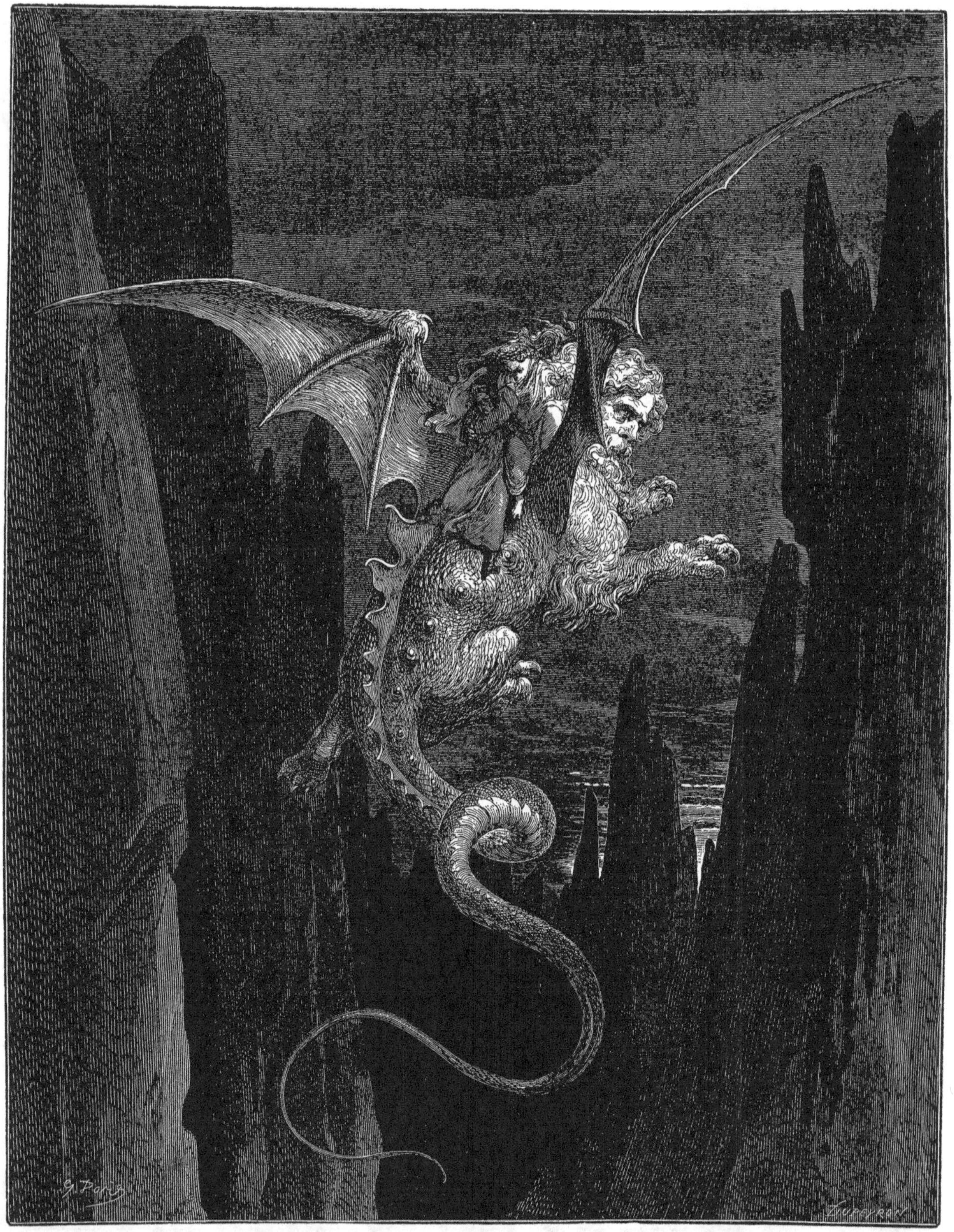

47. New terror I conceived at the steep plunge.
Gustave Doré, 1861

48

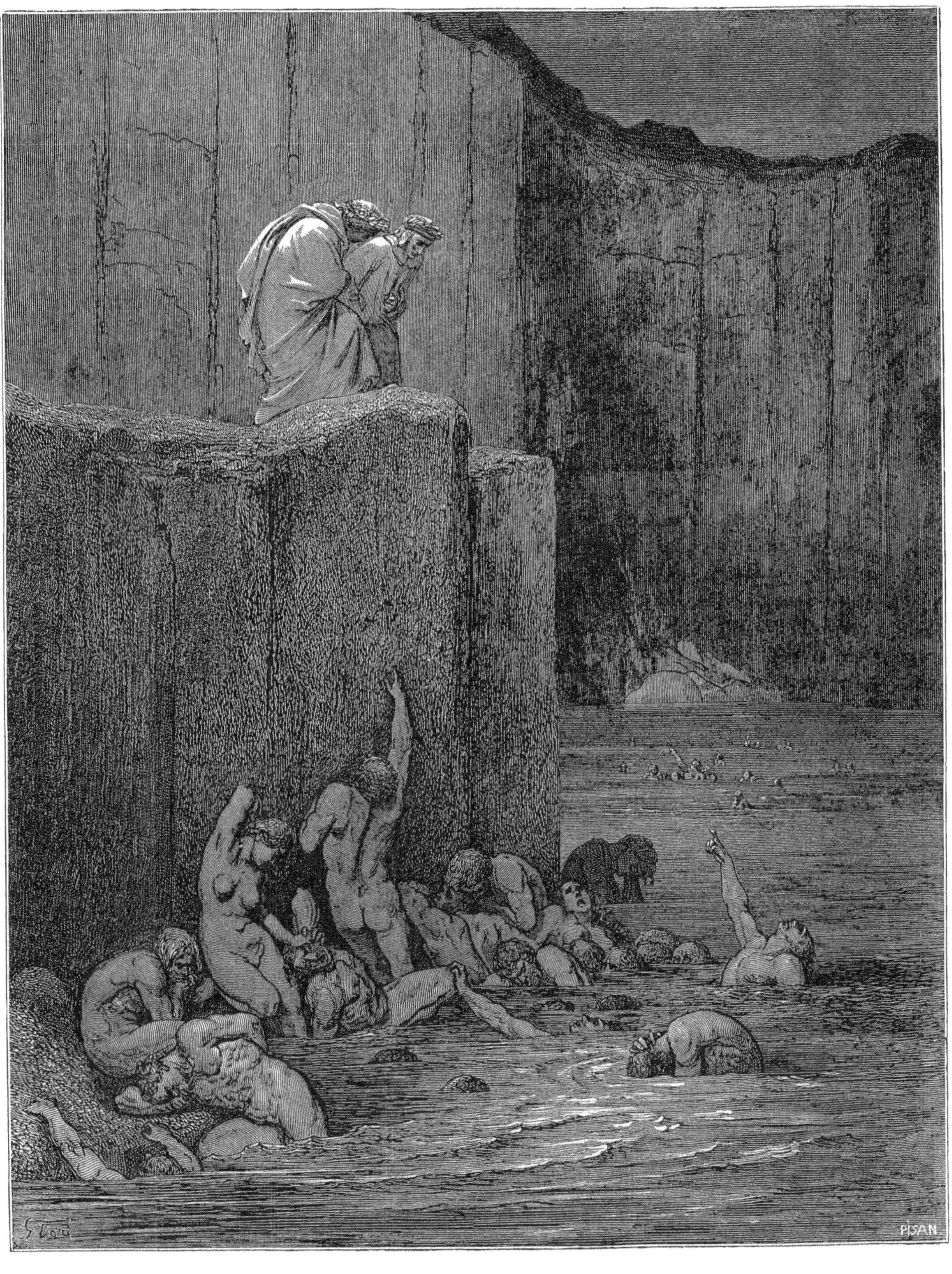

GUSTAVE DORÉ

48. I saw a people smothered in a filth, That out of human privies seemed to flow. Gustave Doré, 1861

49

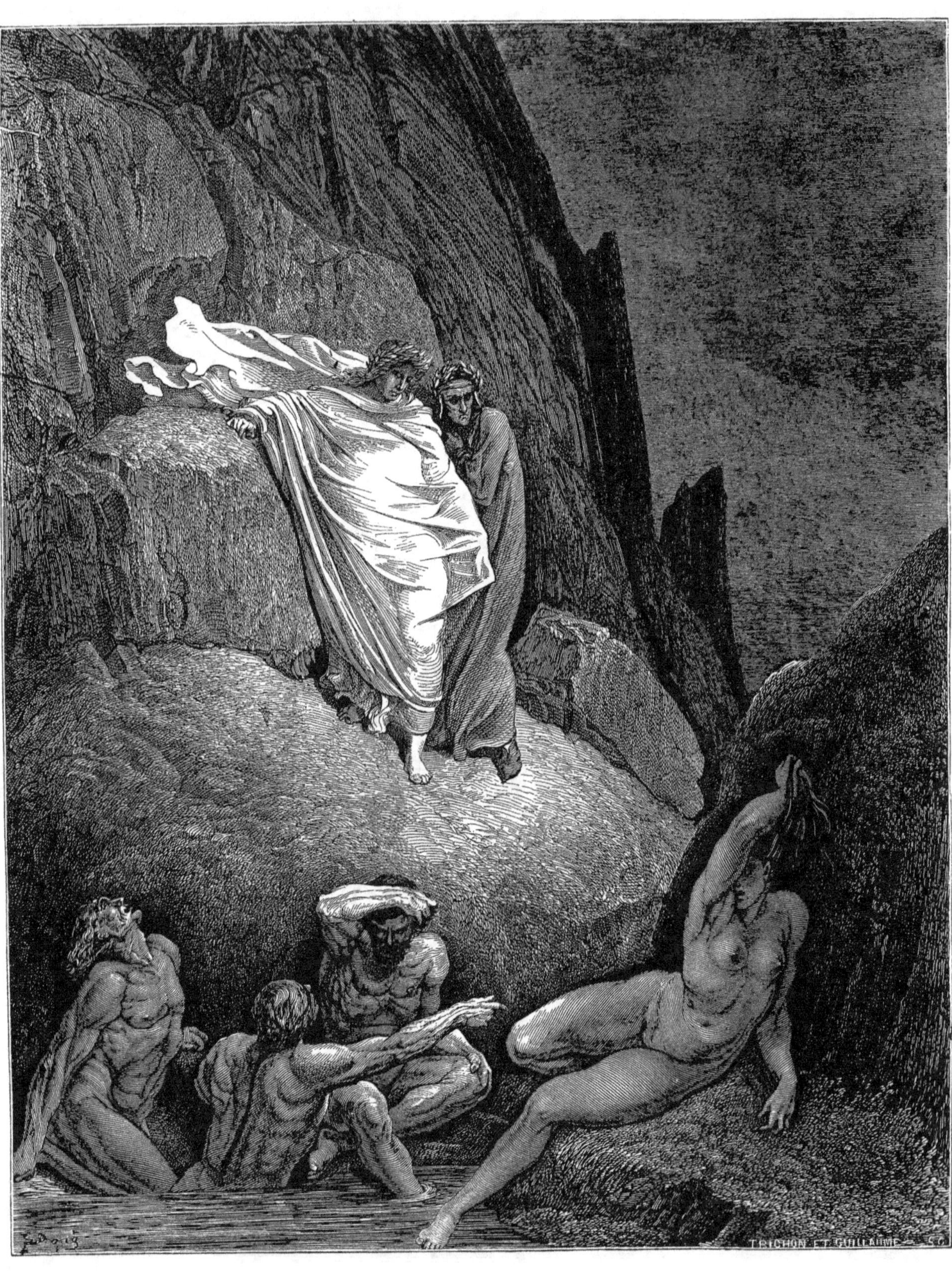

49. Thais the harlot is it, who replied. Unto her
paramour, when he said, 'Have I Great gratitude from
thee?'—'Nay, marvelous.', Gustave Doré, 1861

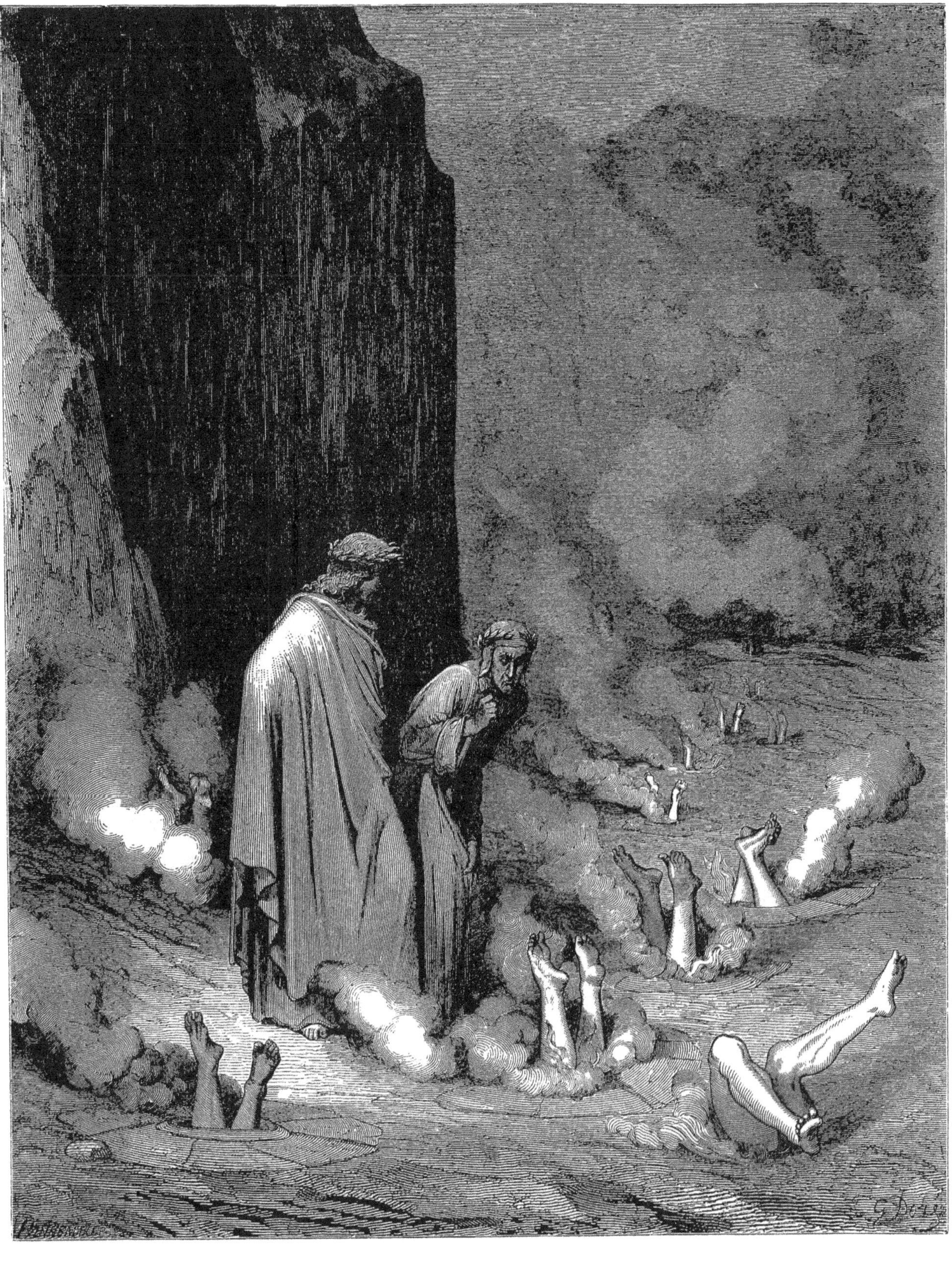

50. 'O doleful soul, implanted like a stake,' To
say began I, 'if thou canst, speak out', Gustave
Doré, 1861

51

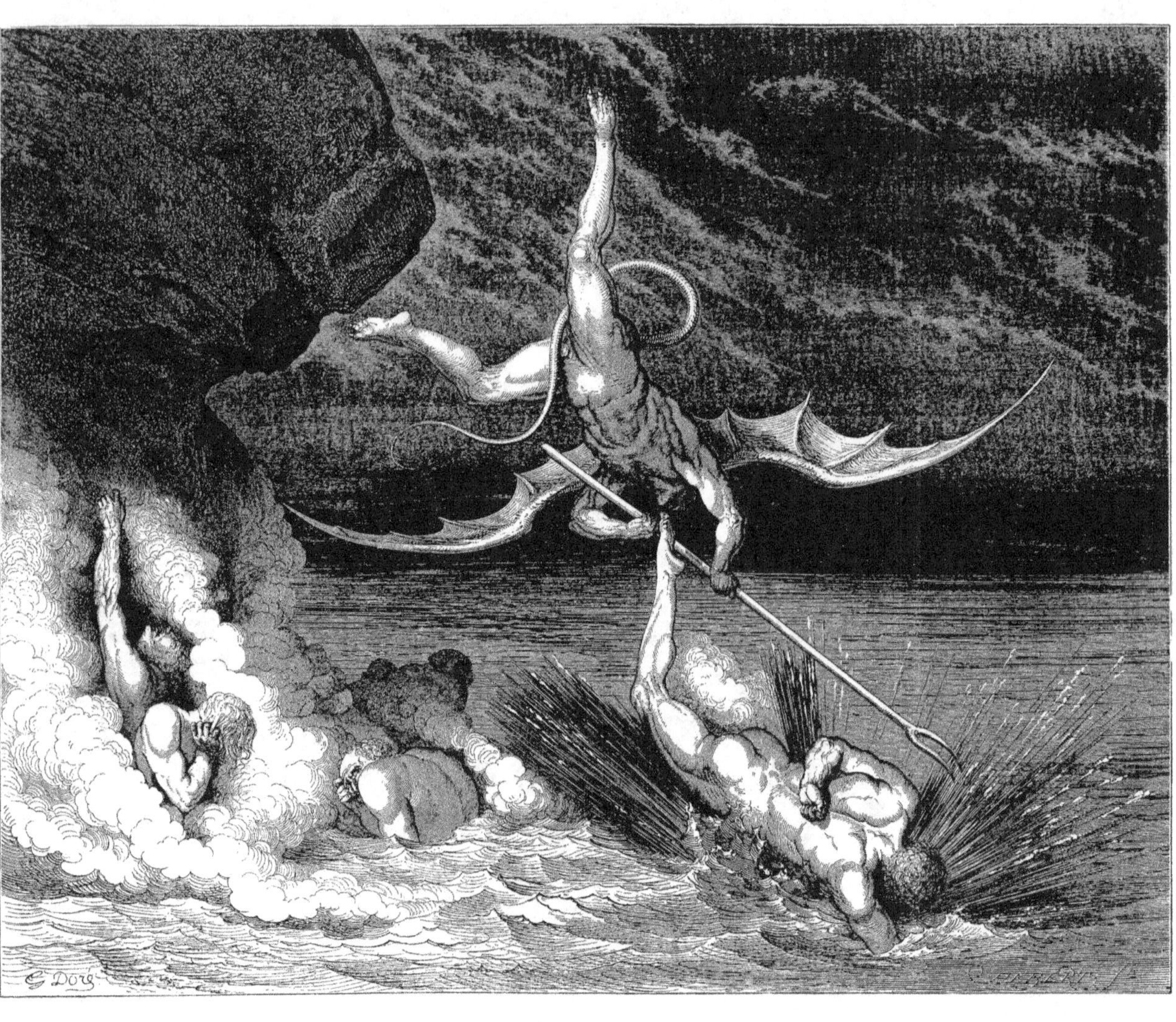

*51. Therefore he moved, and cried- "Thou art
o'ertaken.", Gustave Doré, 1861*

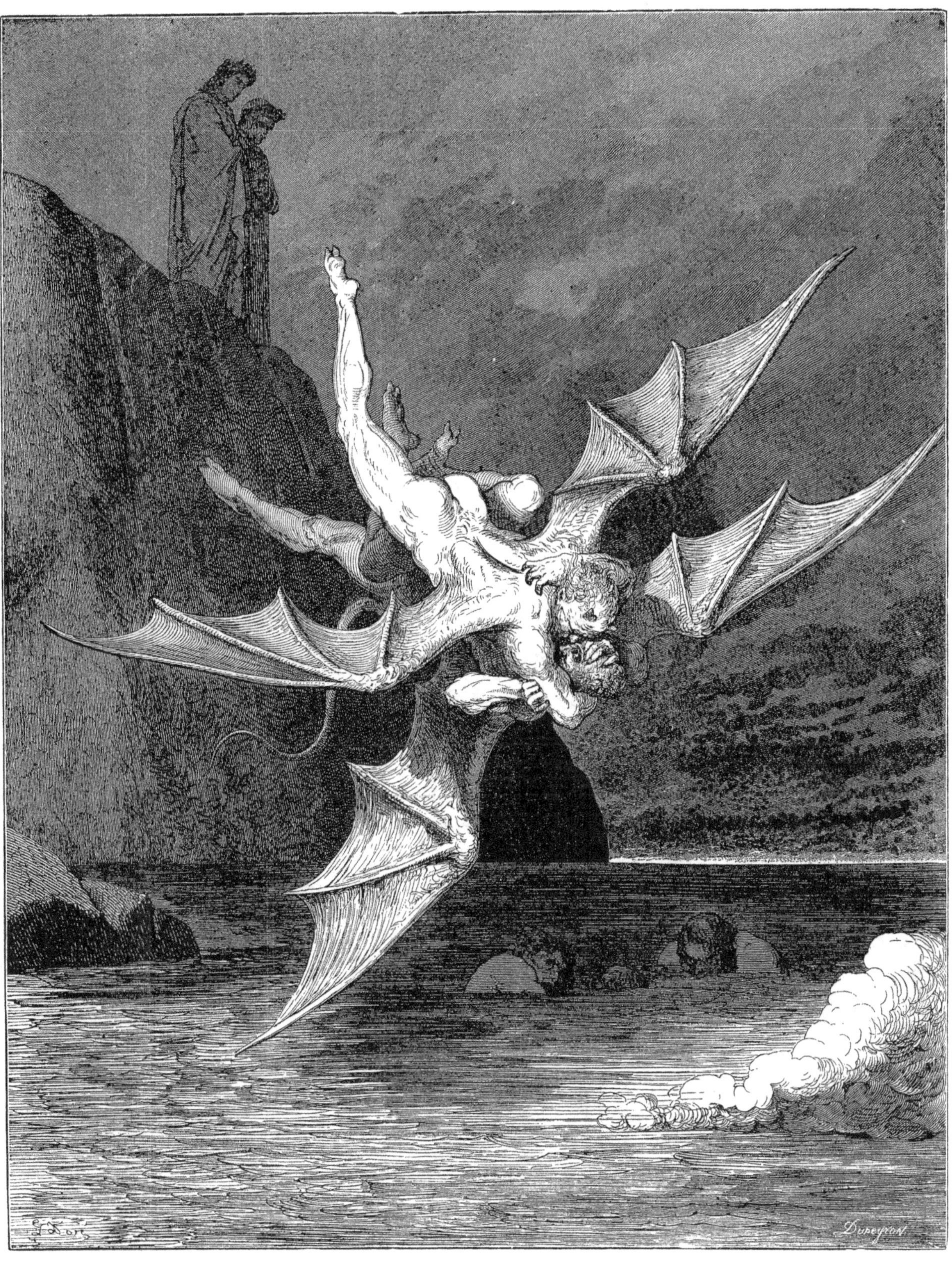

GUSTAVE DORÉ

52 But sooth the other was a doughty sparhawk. To clapperclaw him well, and both of them. Fell in the middle of the boiling pond. Gustave Doré, 1861

GUSTAVE DORÉ

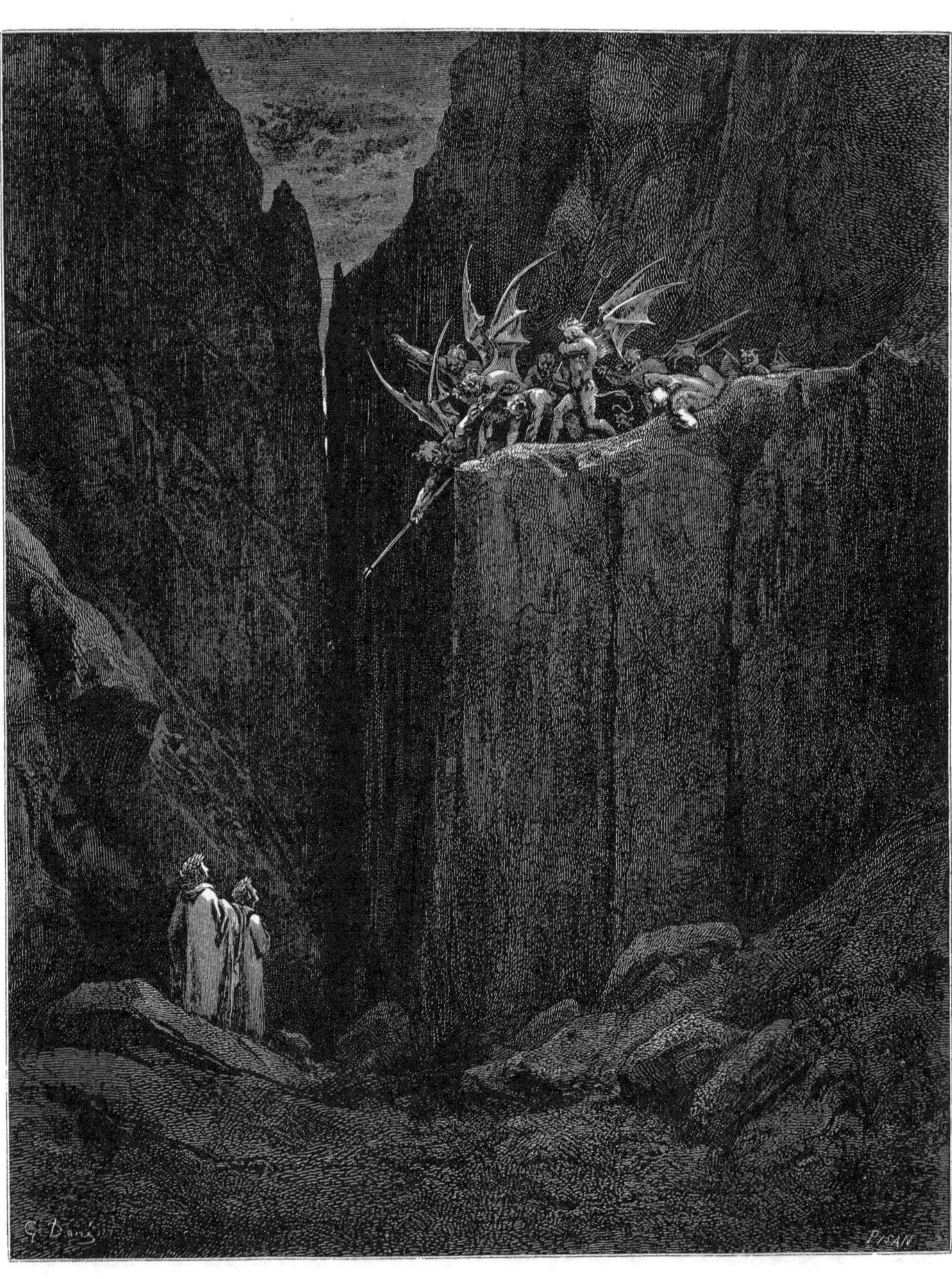

53. Hardly the bed of the ravine below. His feet
had reached, ere they had reached the hill.
Right over us. Gustave Doré. 1861

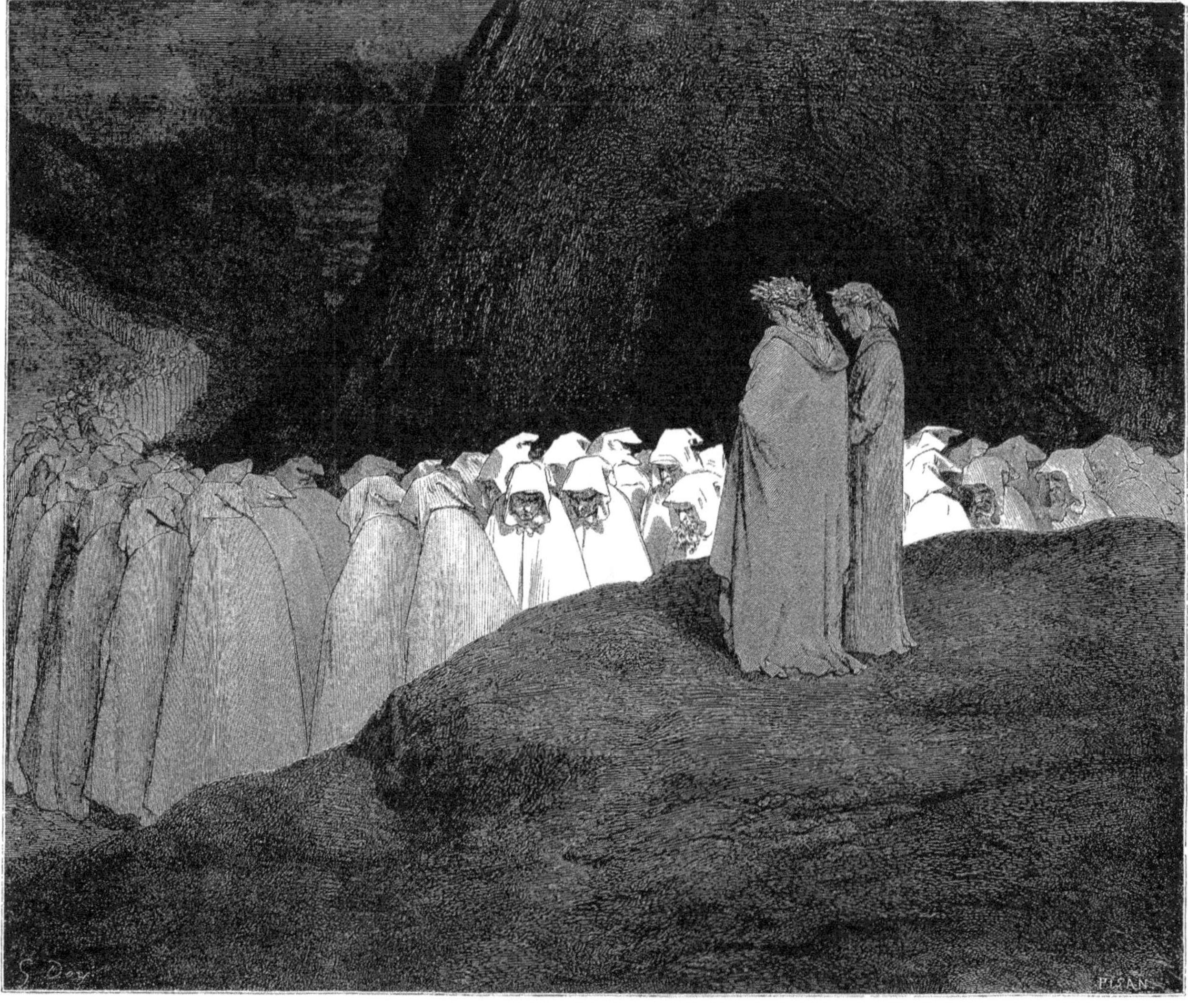

GUSTAVE DORÉ

55

GUSTAVE DORÉ

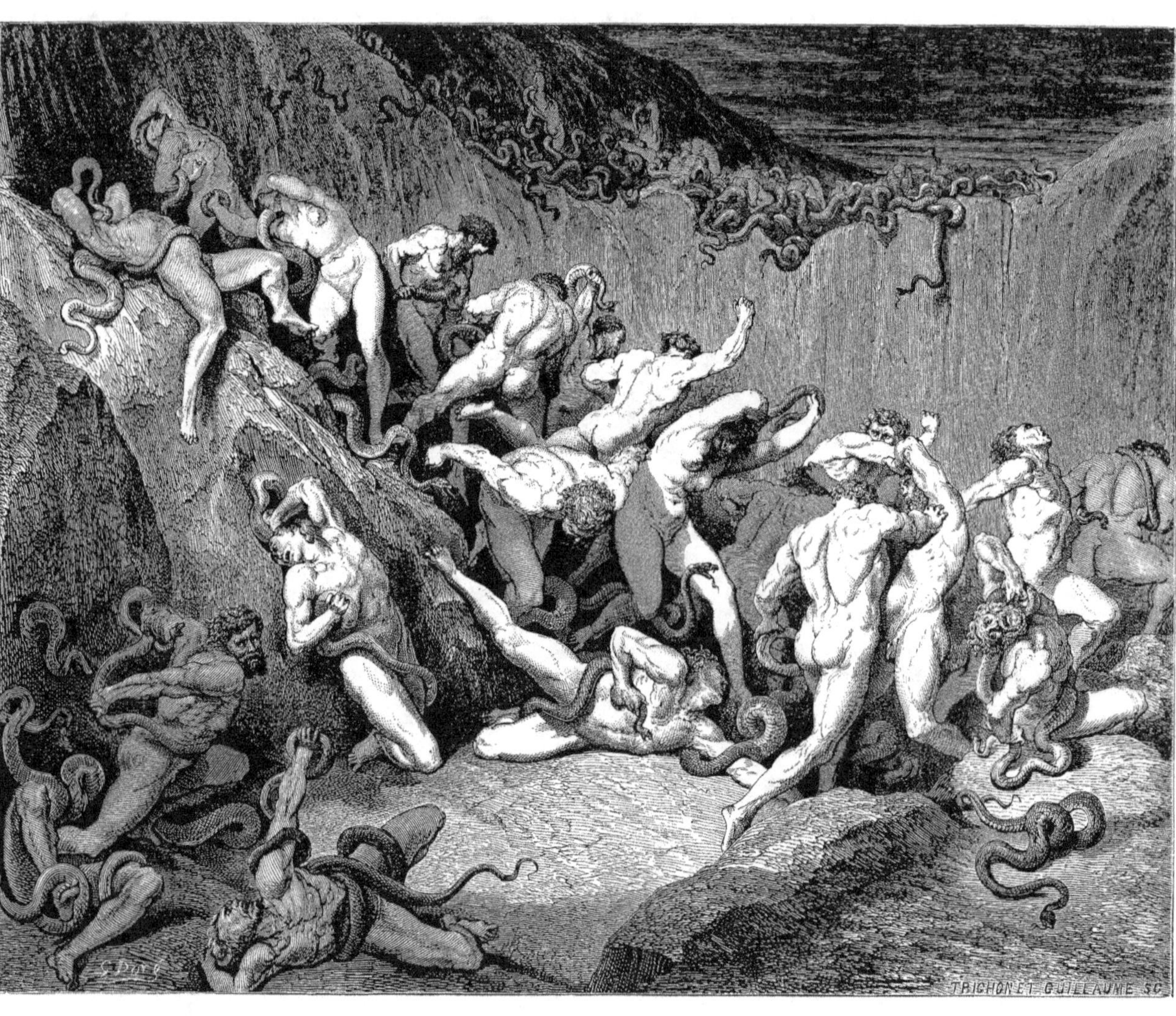

55. Among this cruel and most dismal throng,
People were running naked and affrighted.
Gustave Doré, 1861

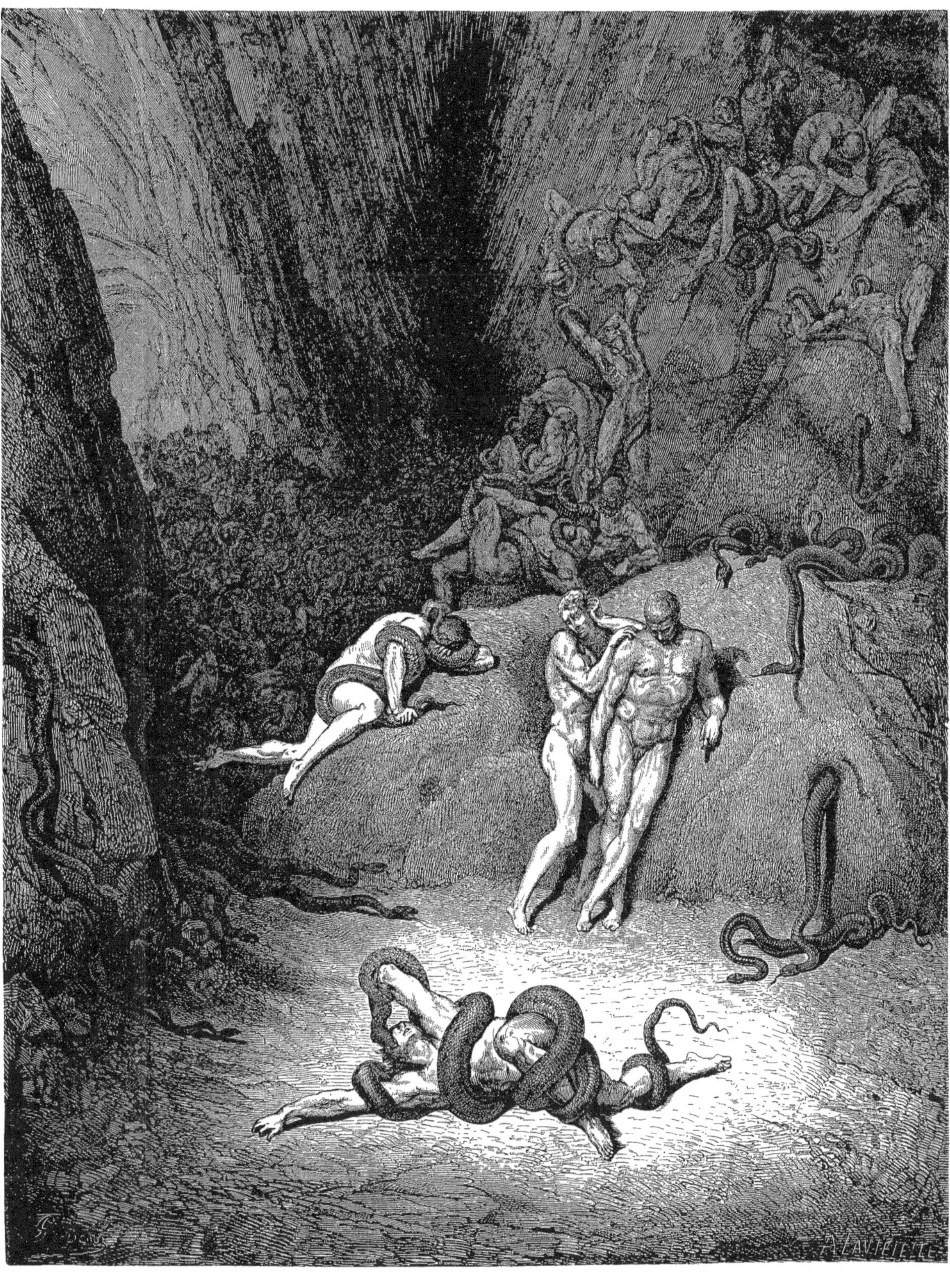

56. O me, Agnello, how thou changest! Behold,
thou now art neither two nor one, Gustave
Doré, 1861

57

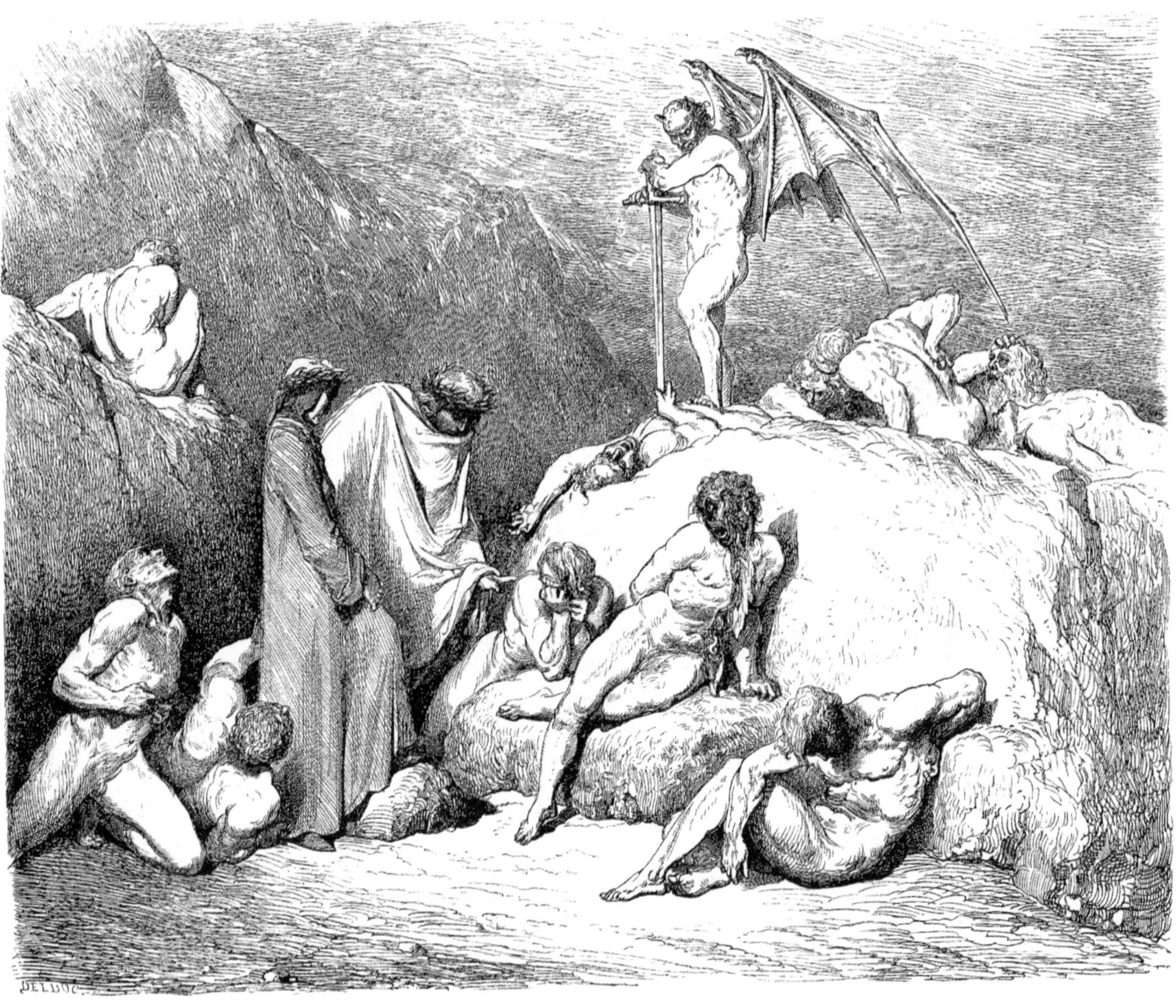

57. Call to rememberance Pier da Medicina.
Gustave Doré. 1861

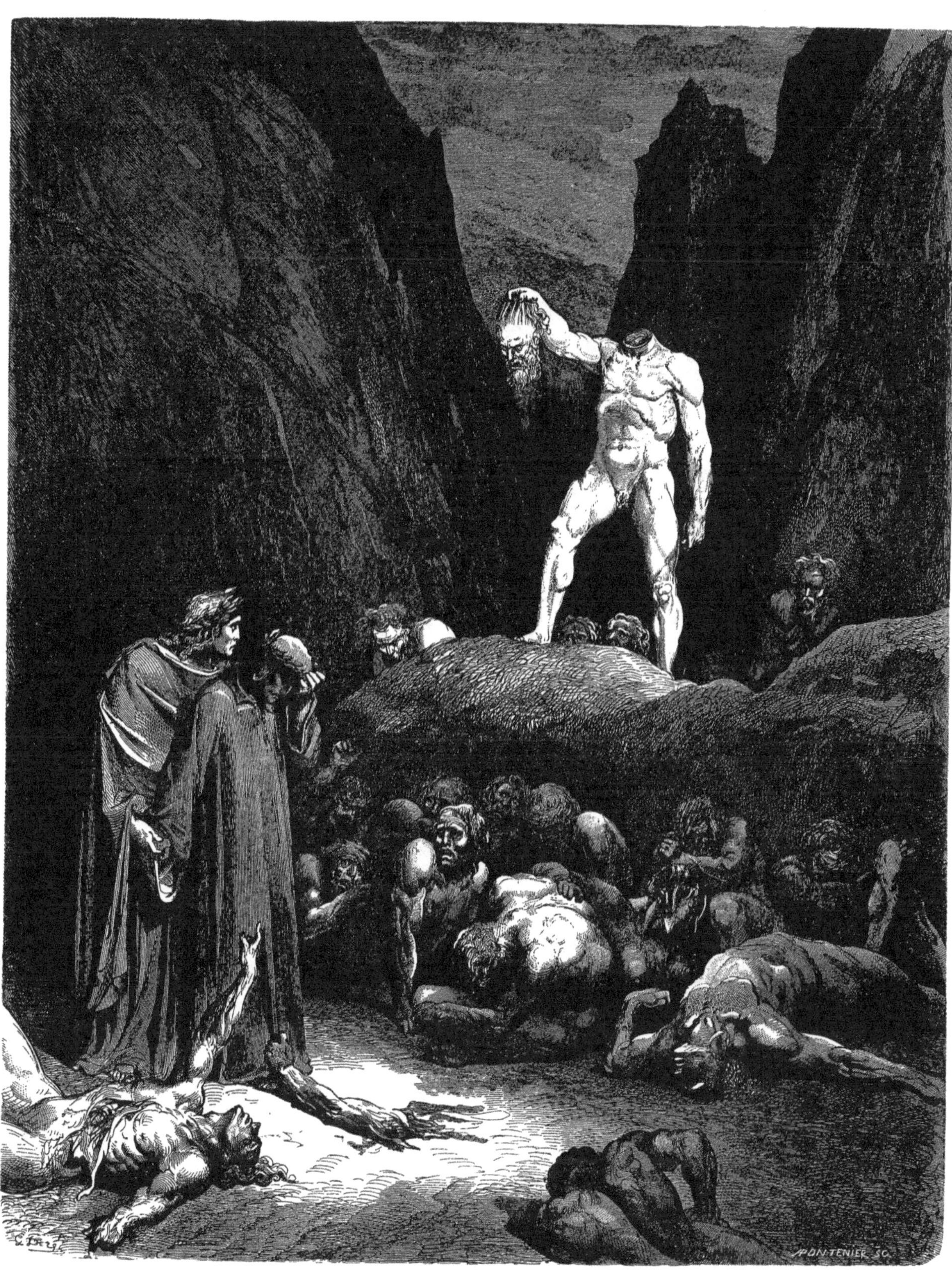

GUSTAVE DORÉ

58. Here stood I like the friar, that doth shrive. A wretch for murder doom'd. Gustave Doré, 1861

59

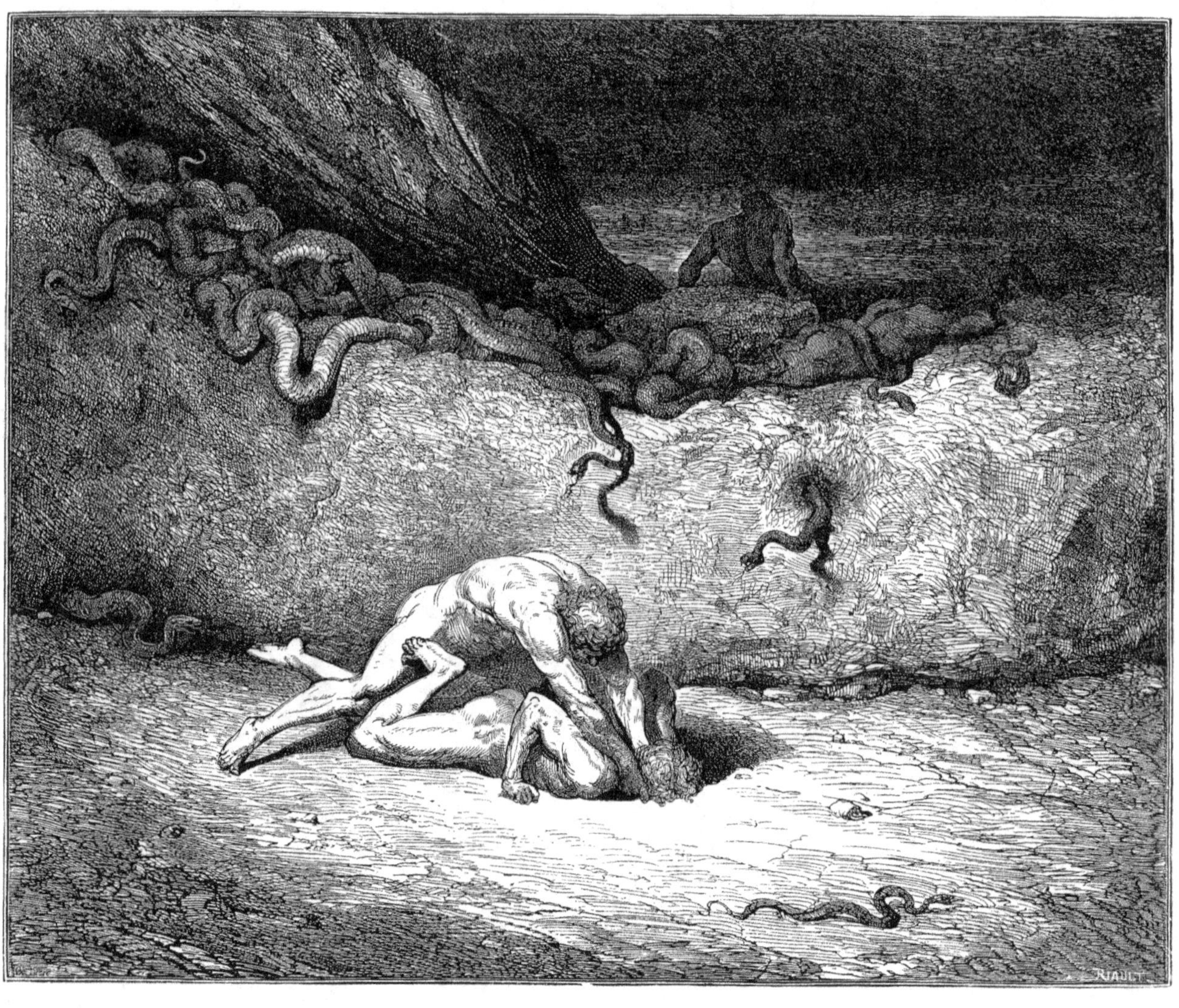

59. 'That mad sprite is Gianni Schicchi, And
raving goes thus harrying other people'.
Gustave Doré, 1861

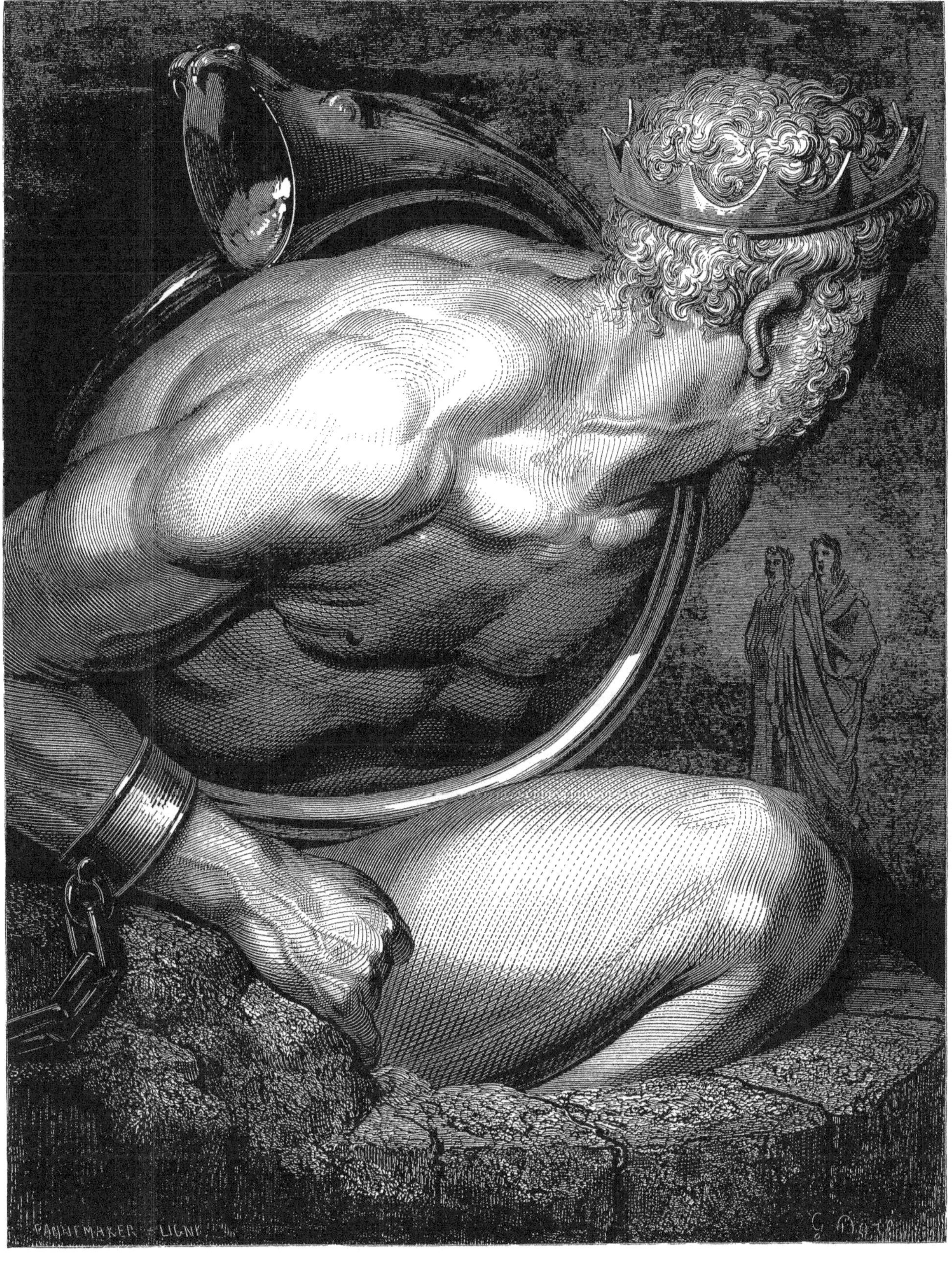

60. Oh, senseless spirit! let thy horn for thee
Interpret, Gustave Doré, 1861

61

GUSTAVE DORÉ

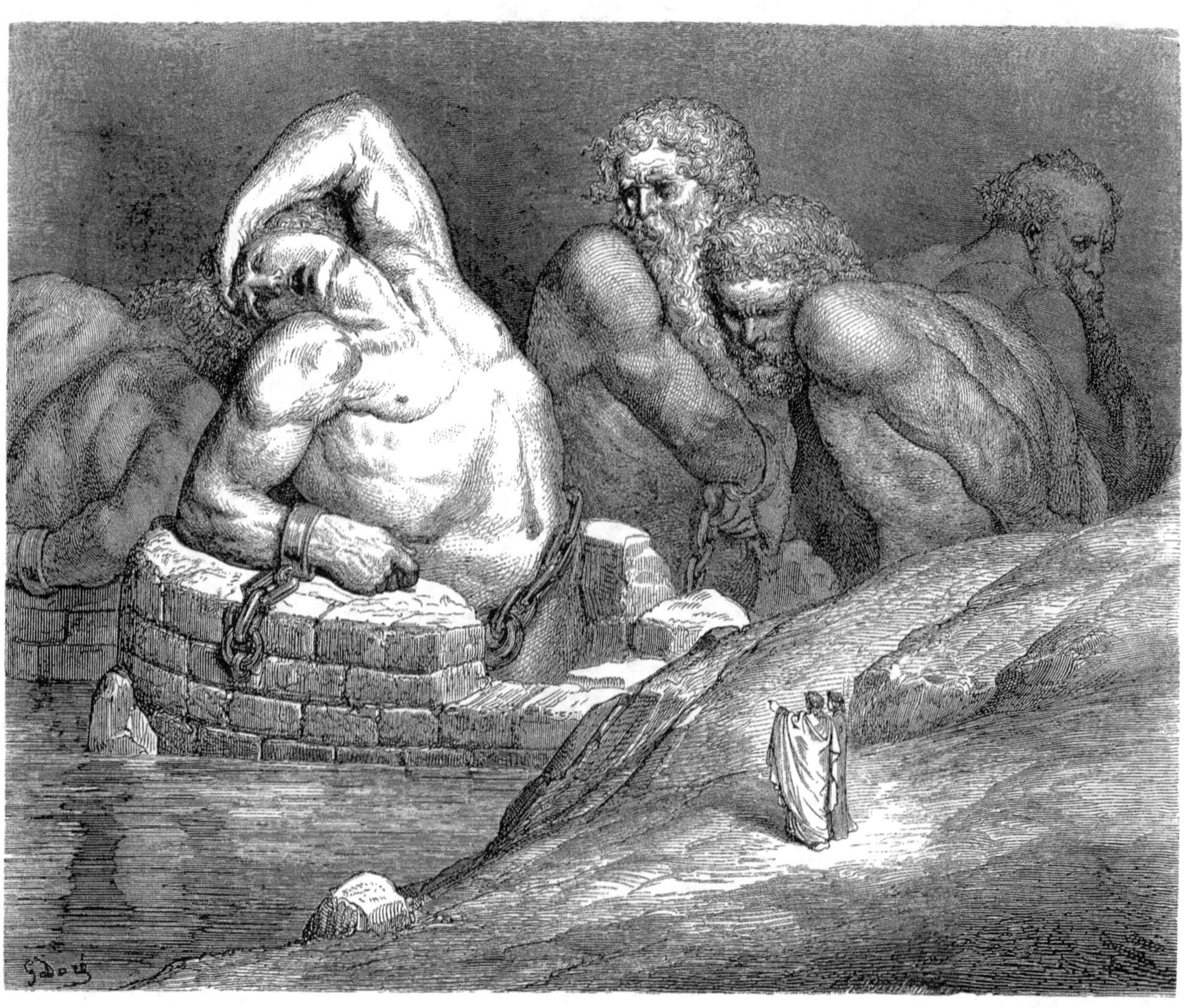

61. 'This proud one wished to make experiment.
Of his own power against the Supreme Jove'.
Gustave Doré, 1861

62

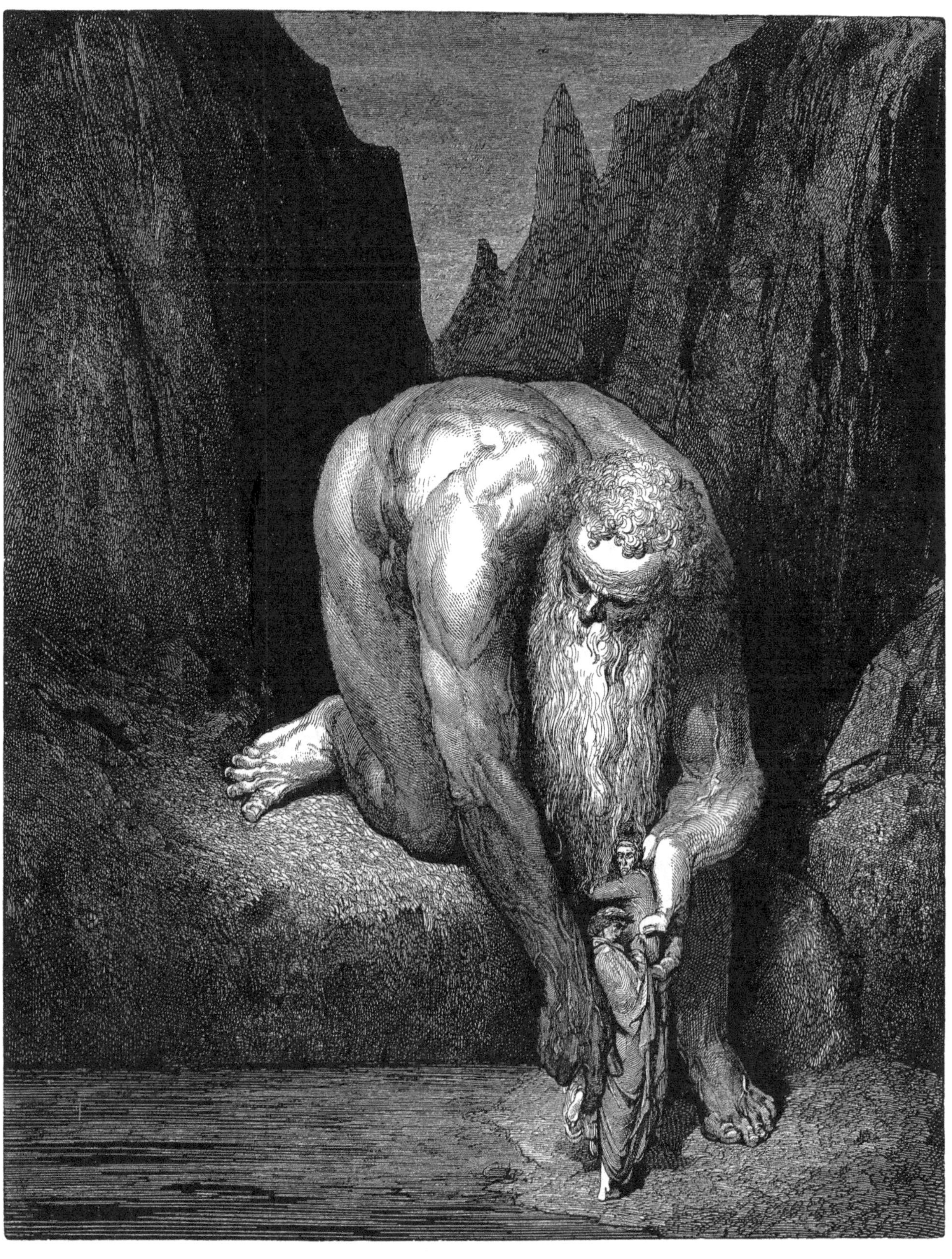

GUSTAVE DORÉ

62. Yet in the abyss, that Lucifer with Judas low
ingulfs, lightly he placed us. Gustave Doré, 1861

63

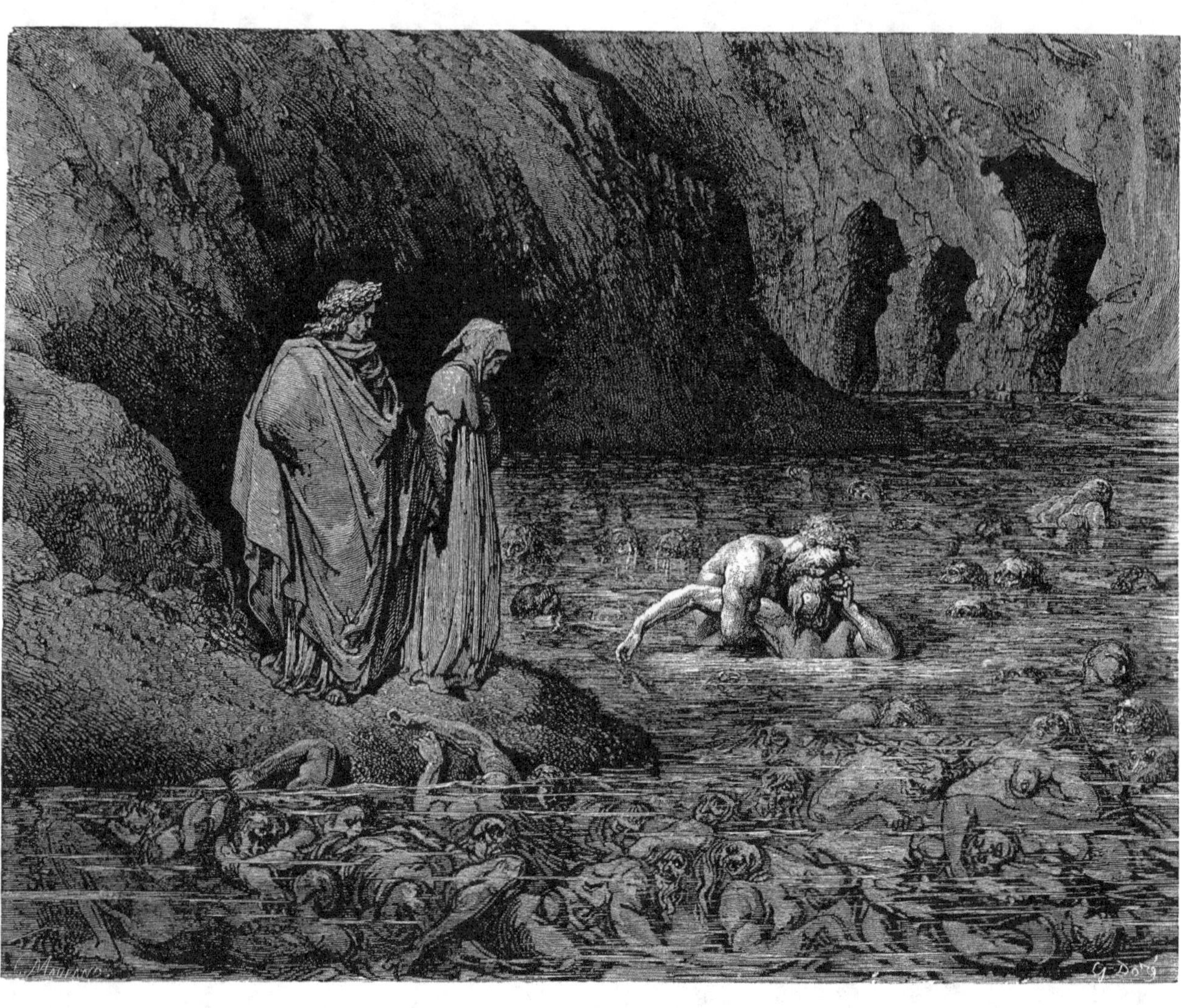

63. The uppermost on the other set his teeth.
Gustave Doré, 1861

64

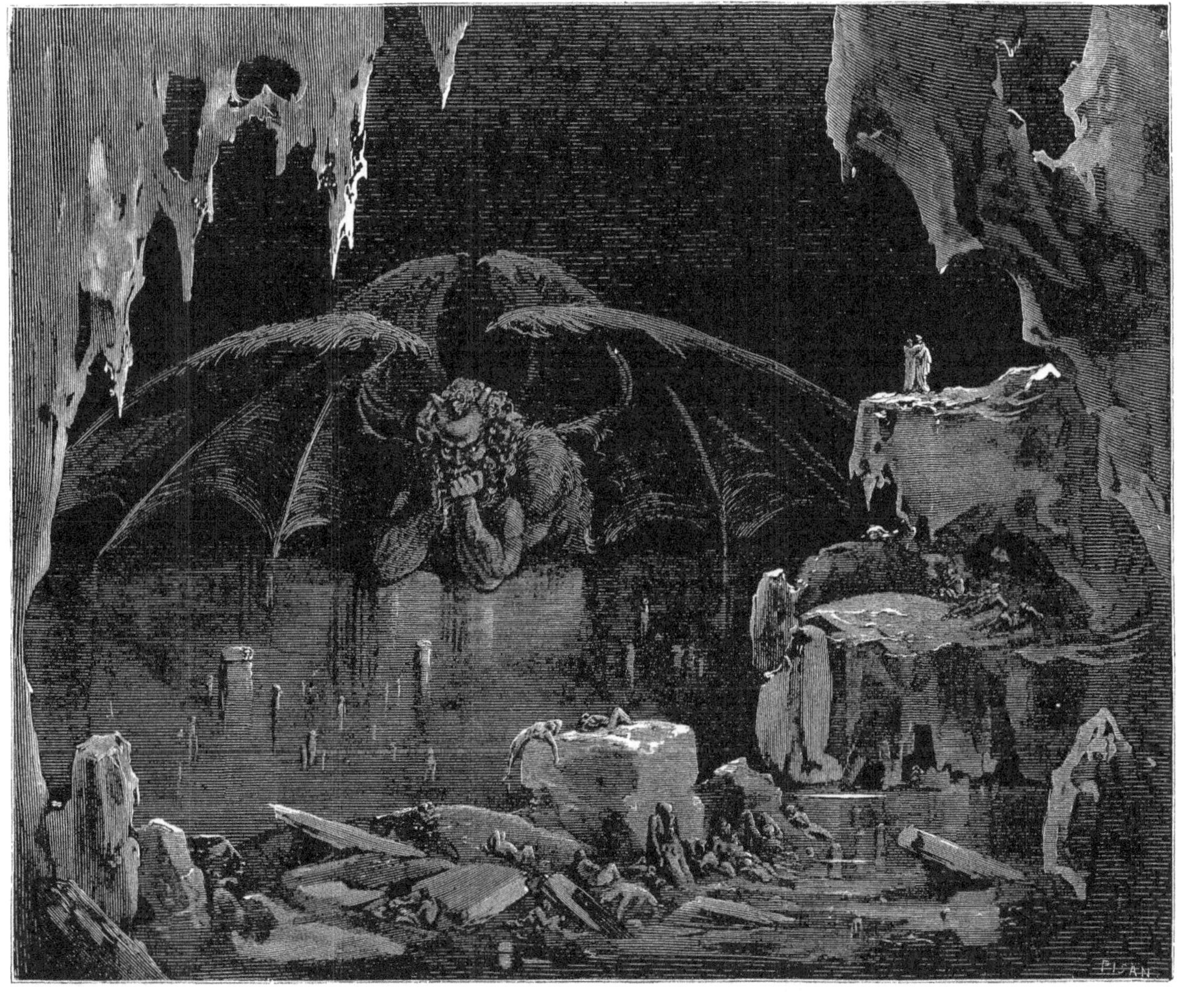

GUSTAVE DORÉ

64 'Behold Dis, and behold the place, Where
thou with fortitude must arm thyself'. Gustave
Doré, 1861

03

PURGATORY

In *Purgatory*, the second part of *The Divine Comedy*, Dante ascends Mount Purgatory, a place for souls who must atone for their sins before entering Heaven. The mountain has seven terraces, each representing one of the seven deadly sins: pride, envy, wrath, sloth, avarice, gluttony, and lust. Souls on each terrace undergo specific punishments designed to cleanse them of their sinful inclinations, with their suffering gradually diminishing as they ascend toward Paradise. On this part of his journey, Dante encounters souls striving for redemption, experiencing penance as a spiritual healing process. Unlike the eternal damnation in Hell, Purgatory offers hope for salvation, and as Dante moves upward, the atmosphere becomes increasingly peaceful.

Throughout *The Divine Comedy* Dante encounters the character of Beatrice, who represents Dante's idealised love. It is a common belief that Beatrice's character is based on a real person called Beatrice Portinari, an acquaintance Dante greatly admired. In the poem, she illustrates divine grace and theology, guiding Dante to spiritual enlightenment in Heaven.

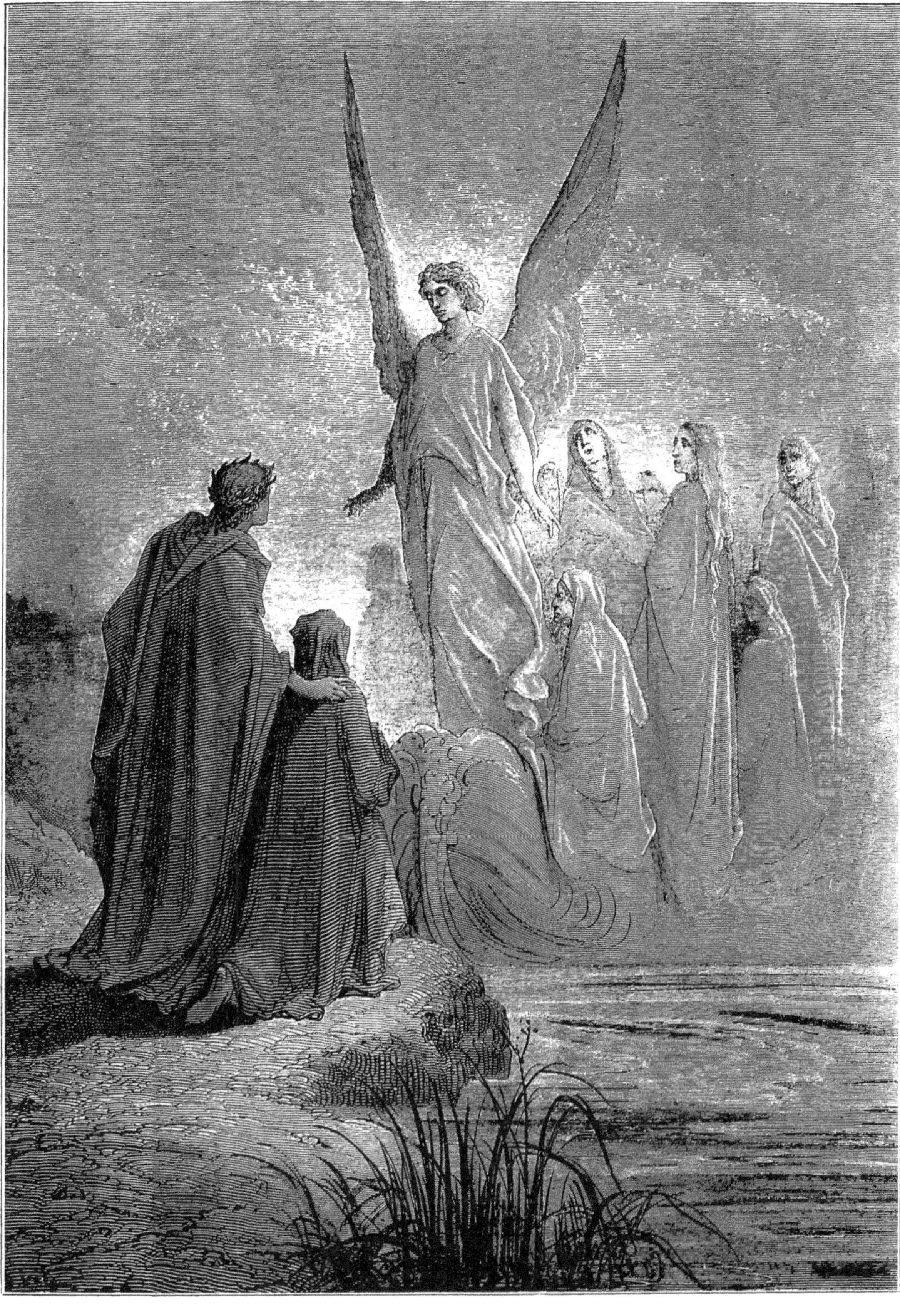

GUSTAVE DORÉ

65. Beatitude seemed written in his face.
Gustave Doré. 1868

66

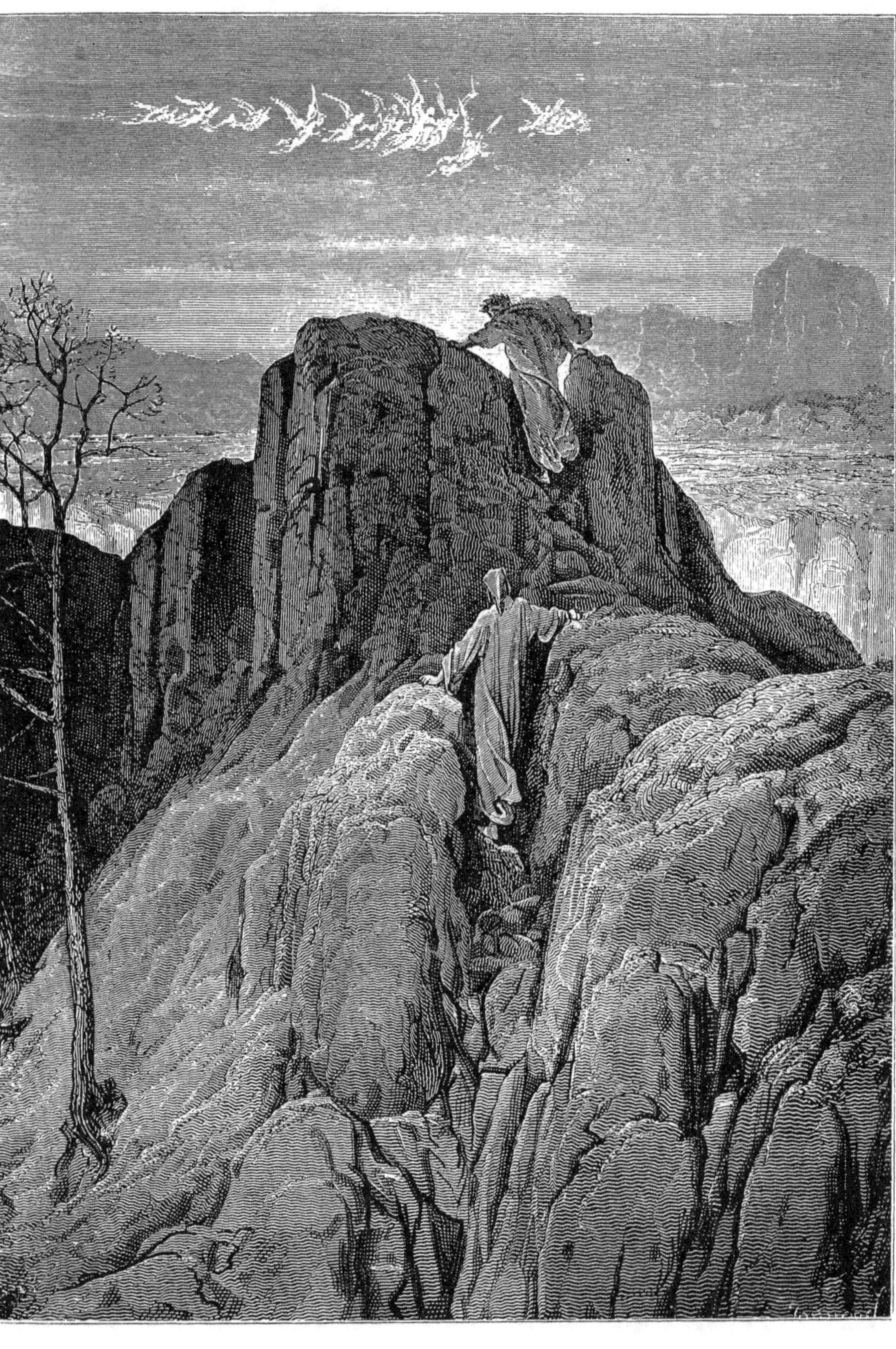

66. We mounted upward through the rifted
rock, And on each side the border pressed
upon us. Gustave Doré, 1868

67

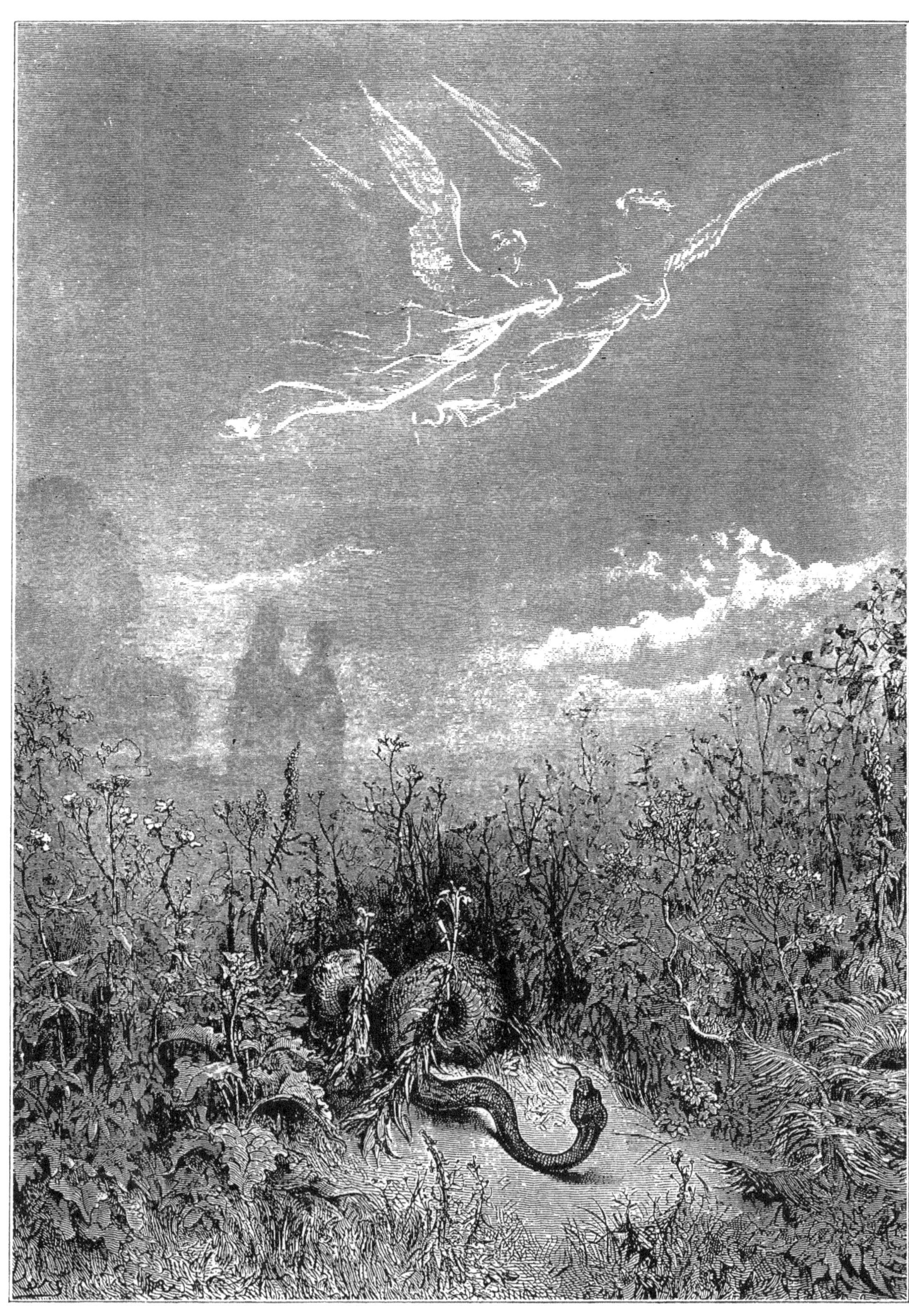

GUSTAVE DORÉ

67 Hearing the air cleft by their verdant wings, The serpent fled, and round the Angels wheeled. Gustave Doré, 1868

68

68. Terrible as the lightning he descended, And
snatched me upward even to the fire, Gustave
Doré, 1868

69

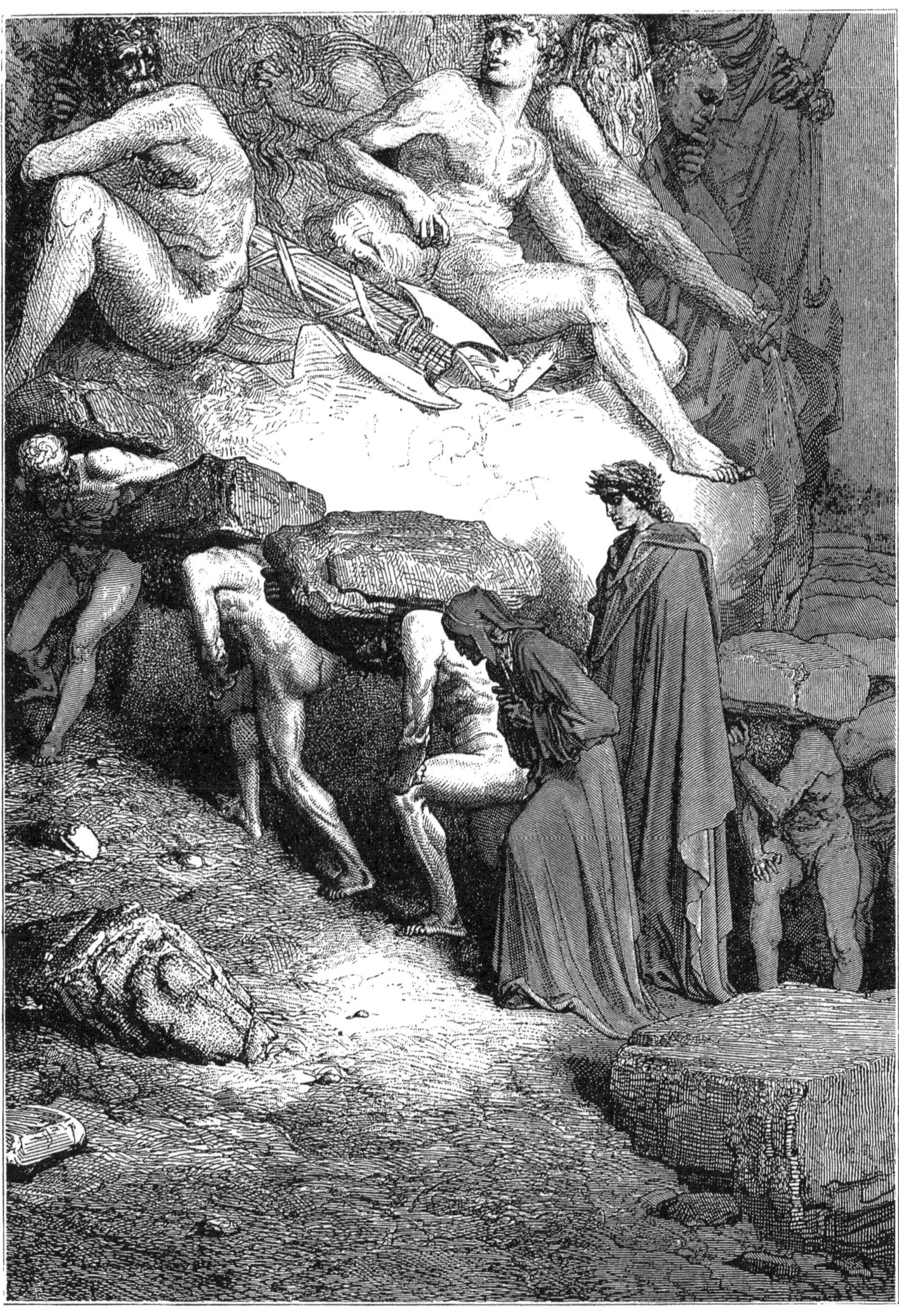

GUSTAVE DORÉ

70

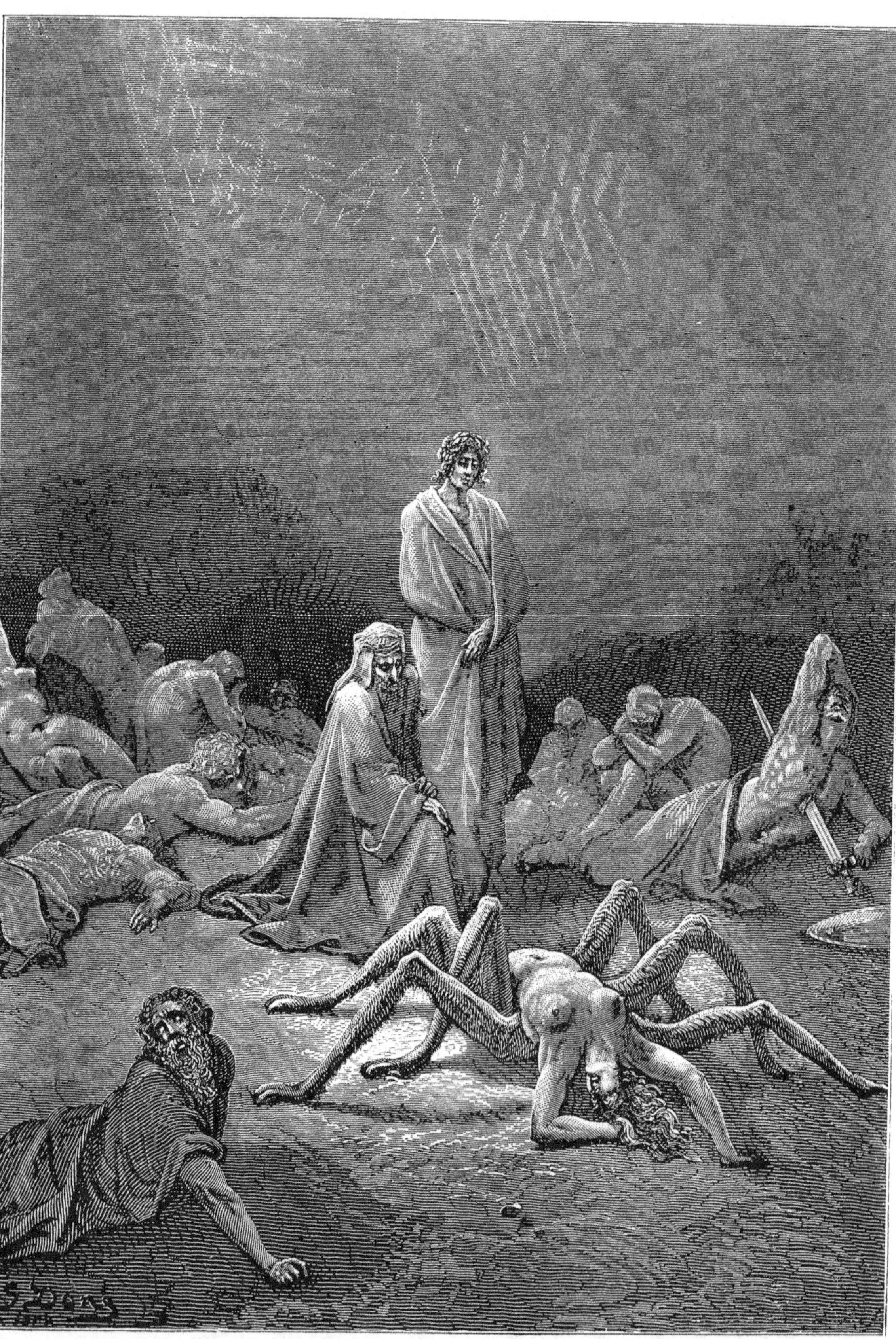

*70. O mad Arachne! so I thee beheld. E'en then
half spider. Gustave Doré, 1868*

71

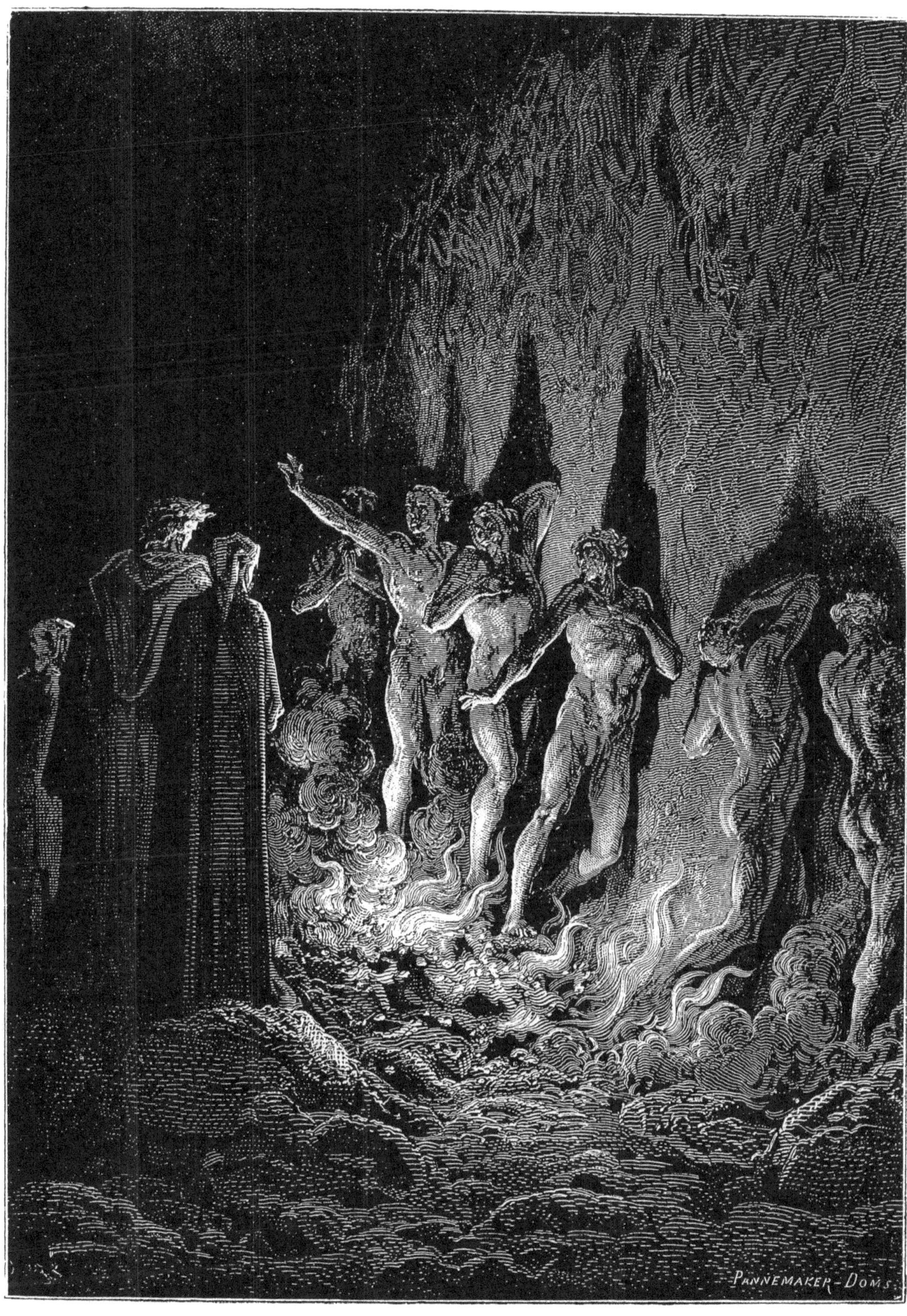

GUSTAVE DORÉ

71. And spirits saw I walking through the flame; Wherefore
I looked, to my own steps and theirs, Apportioning my
sight from time to time, Gustave Doré, 1868

72

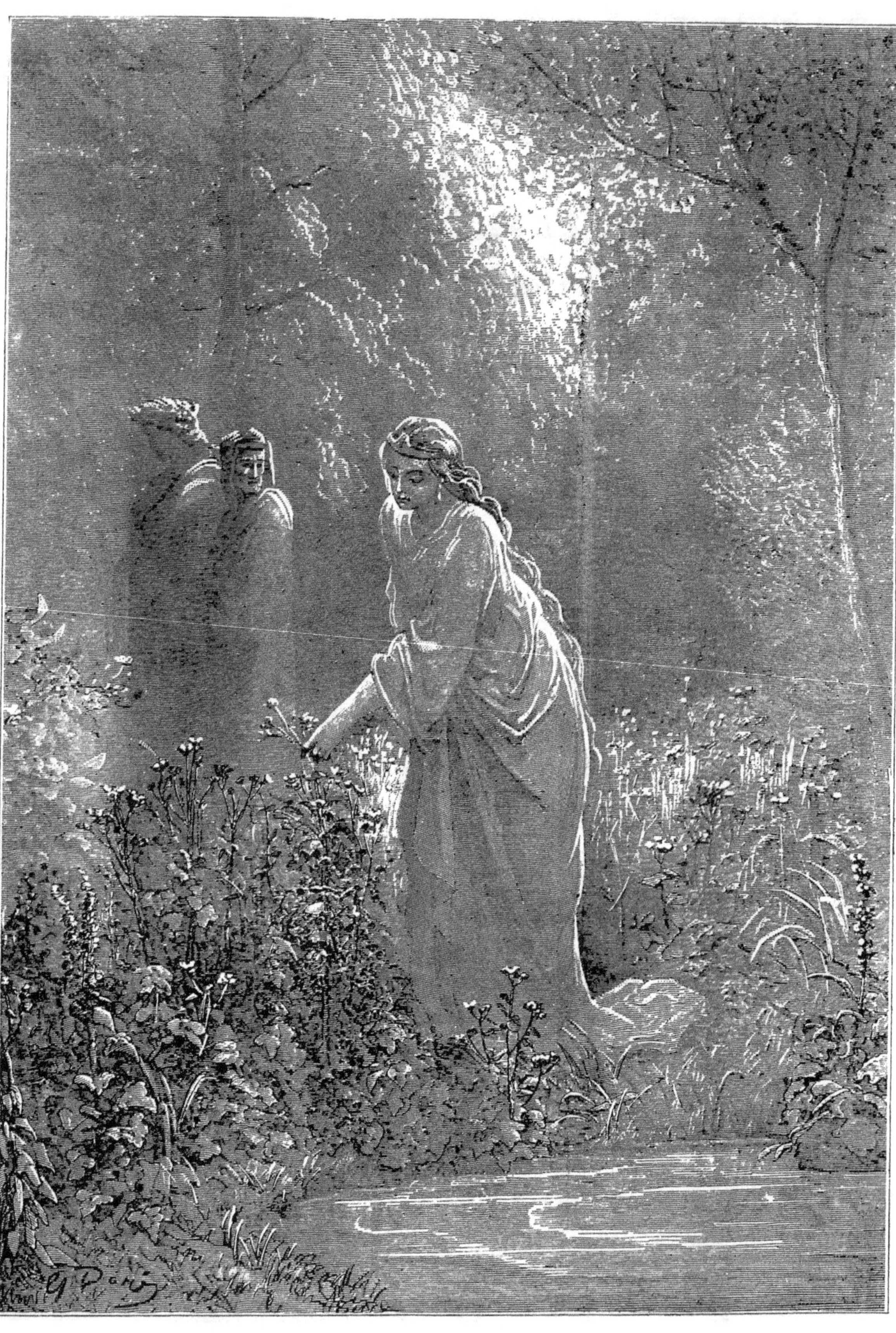

72. Youthful and beautiful in dreams
methought, I sw a lady walking in a meadow.
Gathering flowers. Gustave Doré, 1868

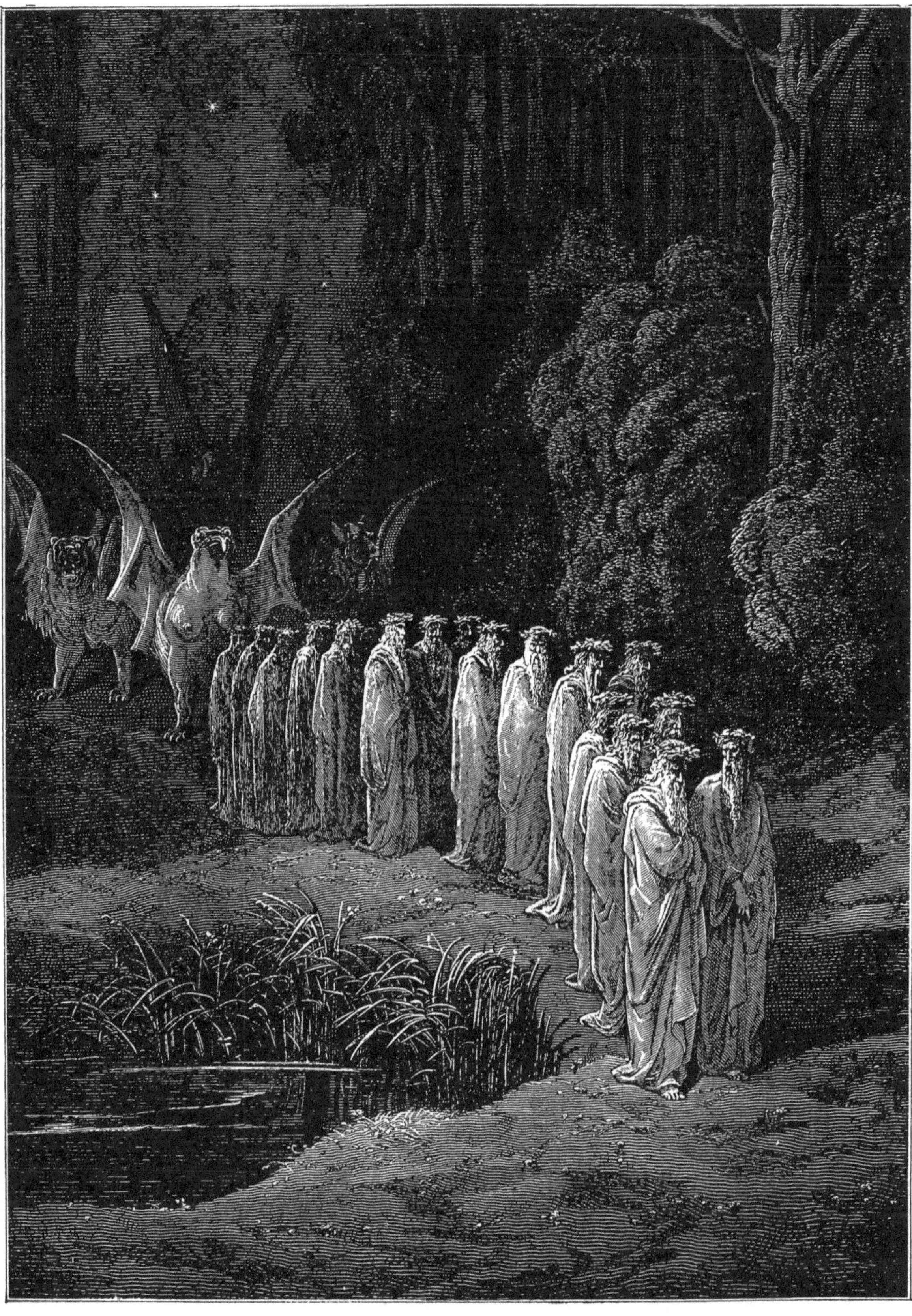

73. The four and twenty Elders, two by two,
Came on incoronate with flower-de-luce.
Gustave Doré, 1868

74

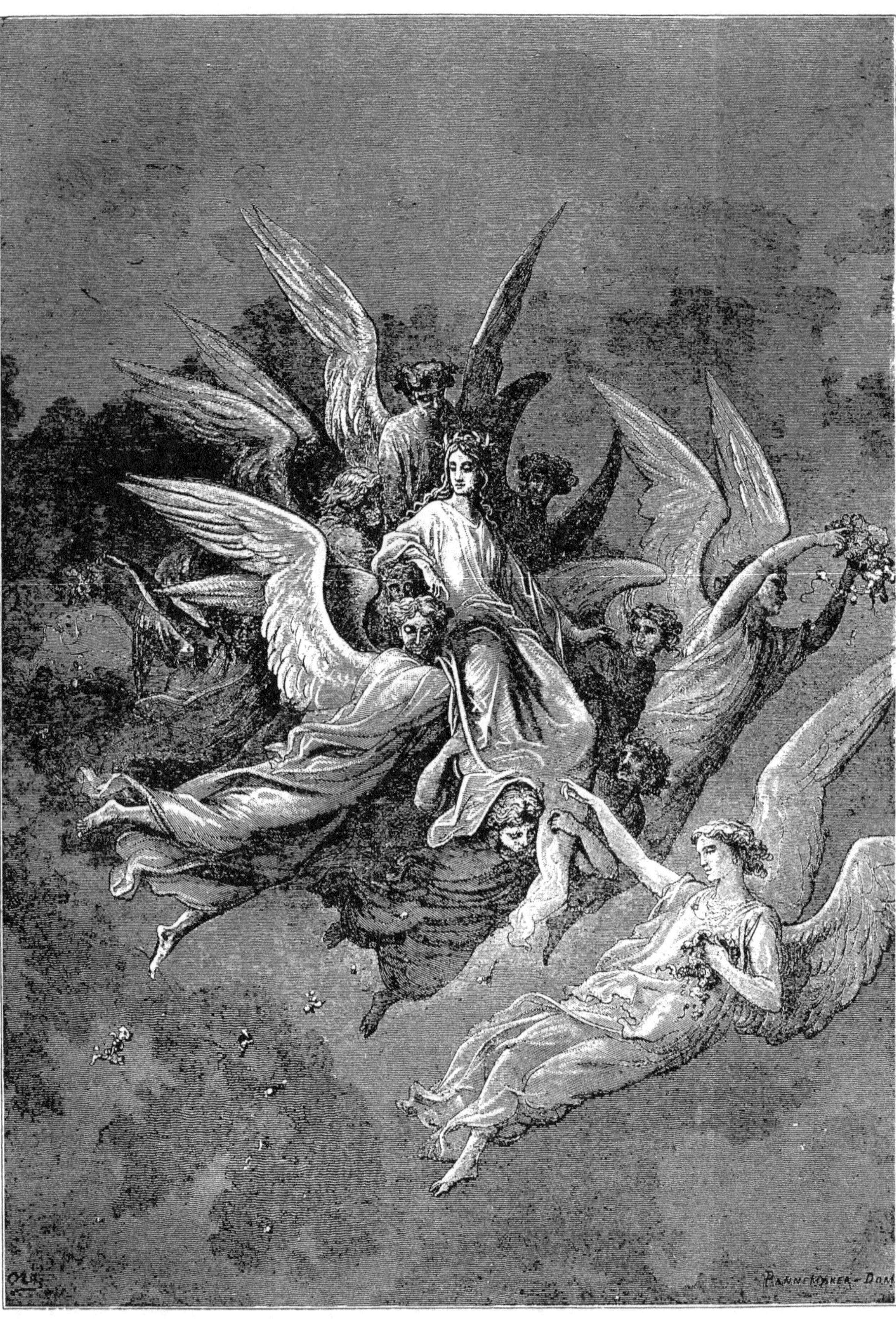

74. *Appeared a lady under a green mantle,*
Vested in colour of the living flame. Gustave
Doré, 1868

75

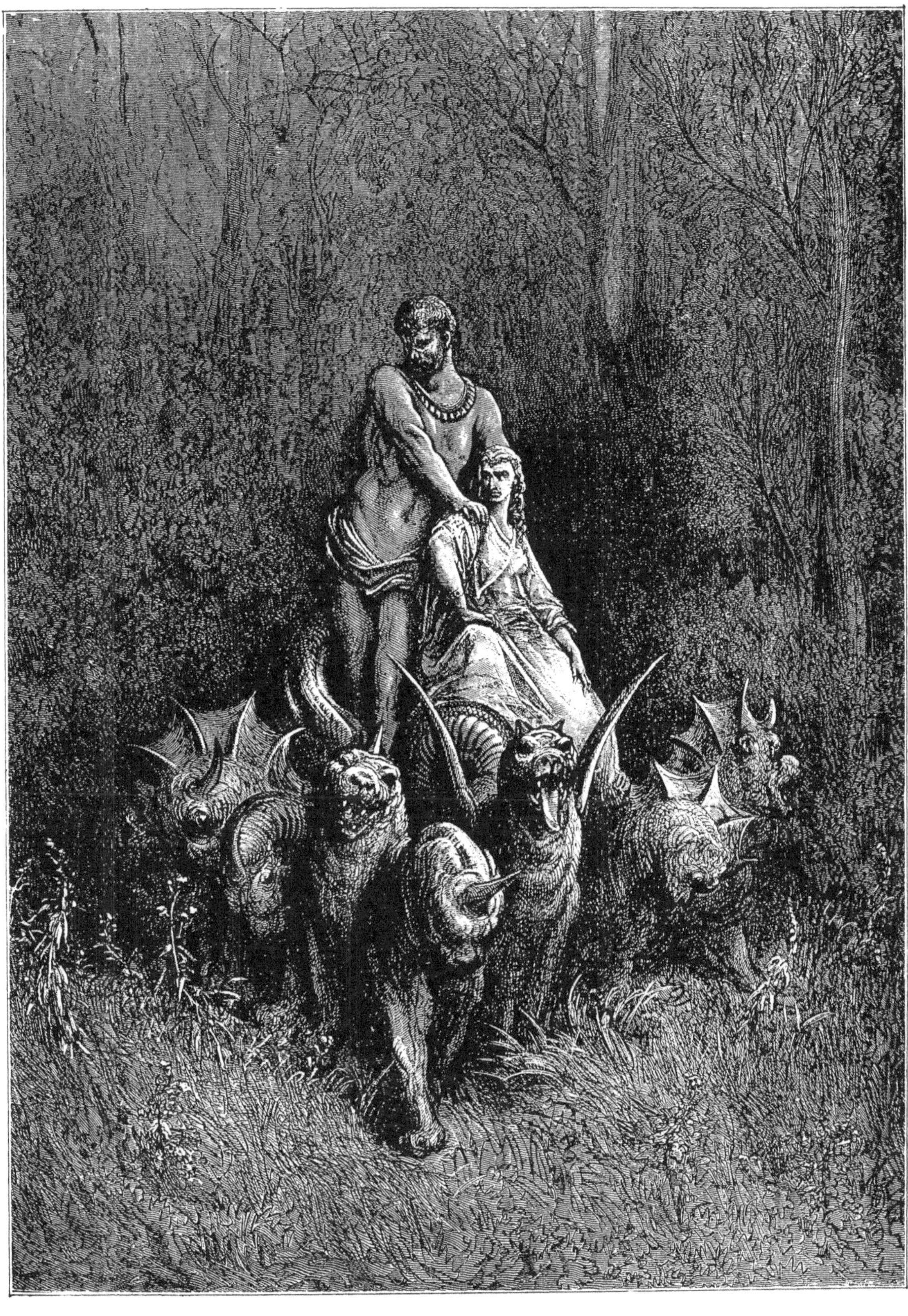

GUSTAVE DORÉ

75. Upright beside her I beheld a giant. And
ever and anon they kissed each other. Gustave
Doré, 1868

04

PARADISE

In *Paradise*, the third part of Dante's *The Divine Comedy*, Dante journeys through the nine celestial spheres of Heaven, guided by Beatrice. Based on the medieval Ptolemaic model of the universe, these spheres represent different virtues and levels of spiritual perfection, each inhabited by souls who exemplified these virtues in life. The journey begins in the sphere of the Moon, representing inconstancy, where souls who failed to keep their vows are found. As Dante ascends, he passes through spheres like Mercury (ambition), Venus (love), the Sun (wisdom), and Mars (fortitude). The higher spheres, including Jupiter (justice), Saturn (temperance), the Fixed Stars (faith, hope, and love), and the Primum Mobile (the angels), lead Dante closer to God. Each sphere becomes more radiant, symbolising increasing divine truth. Beyond the nine spheres is the Empyrean, the realm of pure light, where Dante experiences a direct vision of God and the ultimate union with divine love.

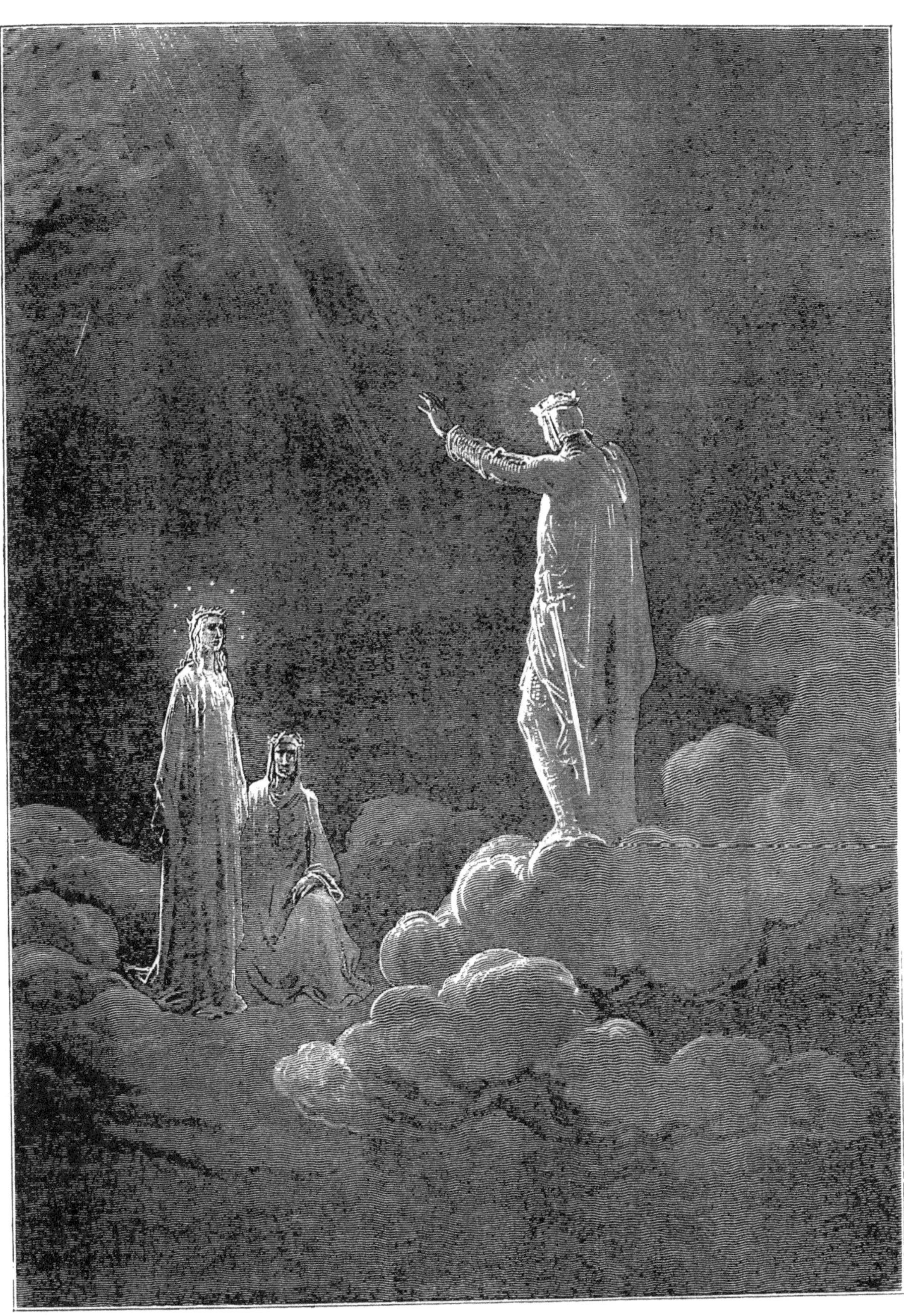

76. *"That left hand margin, which did bathe itself In Rhone, when it is mingled with the Sorgue, Me for its lord awaited in due time". Gustave Doré, 1868*

77

GUSTAVE DORÉ

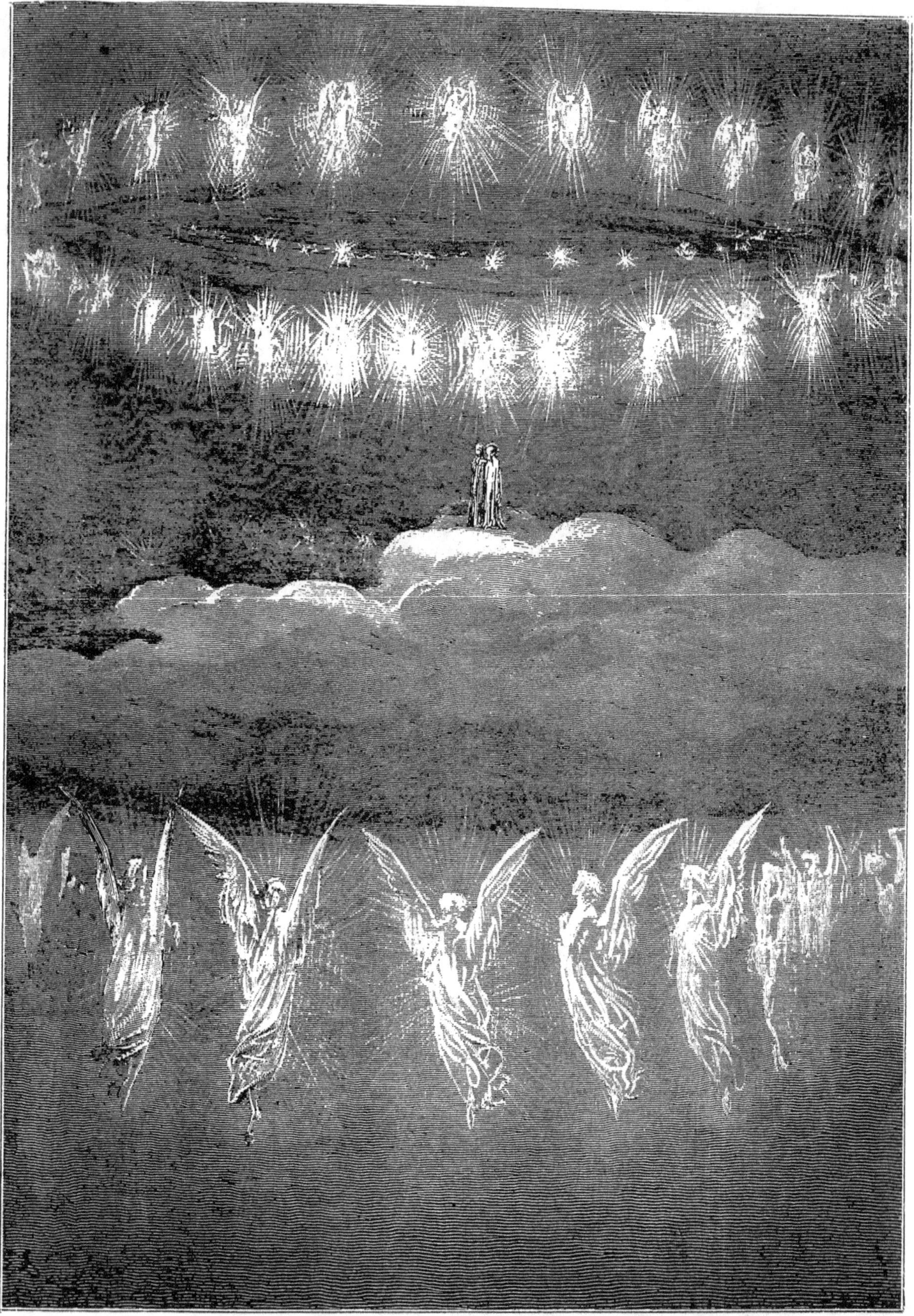

77. In such wise of those sempiternal roses. The garlands twain encompassed us about. And thus the outer to the inner answered. Gustave Doré, 1868

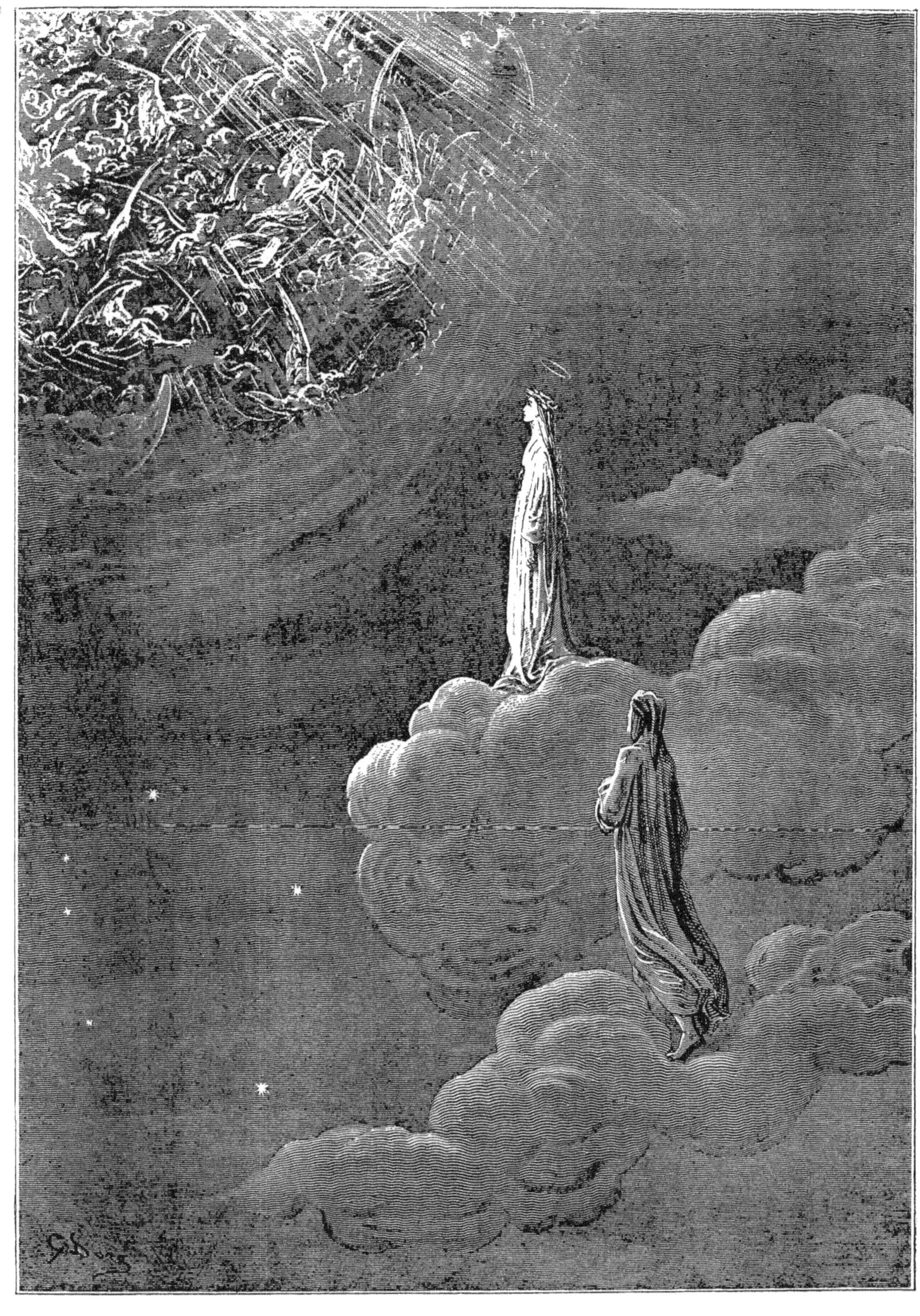

78. Well was I ware that I was more uplifted, By the enkindled smiling of the star, That seemed to me more ruddy than its wont. Gustave Dore, 1868

79

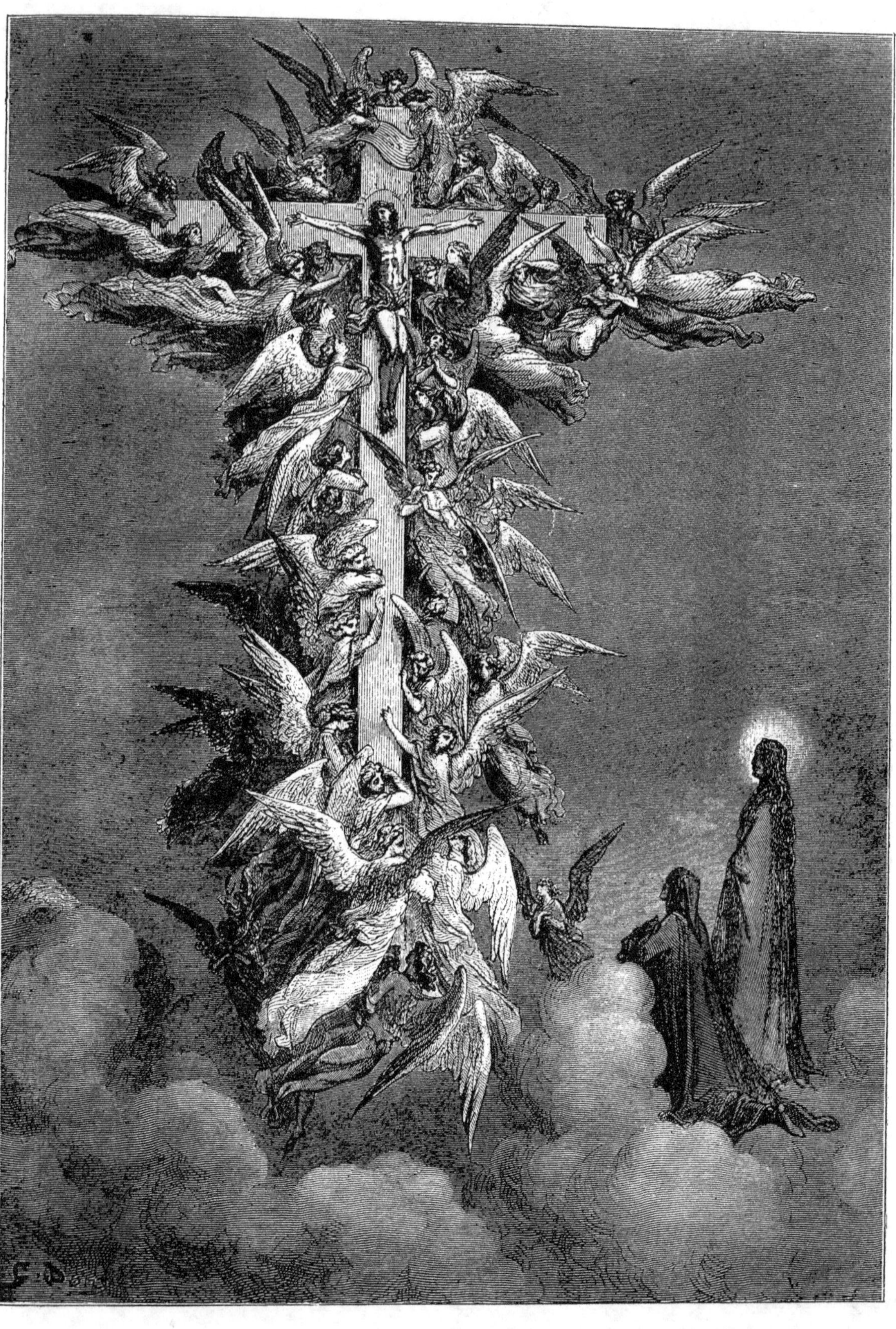

79. Here doth my memory overcome my genius. For
on that cross as levin gleamed forth Christ, So that I
cannot find ensample worthy, Gustave Doré, 1868

80

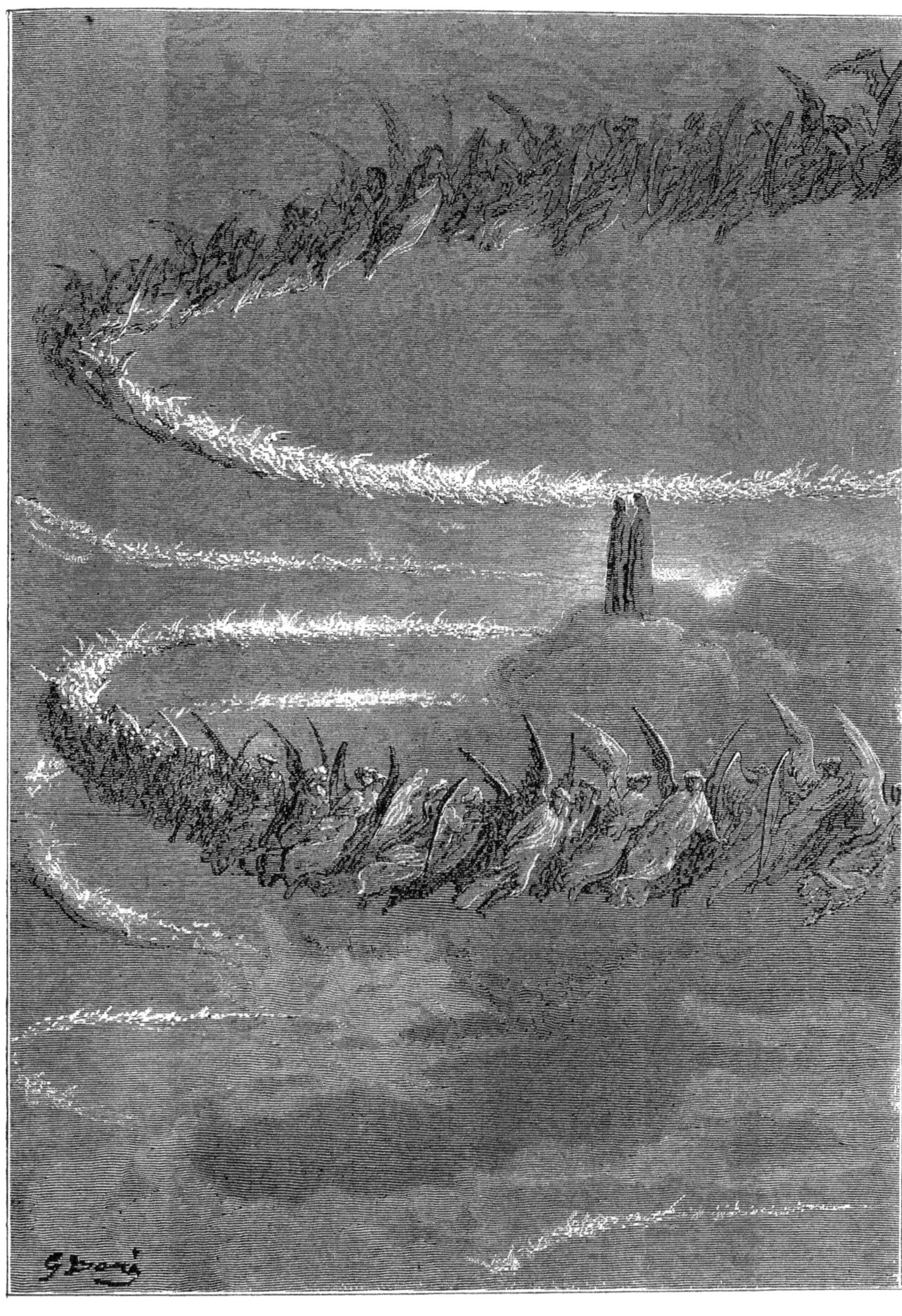

GUSTAVE DORÉ

80. The holy creatures. Sang flying to and fro.
Gustave Doré. 1868

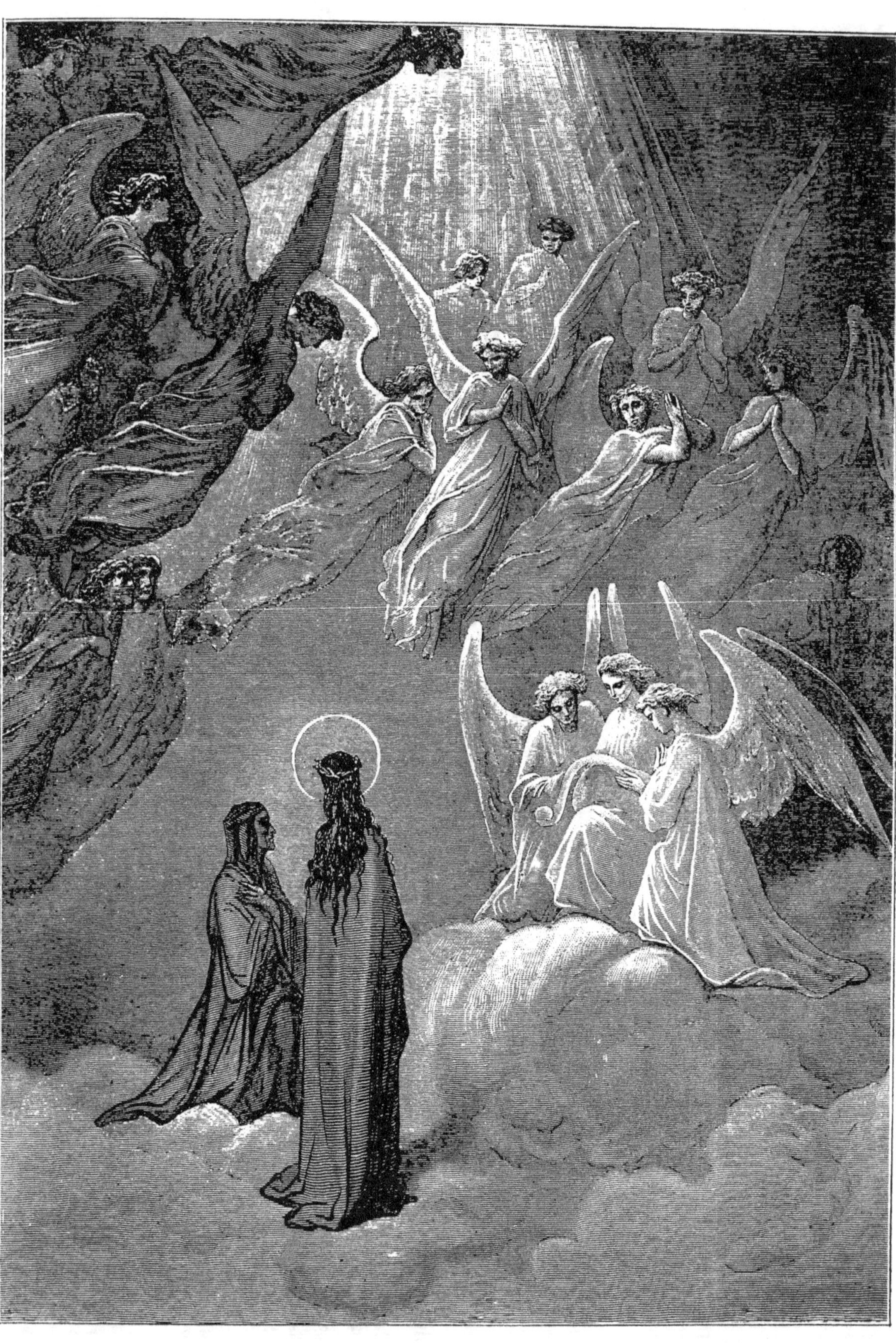

81. Those living luminaries all, By far more luminous, did songs begin, Lapsing and falling from my memory. Gustave Doré, 1868

82

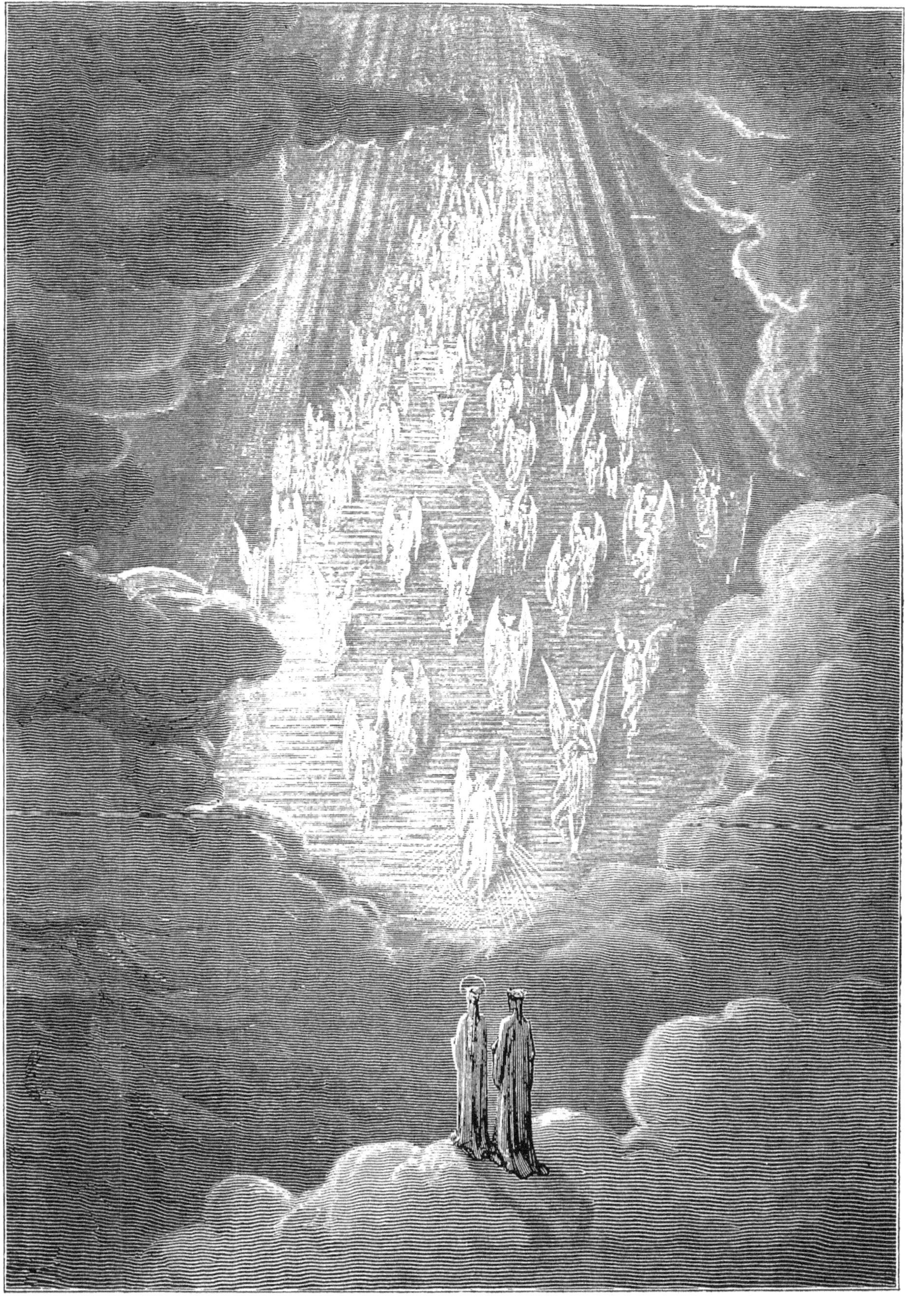

82. A stairway I beheld to such height. Uplifted,
that mine eye pursued it not. Gustave Doré.
1868

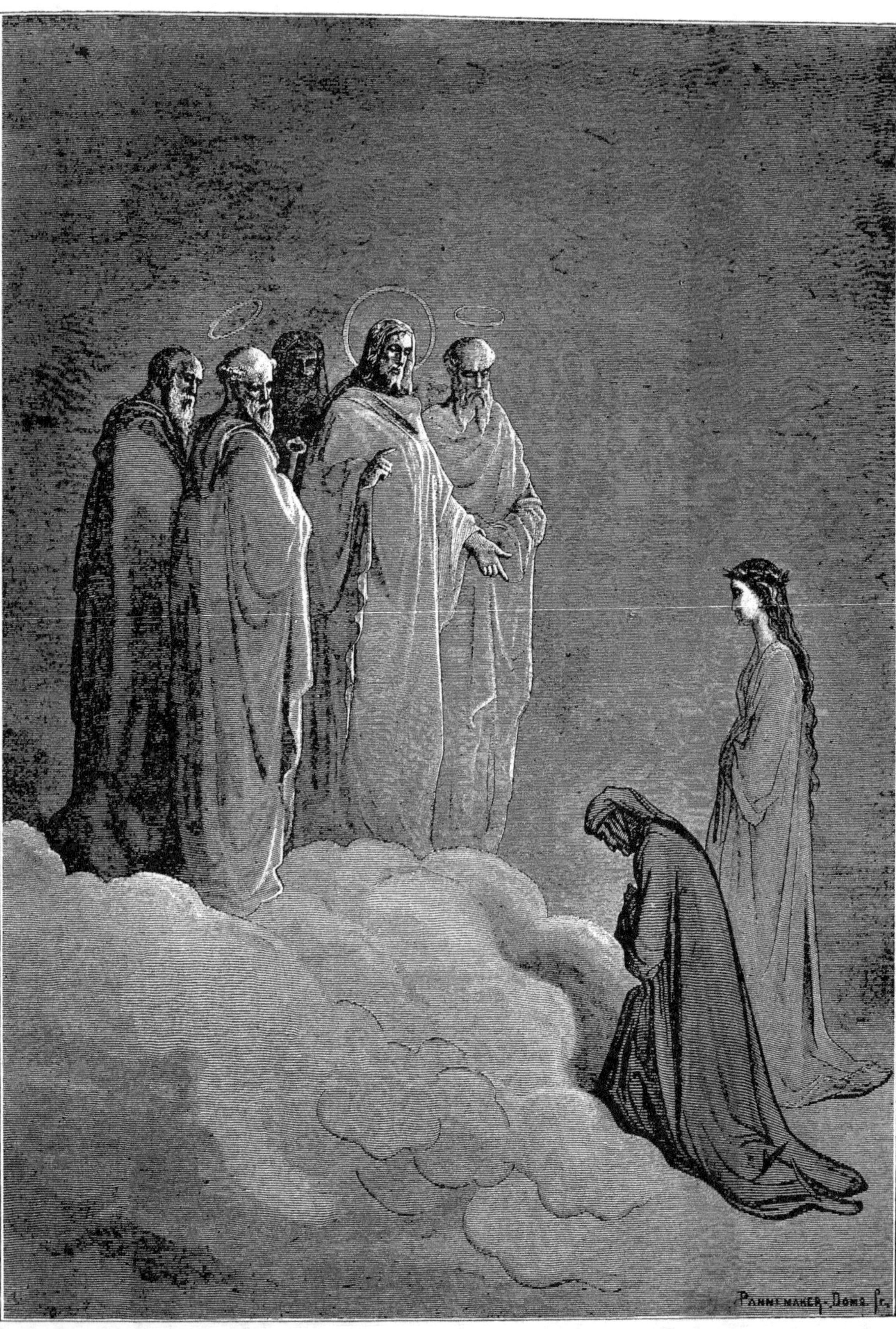

83. "Begin then, and declare to what thy soul, Is aimed, and count it for a certainty, Sight is in thee bewildered and not dead". Gustave Doré, 1868

84

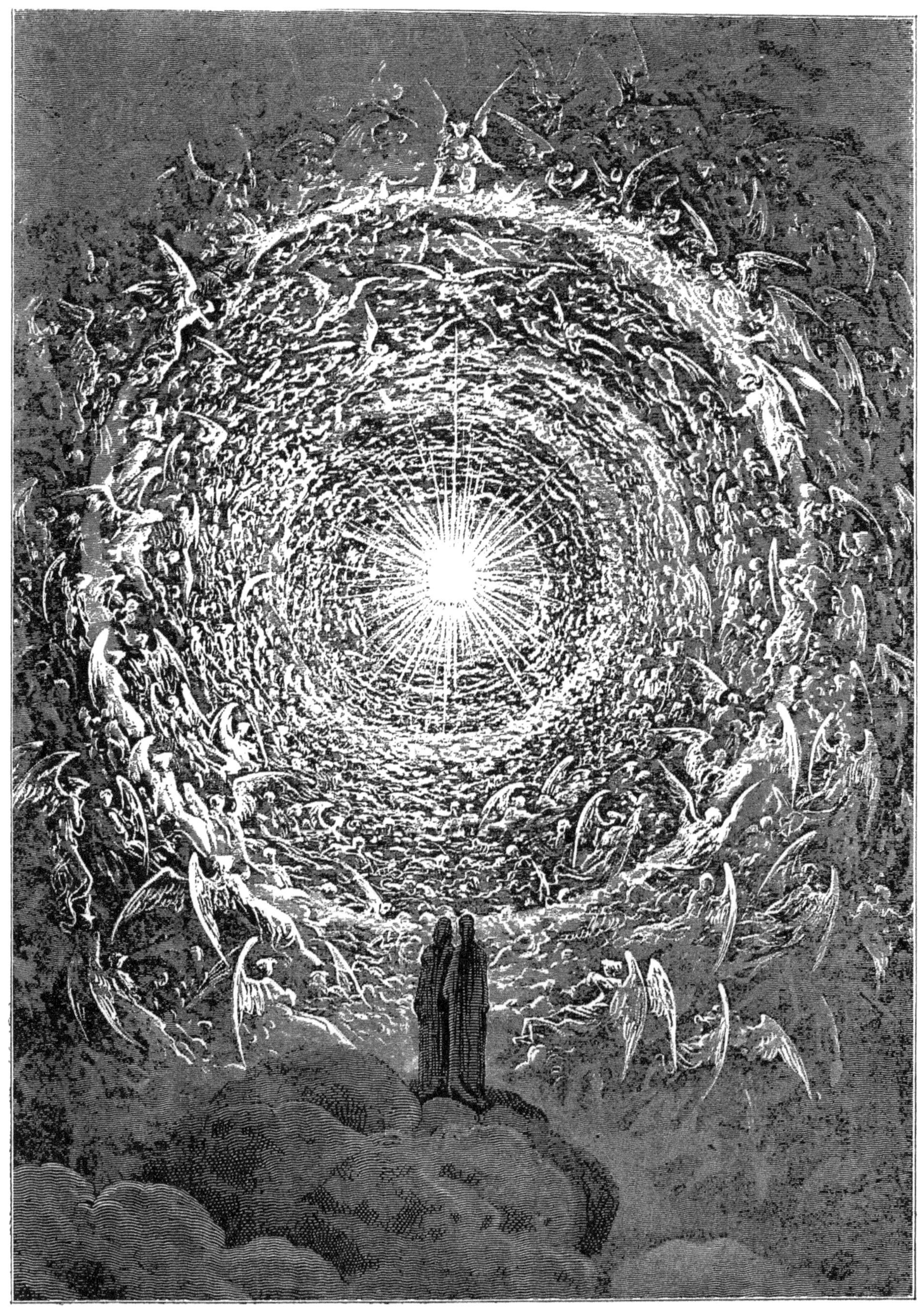

GUSTAVE DORÉ

84. In fashion, as a snow-white rose, lay then Before
my view the saintly multitude, Which in his own
blood Christ espous'd. Gustave Doré, 1868.

05

LONDON A PILGRIMAGE

GUSTAVE DORÉ

London: A Pilgrimage (1872) is a vivid portrayal of Victorian London, designed to show the city's 'shadows and sunlight'. The book presents an in-depth exploration of both the grandeur and the grim realities of the rapidly growing metropolis. It is a collaboration between Gustave Doré and journalist Blanchard Jerrold. Over four years, Jerrold and Doré traversed the streets of London, documenting its diverse social fabric—from the wealthy West End to the squalid slums of the East End. Jerrold's insightful commentary is complemented by Doré's dramatic, haunting engravings, which capture the stark contrasts of wealth and poverty and the human stories behind London's bustling urban life.

More than just a travelogue, *London: A Pilgrimage* is a historical document highlighting the city's complexity while critiquing its social inequalities. Doré's illustrations, in particular, have become iconic representations of Victorian London, influencing how generations have visualised the city. Vincent Van Gogh was one of Doré's admirers and made his coloured version of Doré's engraving *'Newgate – exercise yard'*, known as *'Prisoners'* Round (after Gustave Doré). The powerful combination of words and images in *London: A Pilgrimage* still resonates with contemporary readers and scholars as a first-hand record of urban life in the 19th century.

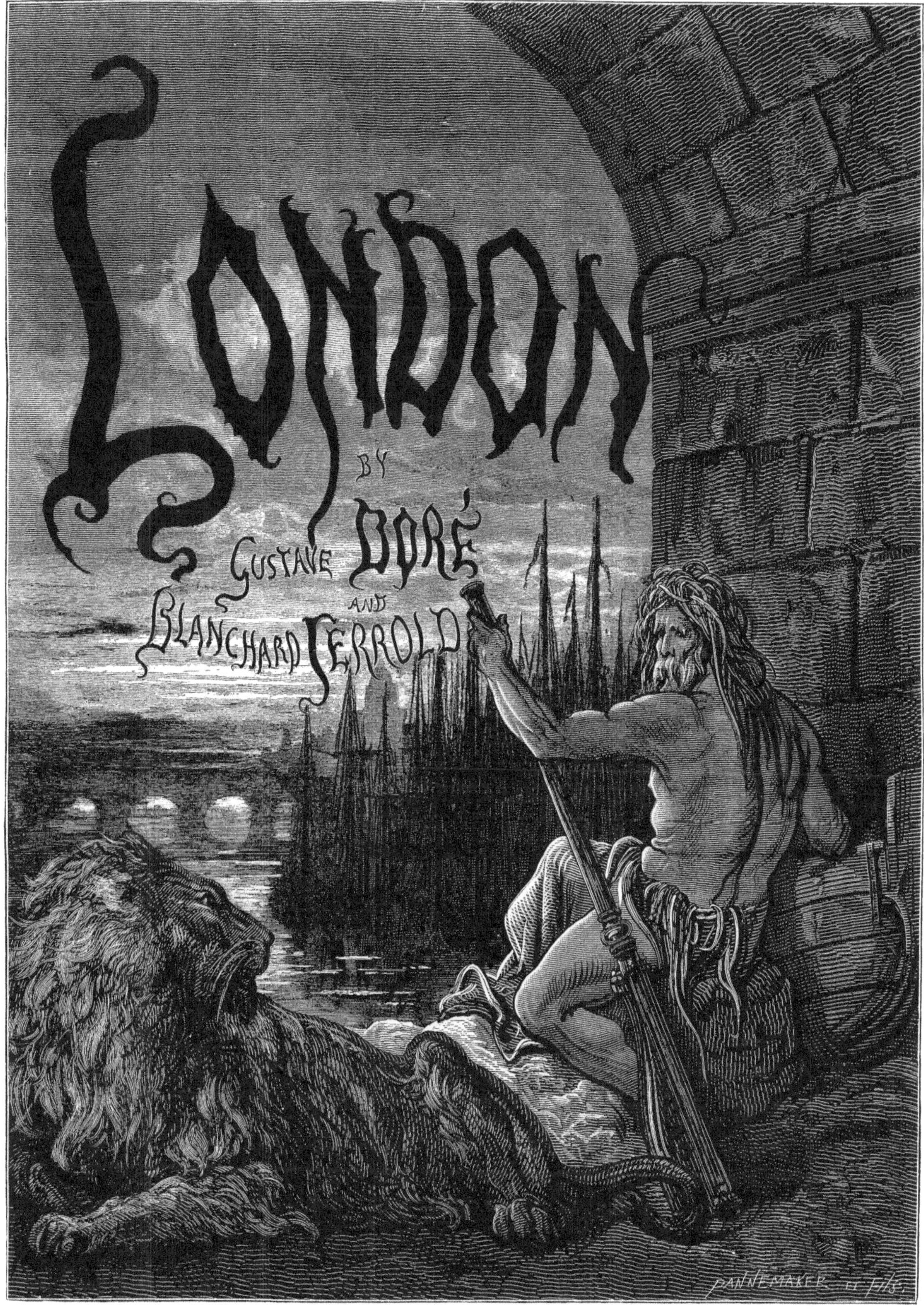

85. Father Thames, Gustave Doré, 1872

86

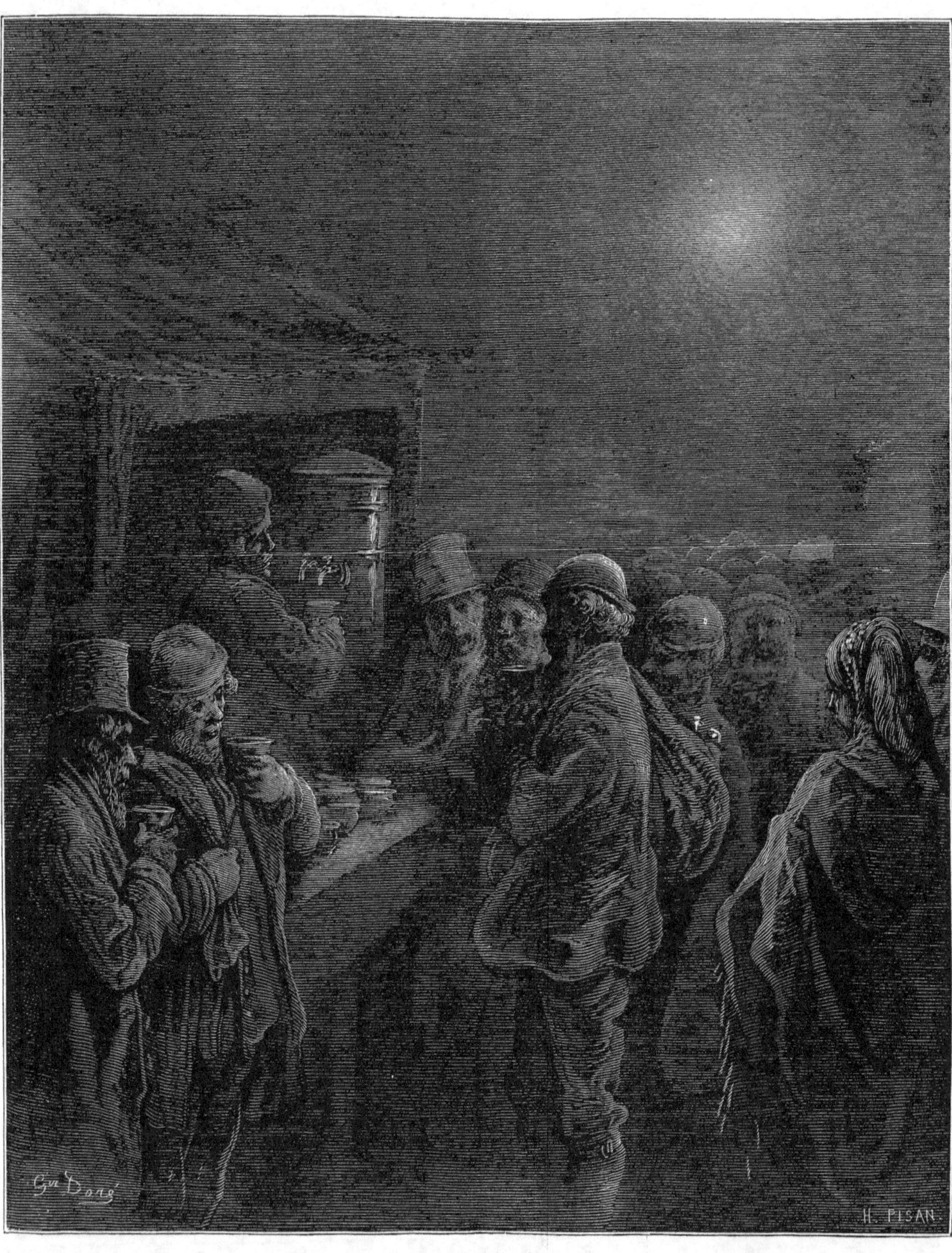

86. Coffee Stall - Early Morning, Gustave Doré, 1872

87

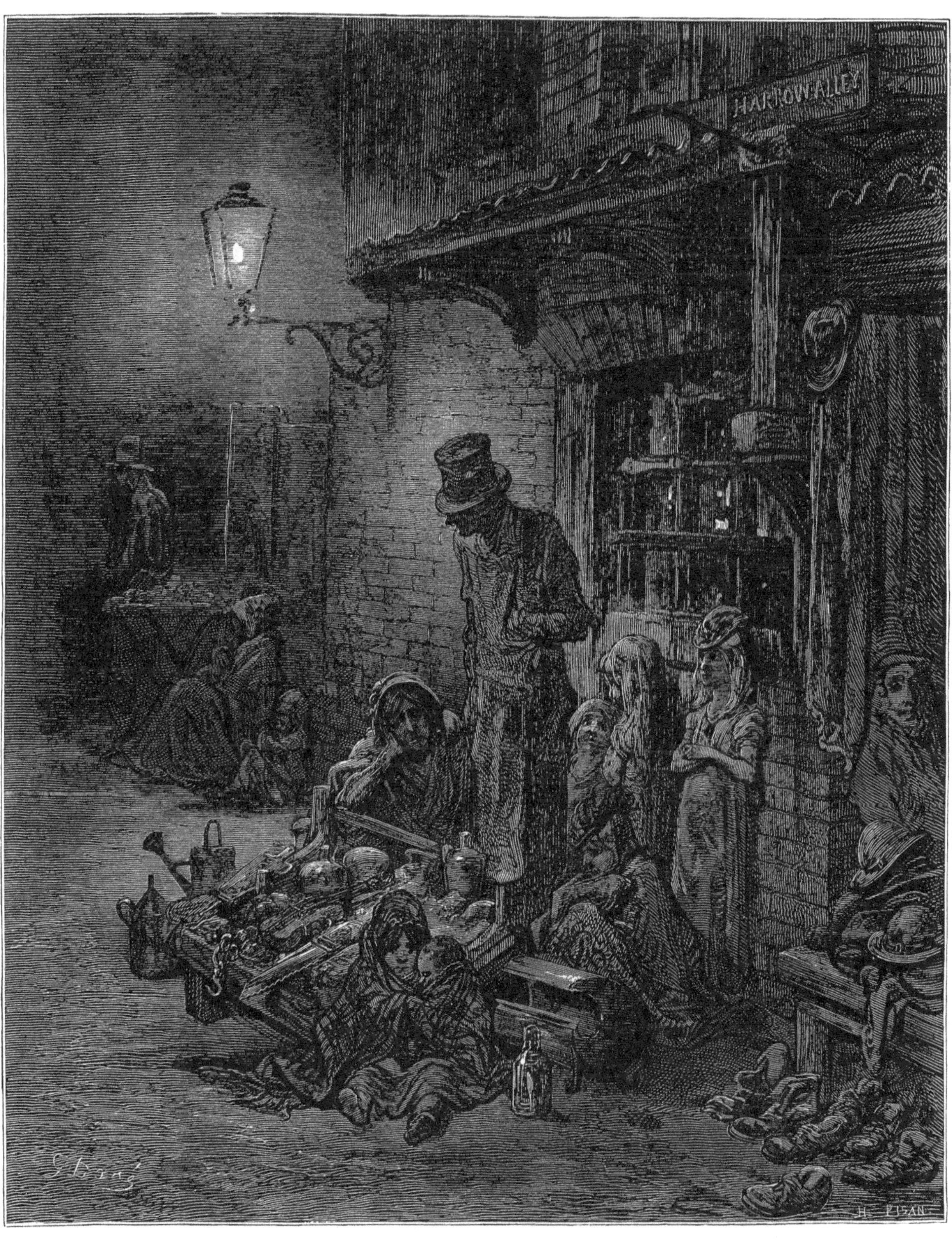

GUSTAVE DORÉ

87. Wentworth Street, Whitechapel, Gustave Doré,
1872

88

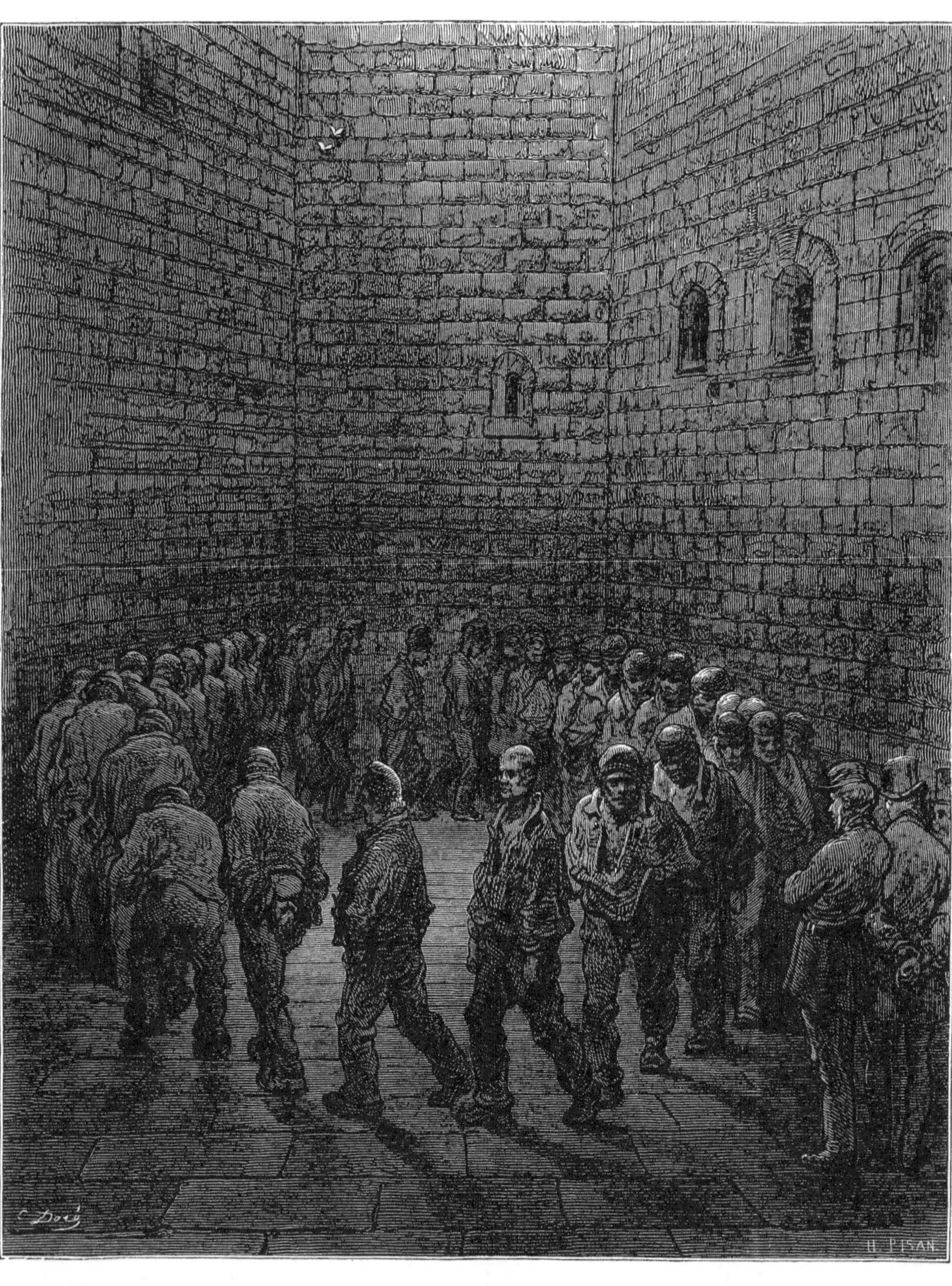

88. Newgate - Exercise Yard, Gustave Doré, 1872

89

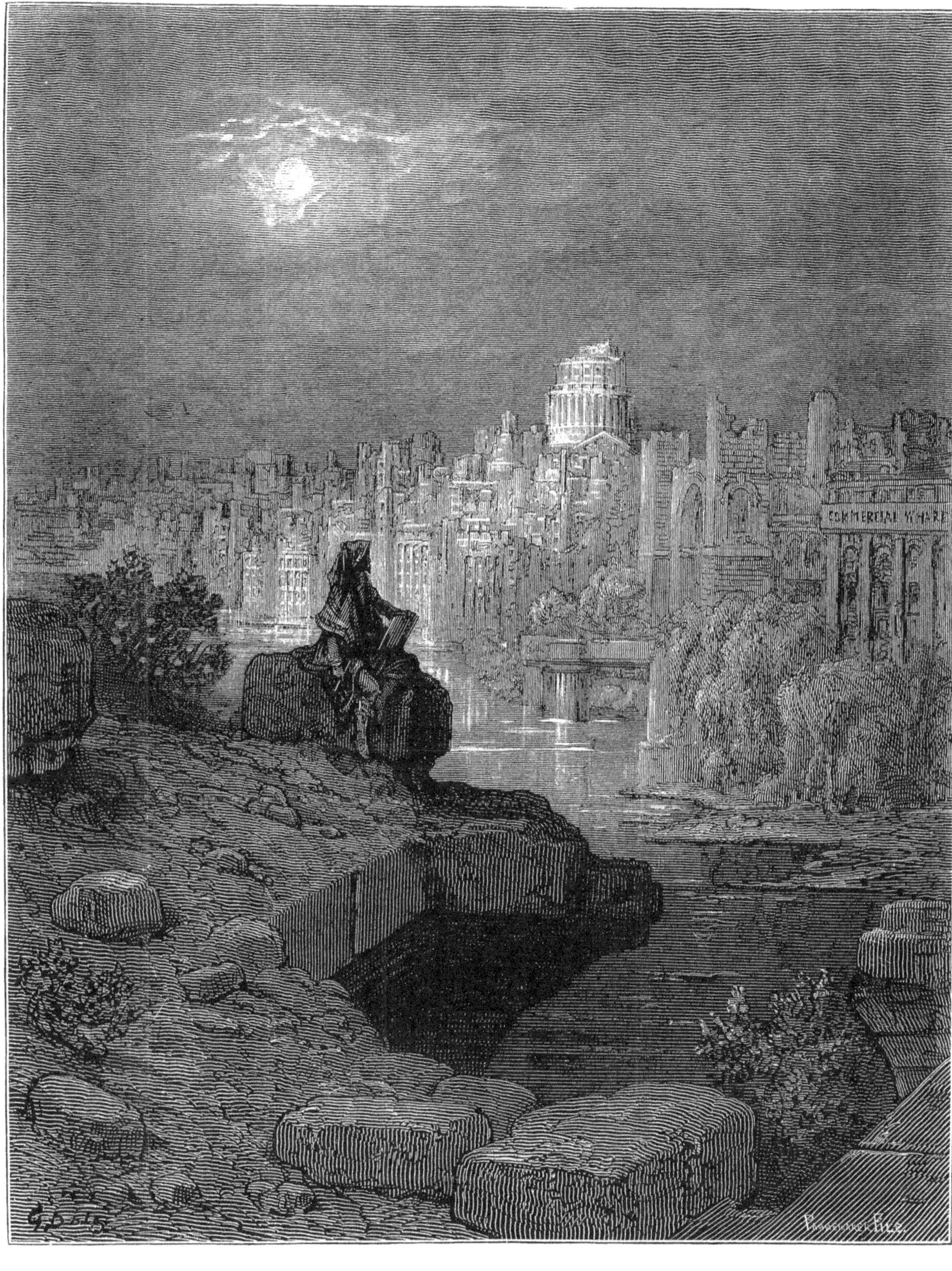

GUSTAVE DORÉ

89. The New Zealander, Gustave Doré, 1872

GUSTAVE DORÉ

06

DON QUIXOTE

Miguel de Cervantes wrote *Don Quixote*, which was first published in two parts in 1605 and 1615. It is considered by literary historians to be the first modern novel. The book tells the story of Don Quixote, an ageing nobleman captivated by tales of chivalry who transforms into a wandering knight in pursuit of adventure. Accompanied by his loyal squire, Sancho Panza, he embarks on a series of remarkable and often misguided exploits. Quixote's vivid imagination frequently leads him astray; meanwhile, Sancho Panza, despite his simplicity, grows wiser and more practical. Over time, Don Quixote's true character is revealed—beneath his delusions, he is noble and kind, gradually earning Sancho Panza's respect and loyalty. After facing many humiliations throughout their journey, Quixote ultimately lets go of his grand illusions. Returning home, he renounces his fantasies of knighthood and passes away.

Don Quixote is a satire of the chivalric stories popular at the time. Through Quixote's journey, Cervantes critiques the outdated notions of knighthood and satirises the human condition, making *Don Quixote* a humorous tale and a timeless meditation on dreams, delusion, and disillusionment.

Gustave Doré's illustrations for *Don Quixote*, published in 1863, have become the most iconic visual accompaniment to Cervantes' classic novel. Doré masterfully captured the humour, pathos, and drama of Don Quixote's journey, from his battle with the windmills to his adventures on the road with Sancho Panza. His artwork brings out both the absurdity and the deeper themes of the story, making it the definitive illustrative edition of the book.

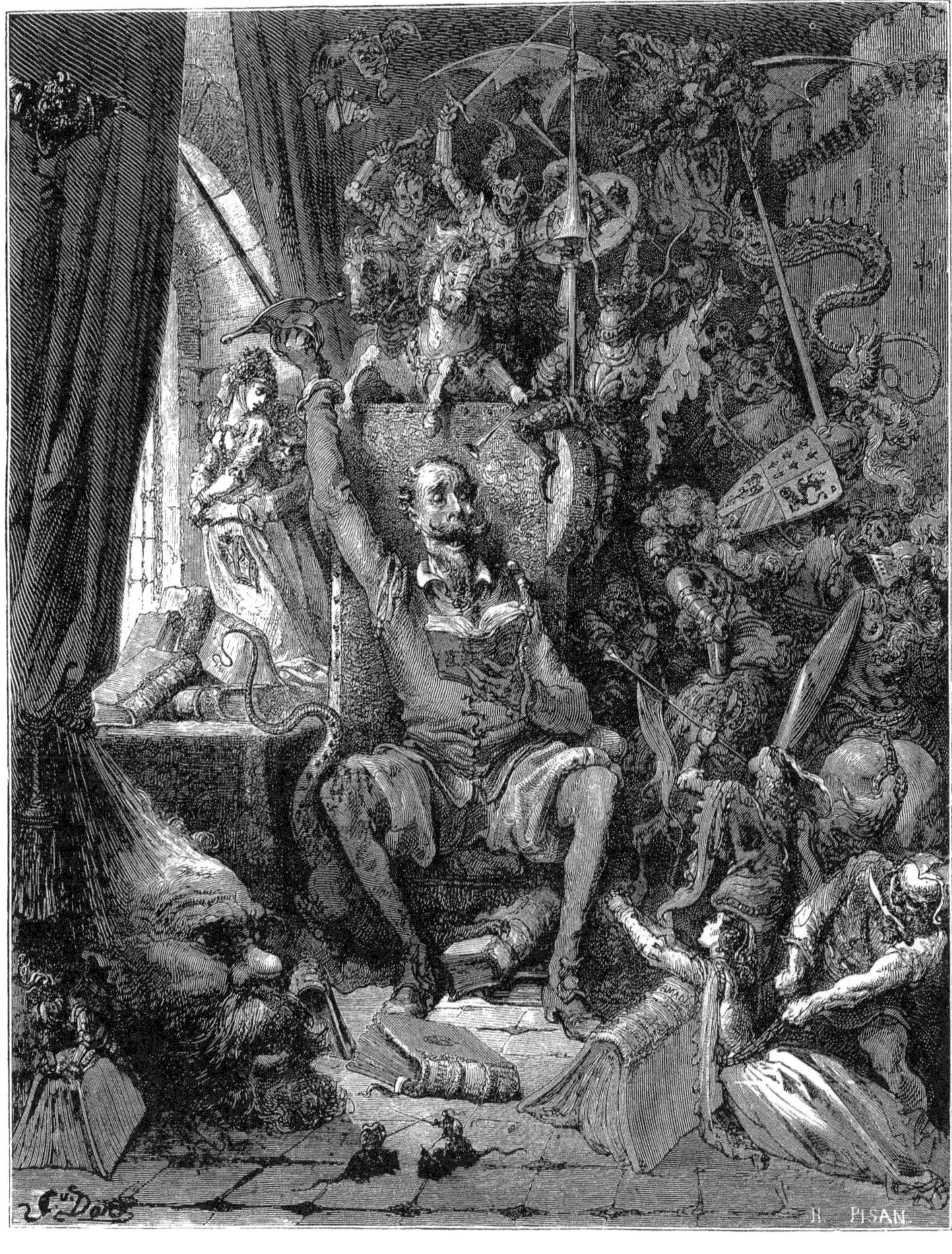

90 A world of disorderly notions, picked out of
his books, crowded into his imagination. Gustave
Doré, 1863

91

GUSTAVE DORÉ

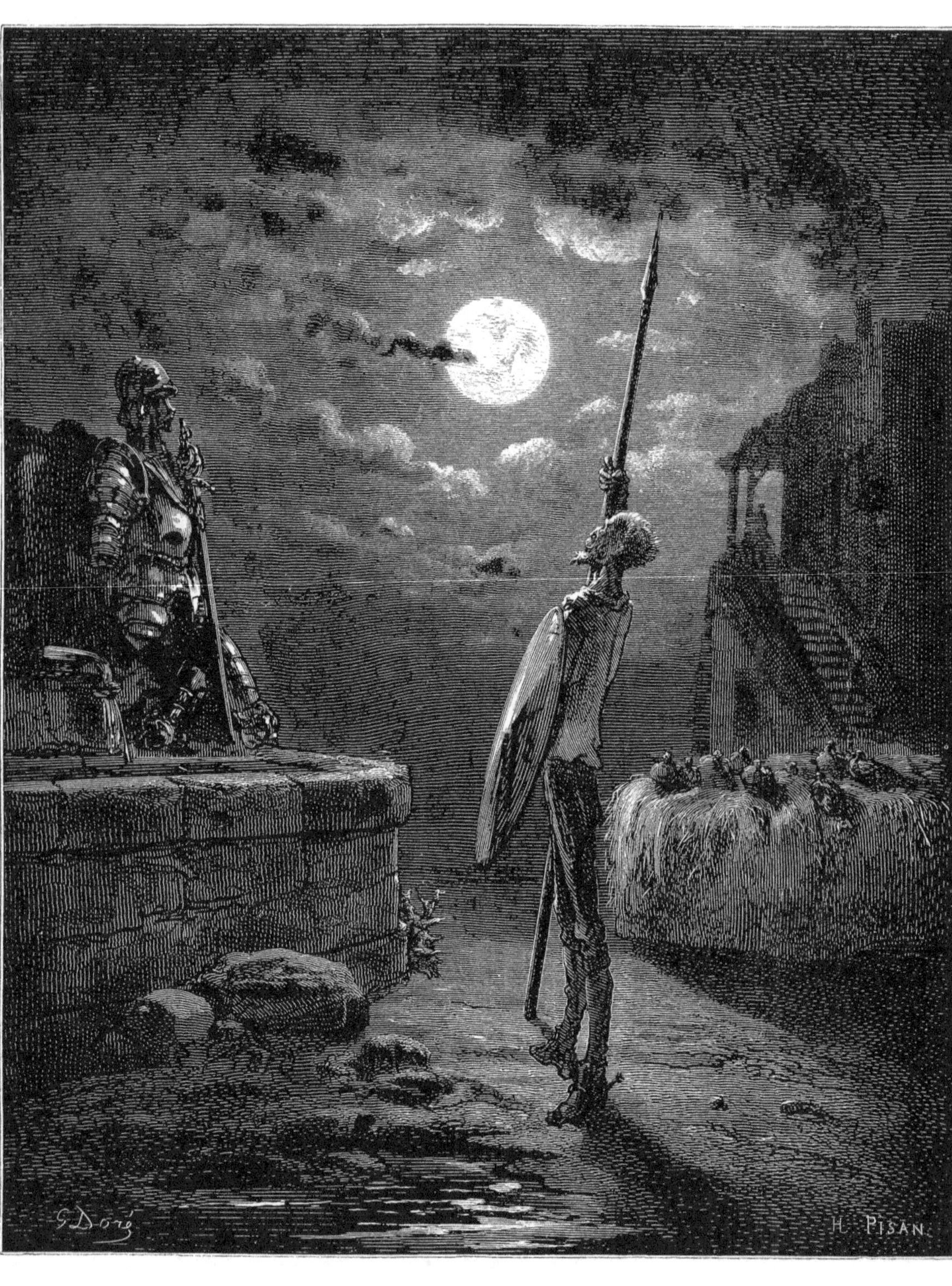

91. He began to walk about by the horse-trough with
a graceful deportment, Gustave Doré, 1863

92

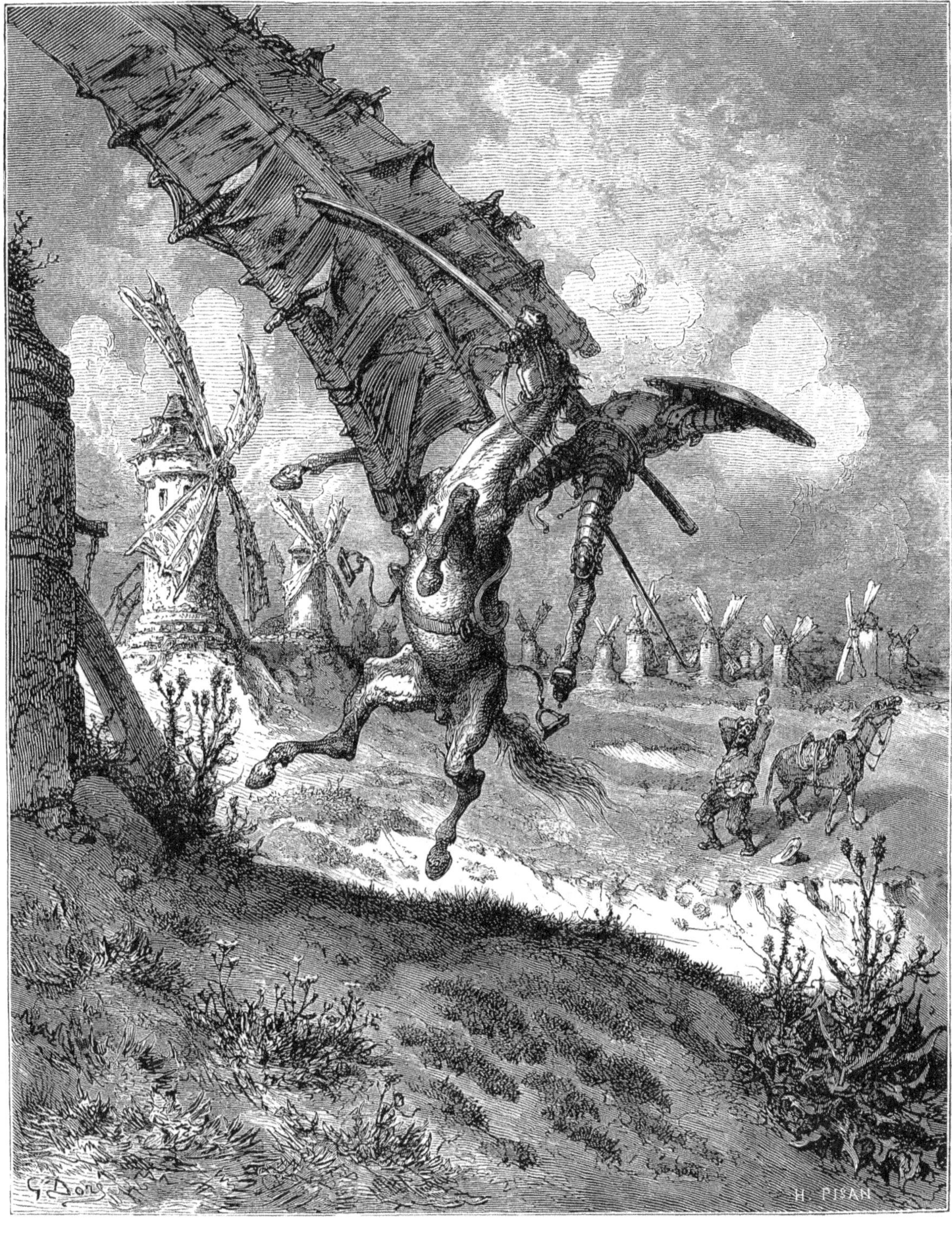

GUSTAVE DORÉ

92. The sail hurled away both knight and horse along
with it. Gustave Doré, 1863

93.

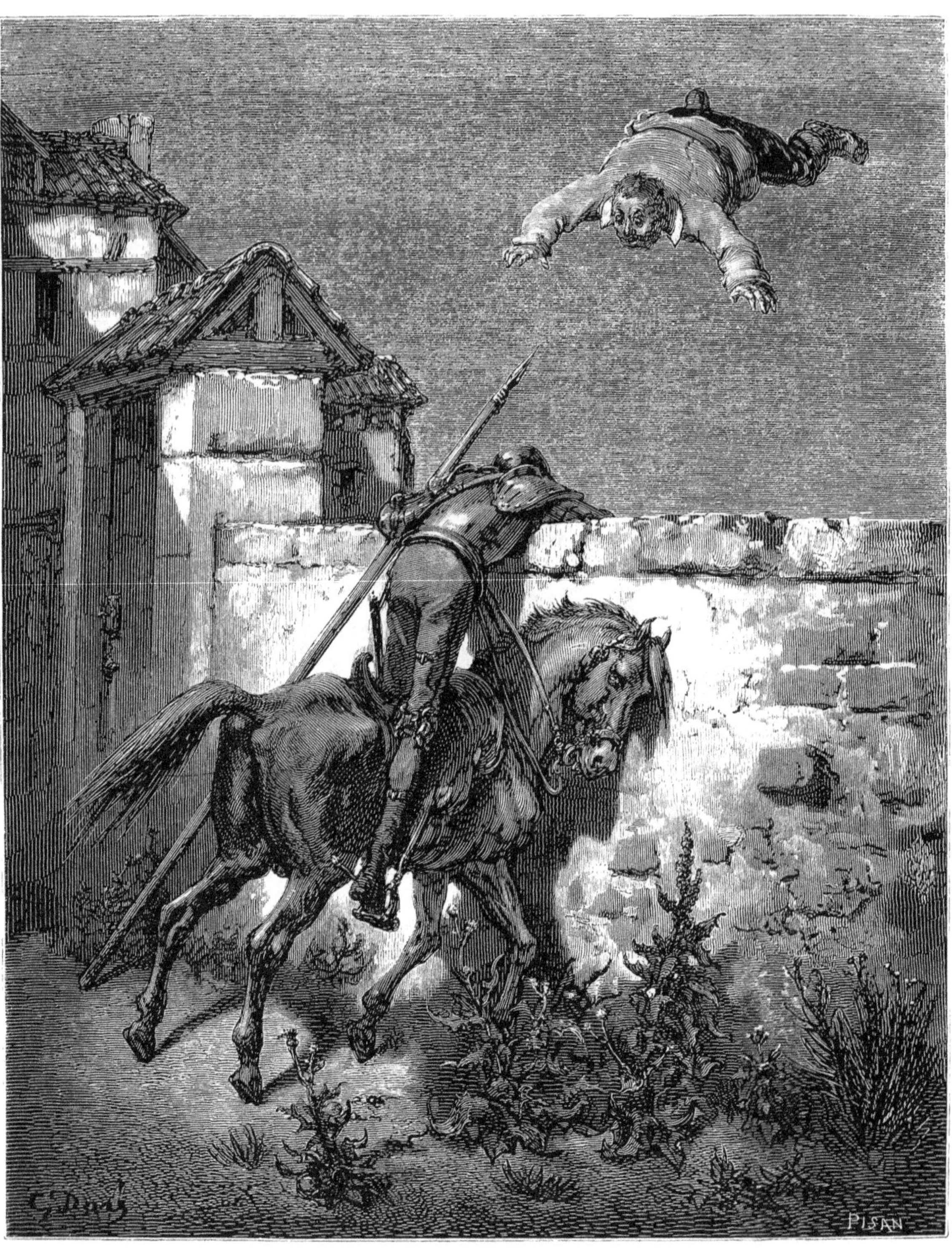

93. The more he stormed, the more they tossed and
laughed. Gustave Doré, 1863

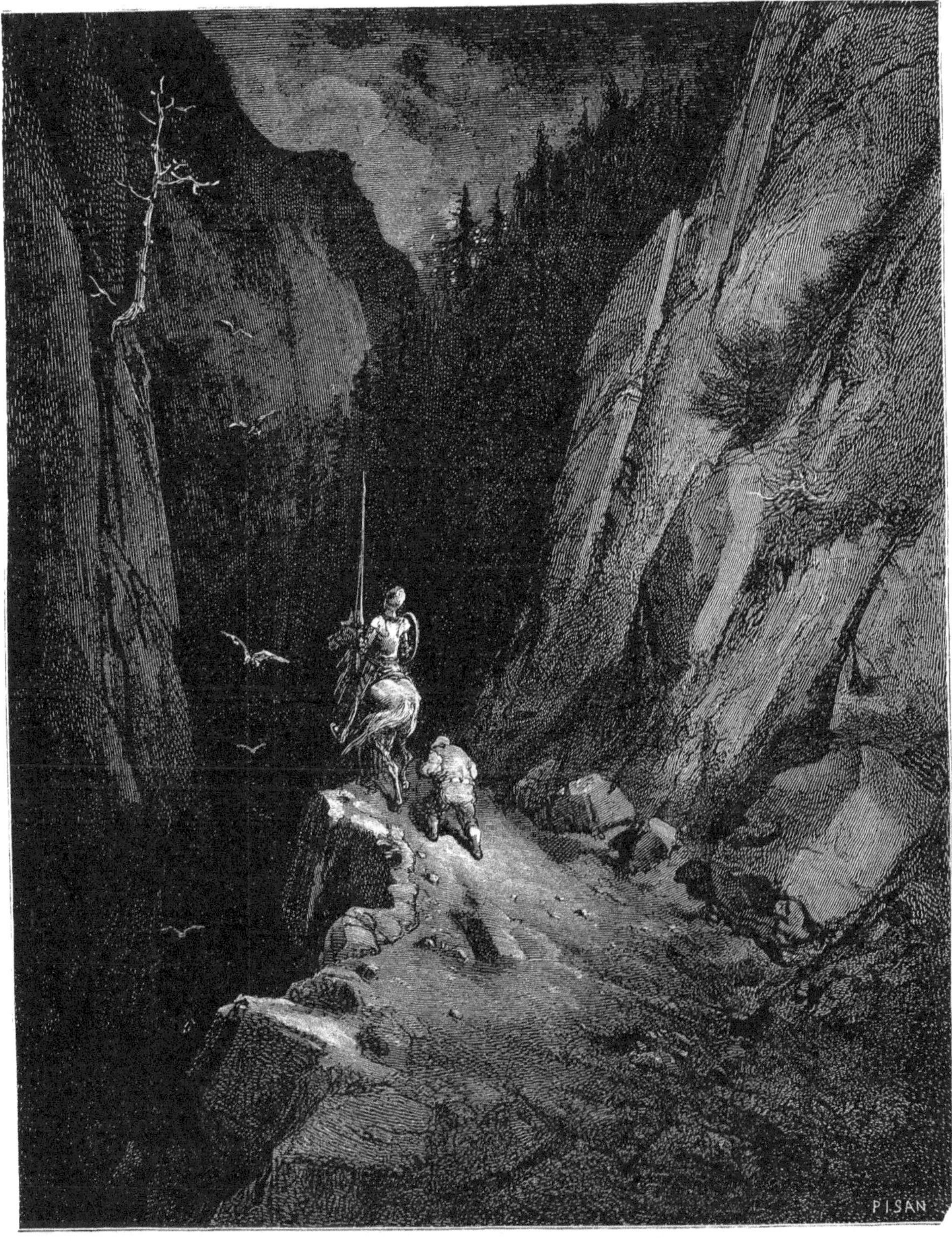

94 Don Quixote was transported with joy to find
himself where he might flatter his ambition with the
hopes of fresh adventures, Gustave Doré, 1863

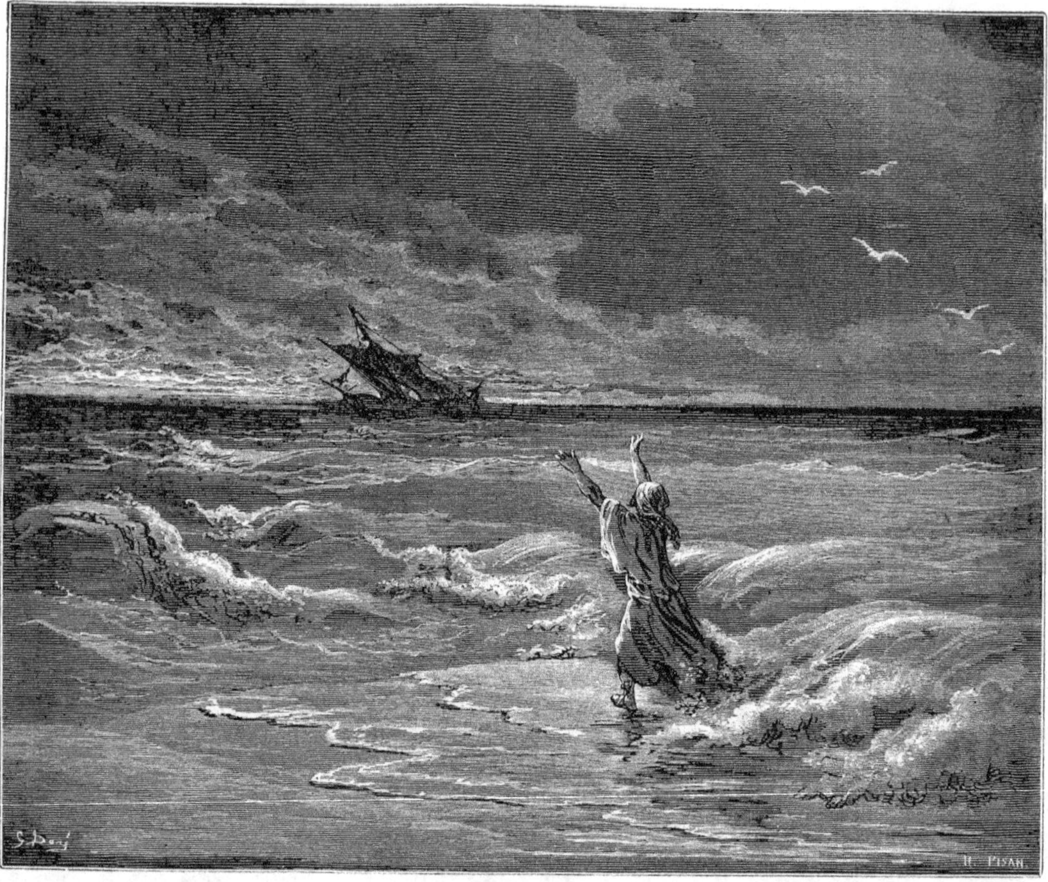

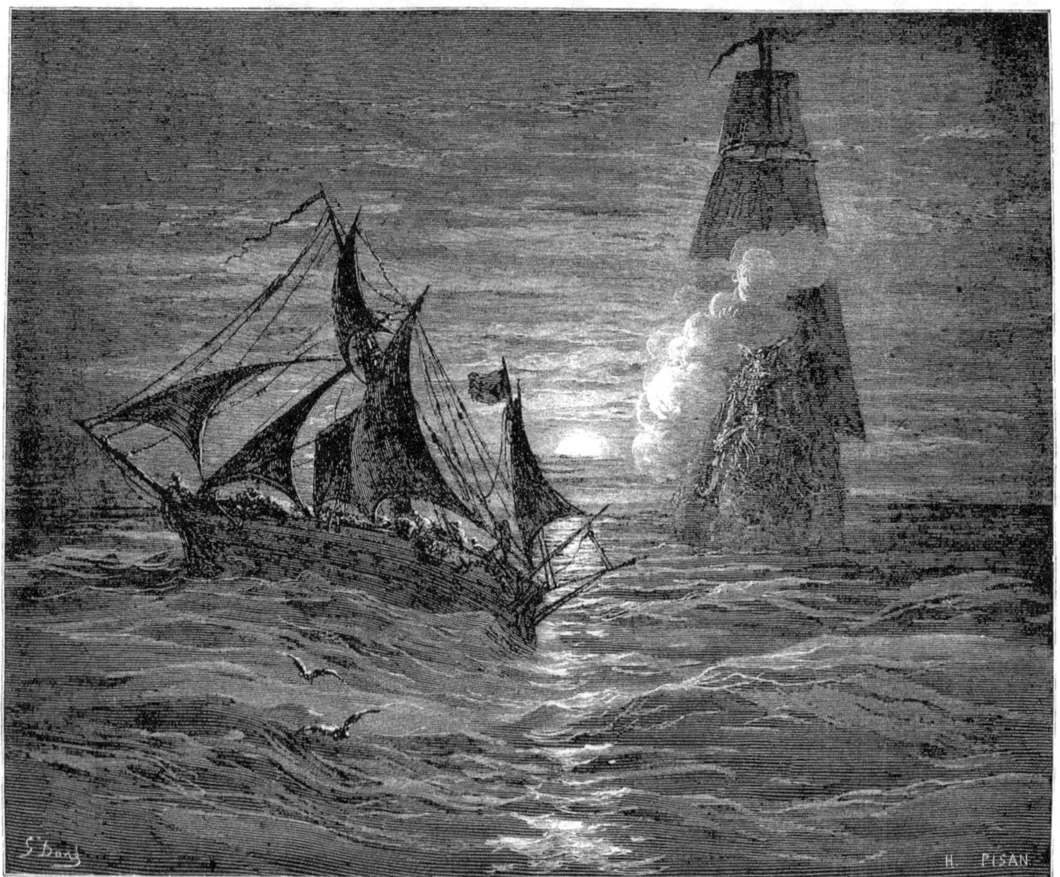

95. 'Come back, my dear daughter, for I forgive thee all', Gustave Doré, 1863

96. They being under the wind, fired two guns at us, Gustave Doré, 1863

97

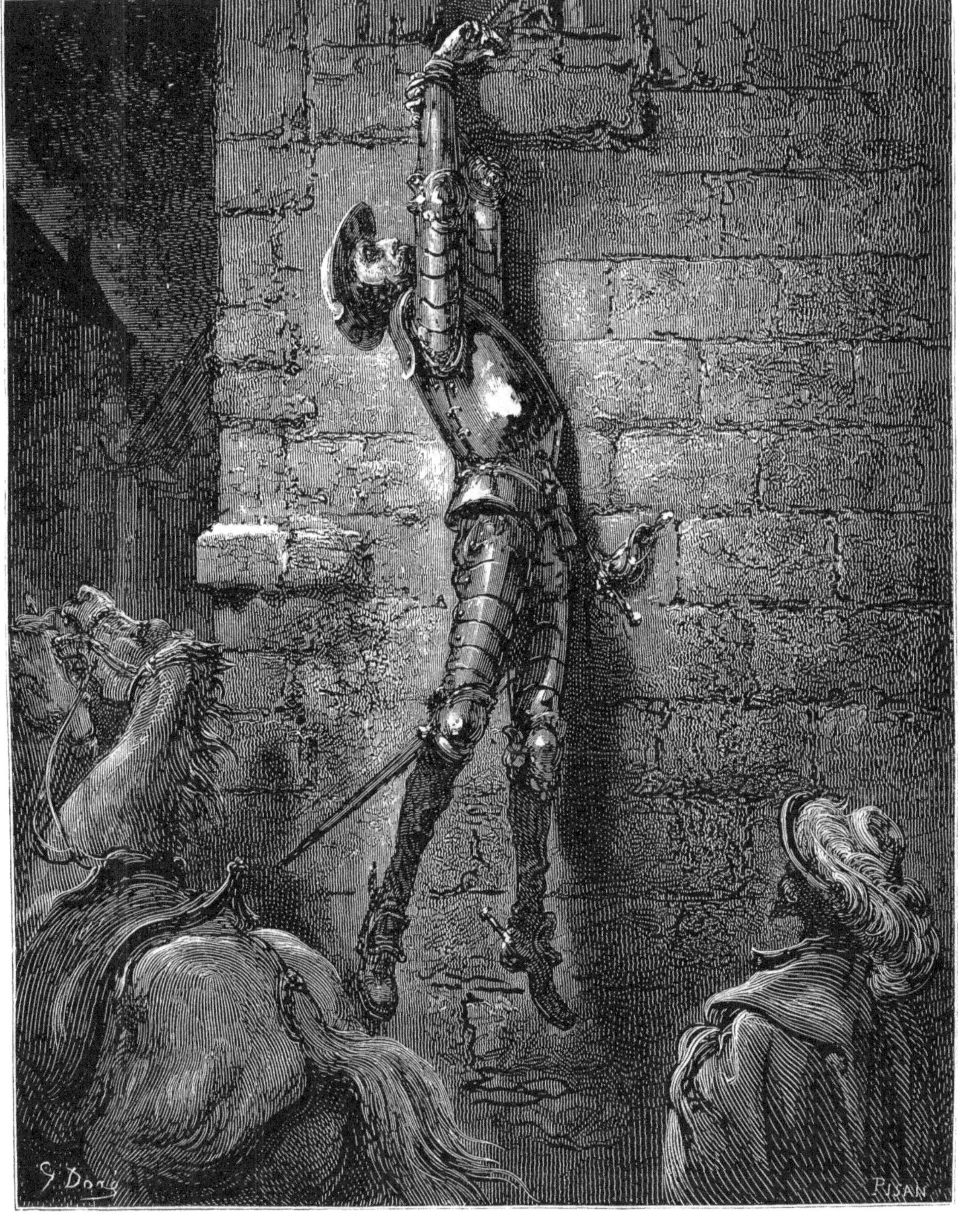

GUSTAVE DORÉ

97. He had inevitably fallen to the ground, had
not his wrist been securely fastened to the rope.
Gustave Doré, 1863

98

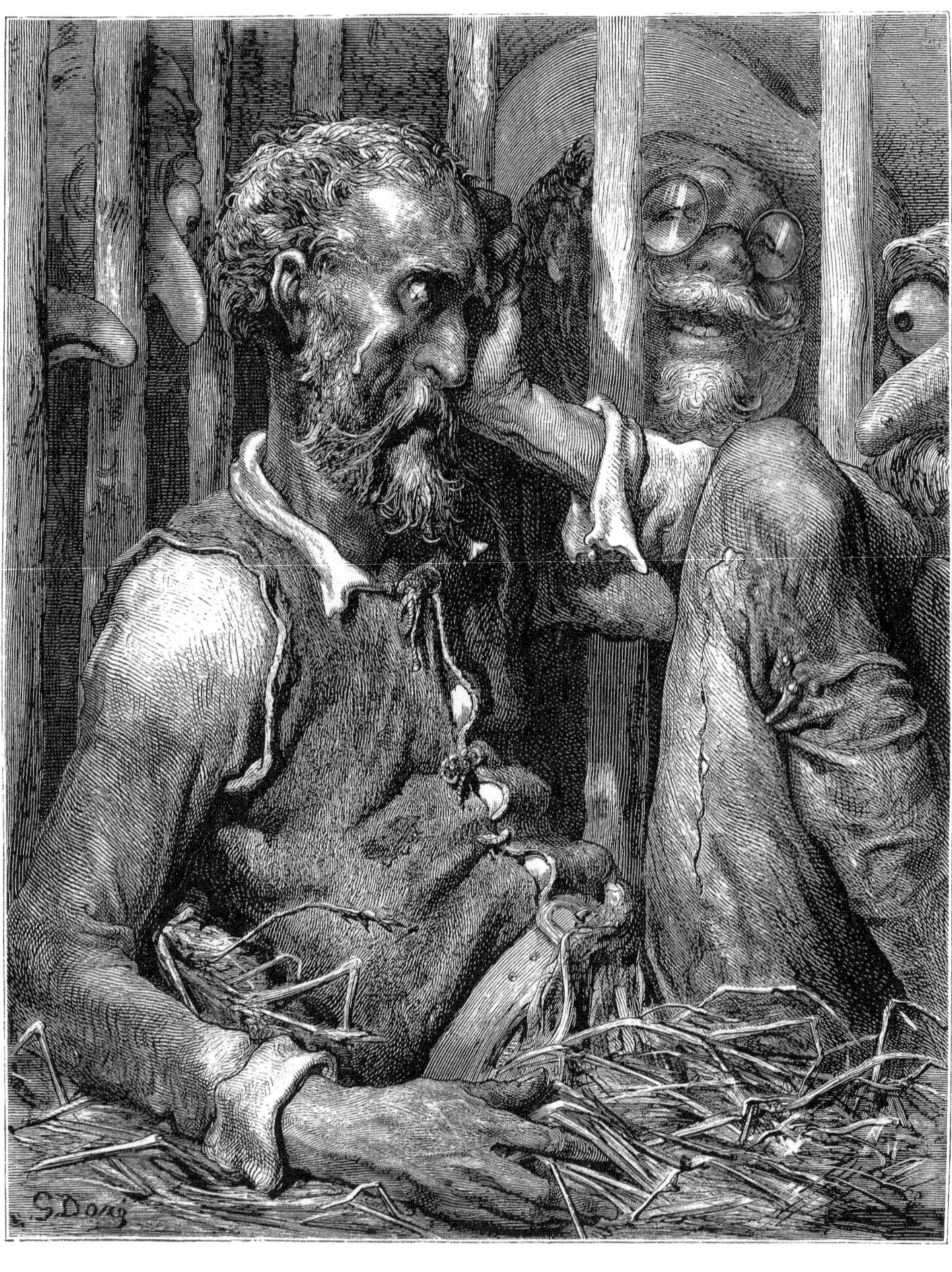

98. Don Quixote was not so much amazed
at his enchantment as at the manner of it.
Gustave Doré, 1863

99

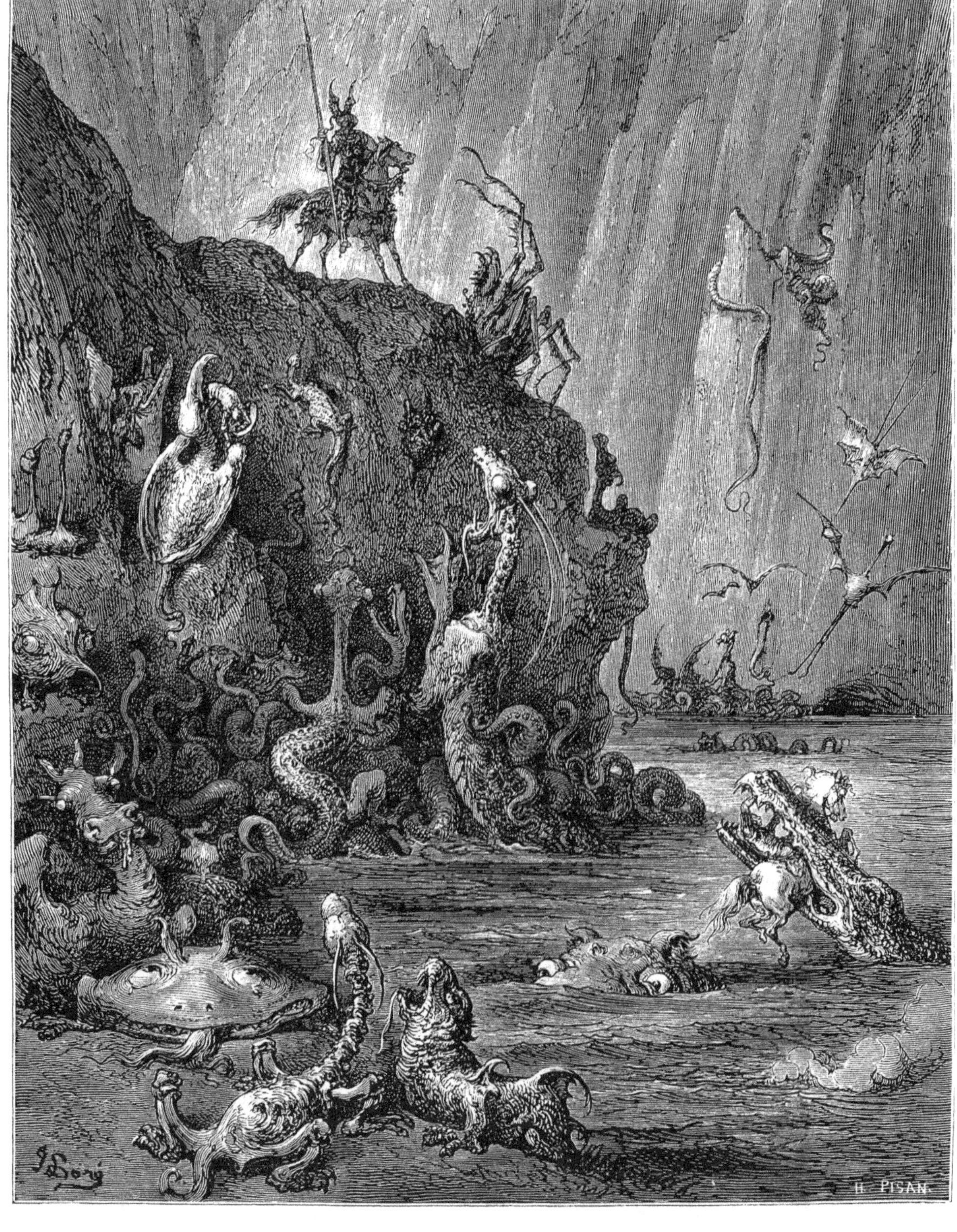

GUSTAVE DORÉ

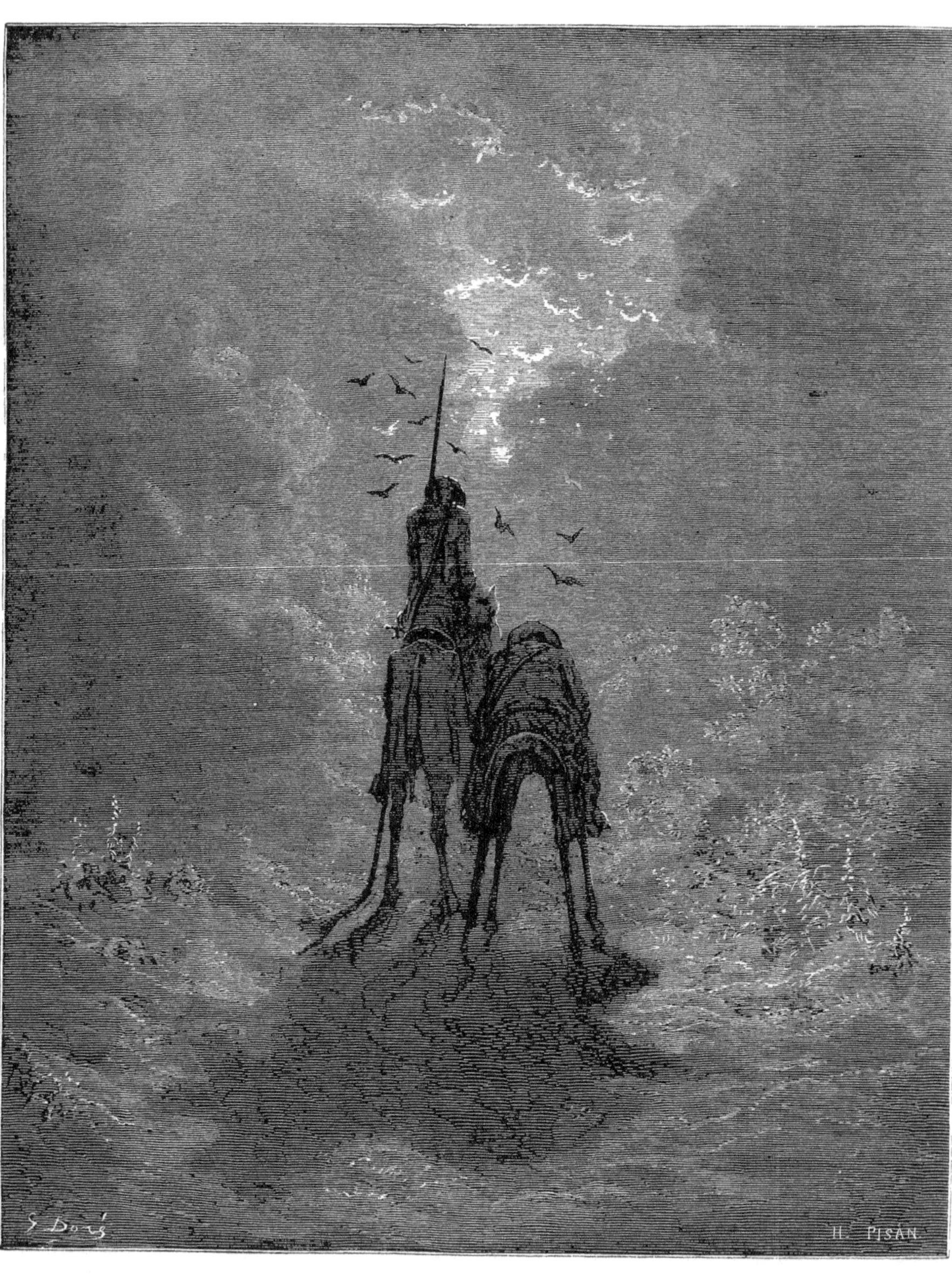

100. We slept as soundly as if we had four feather beds under us. Gustave Doré, 1863

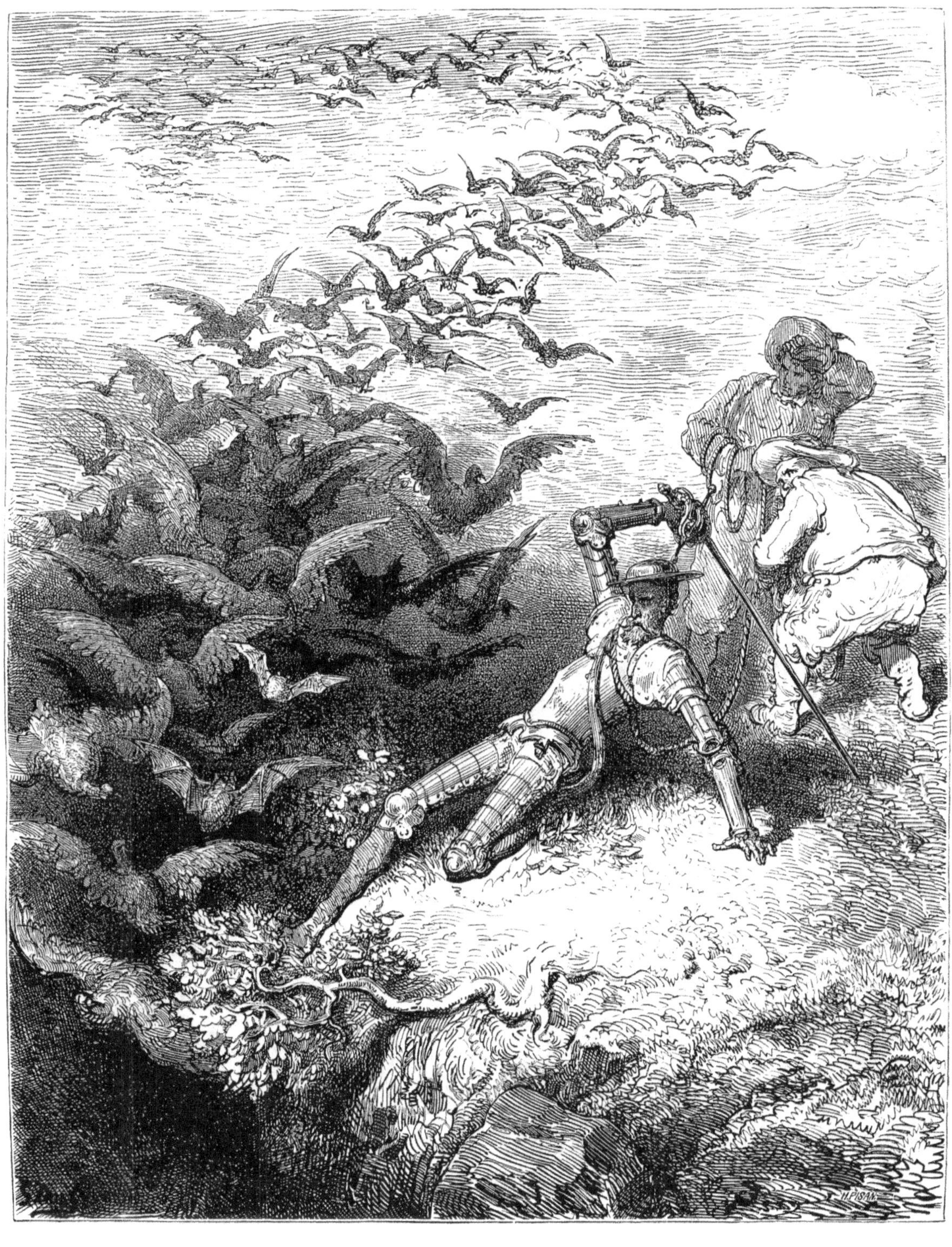

101. 'An infinite number of overgrown crows
and daws came rushing and fluttering out of
the cave'. Gustave Doré, 1863

102

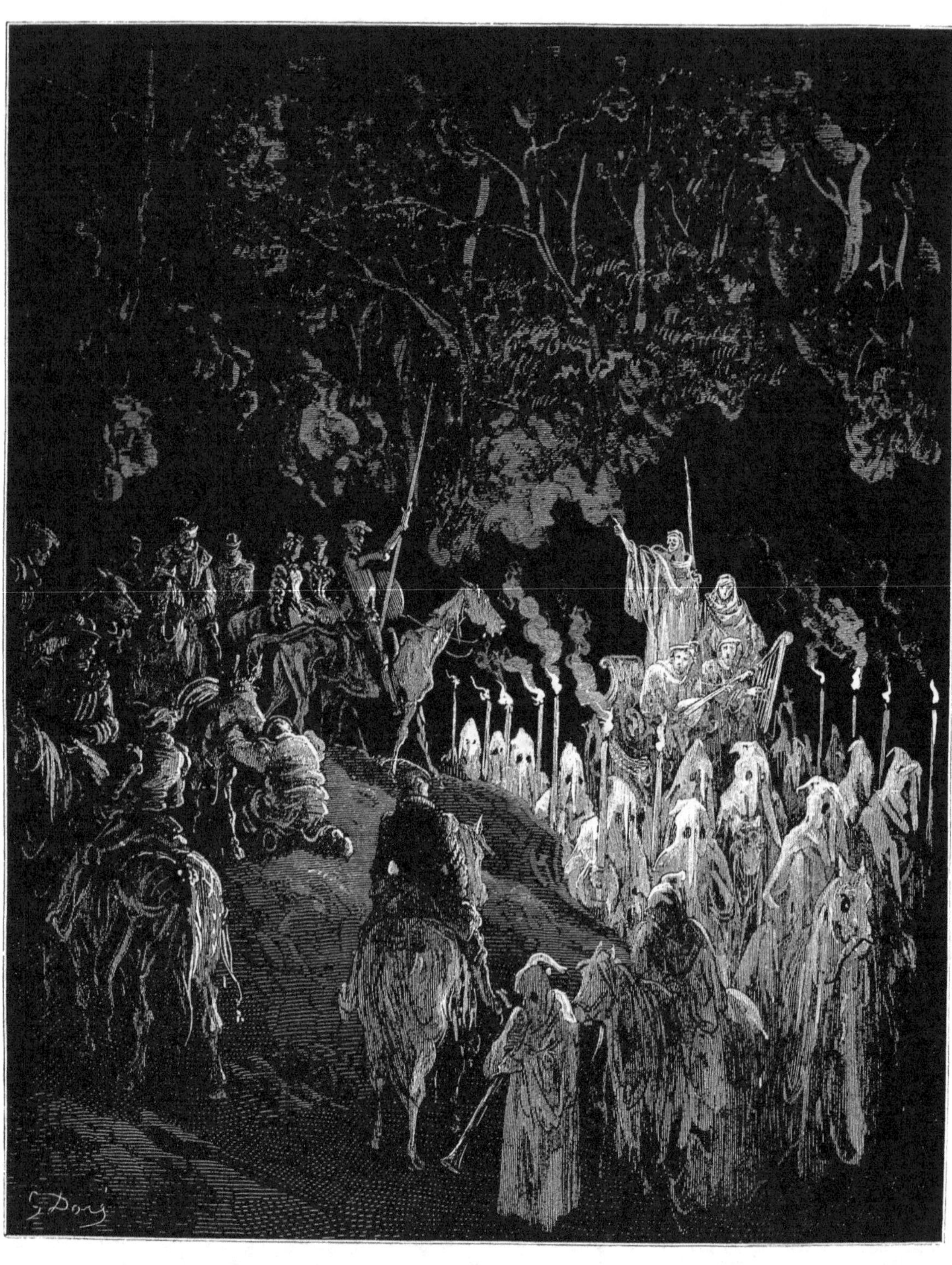

102. The figure in the gown stood up. Gustave
Doré, 1863

103

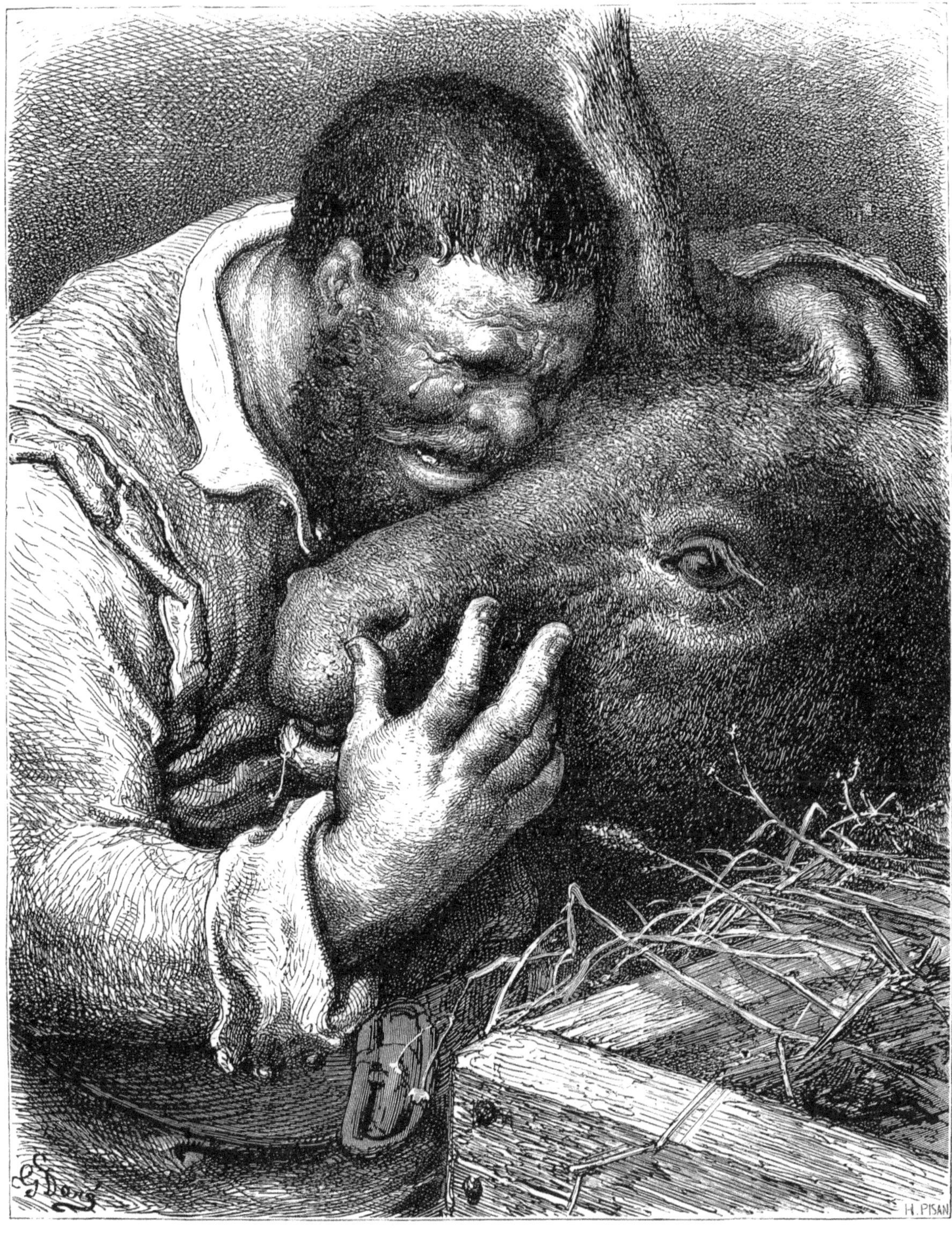

GUSTAVE DORÉ

103. "Come hither," said he, "my friend, thou
faithful companion and fellow-sharer in all my
travels and miseries", Gustave Doré, 1863

07

THE RAVEN

Edgar Allan Poe's *The Raven*, first published in 1845, is a masterful exploration of grief, loss, and the haunting persistence of memory. The poem tells the story of a troubled man visited by a mysterious raven who speaks only the word *"Nevermore."* The poem is set against a dark, atmospheric backdrop and delves into the narrator's descent into despair as he grapples with the death of his beloved Lenore. Poe uses melancholic rhythm, rich symbolism, and alliteration to create a sense of foreboding and psychological torment, making *The Raven* one of American literature's most celebrated and analysed works.

The Raven was one of Gustave Doré's final projects. His atmospheric and dramatic illustrations enhance the poem's themes of loss, madness, and the supernatural. Doré completed the 26 images for the poem in 1883, and the book was published posthumously in 1884. His rendition of *The Raven* remains one of the most visually iconic representations of Poe's timeless masterpiece.

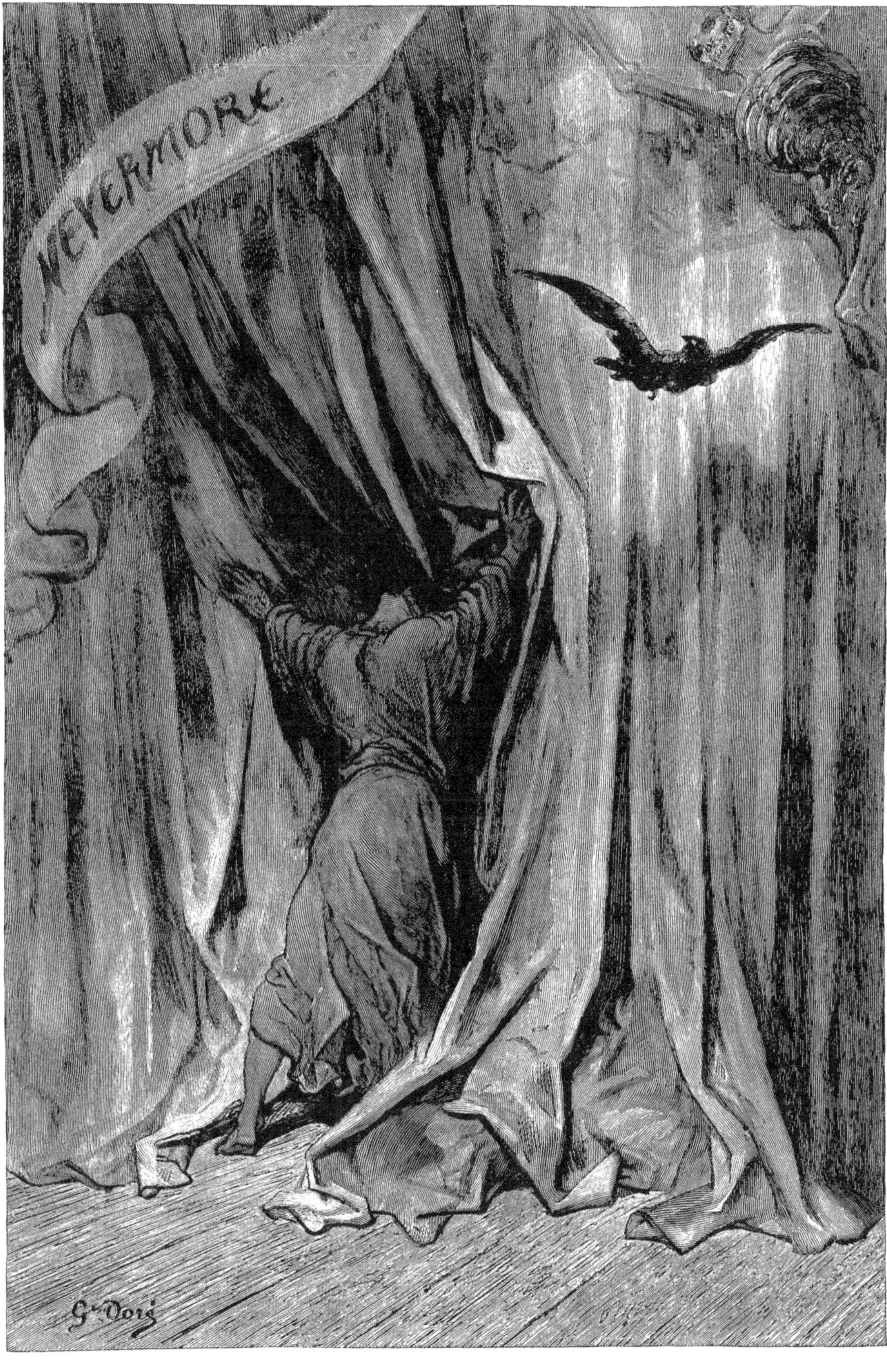

104. Nevermore, Gustave Doré, 1884

105.

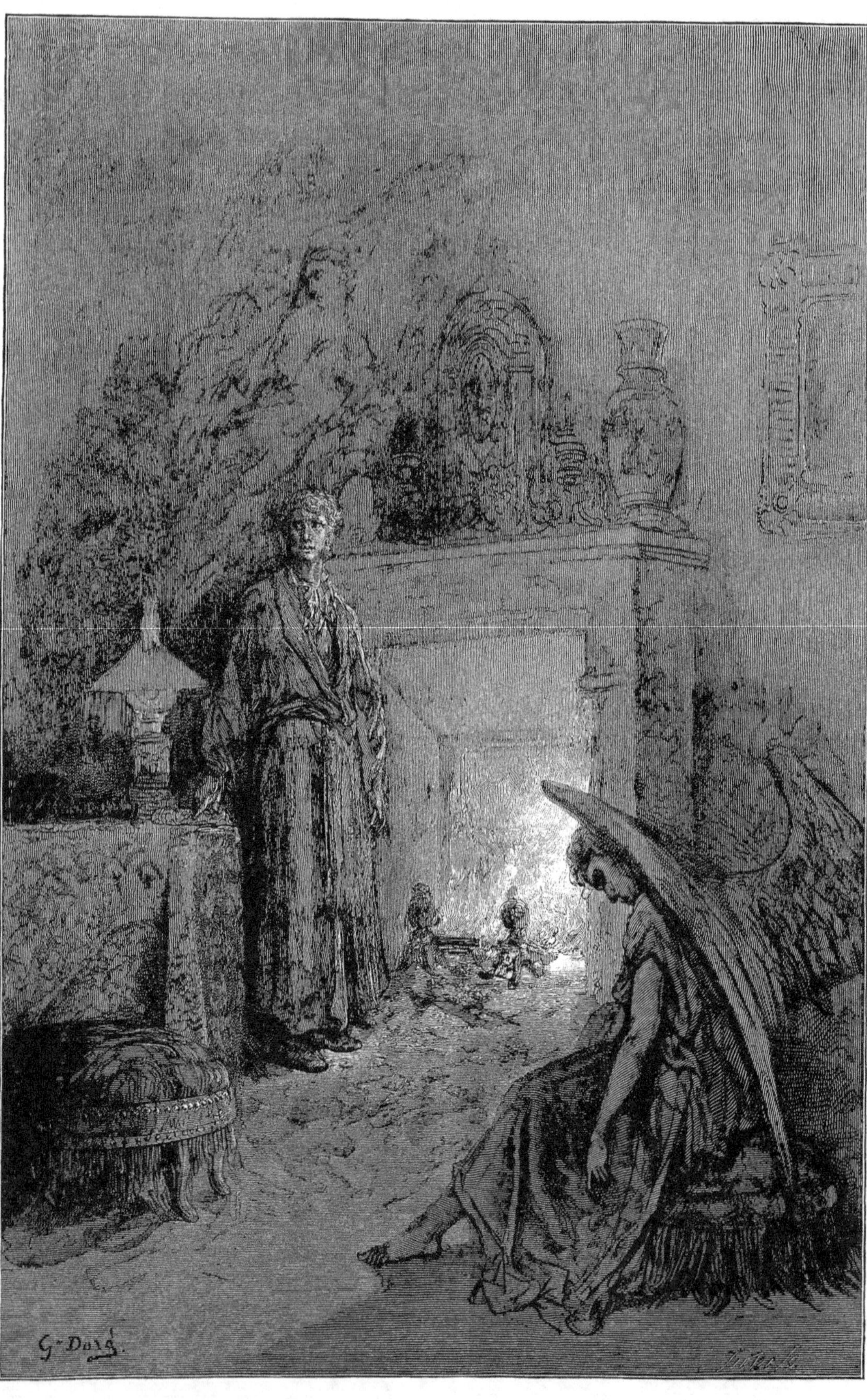

105. *Ah, distinctly I remember, it was in the bleak December, Gustave Doré, 1884*

106.

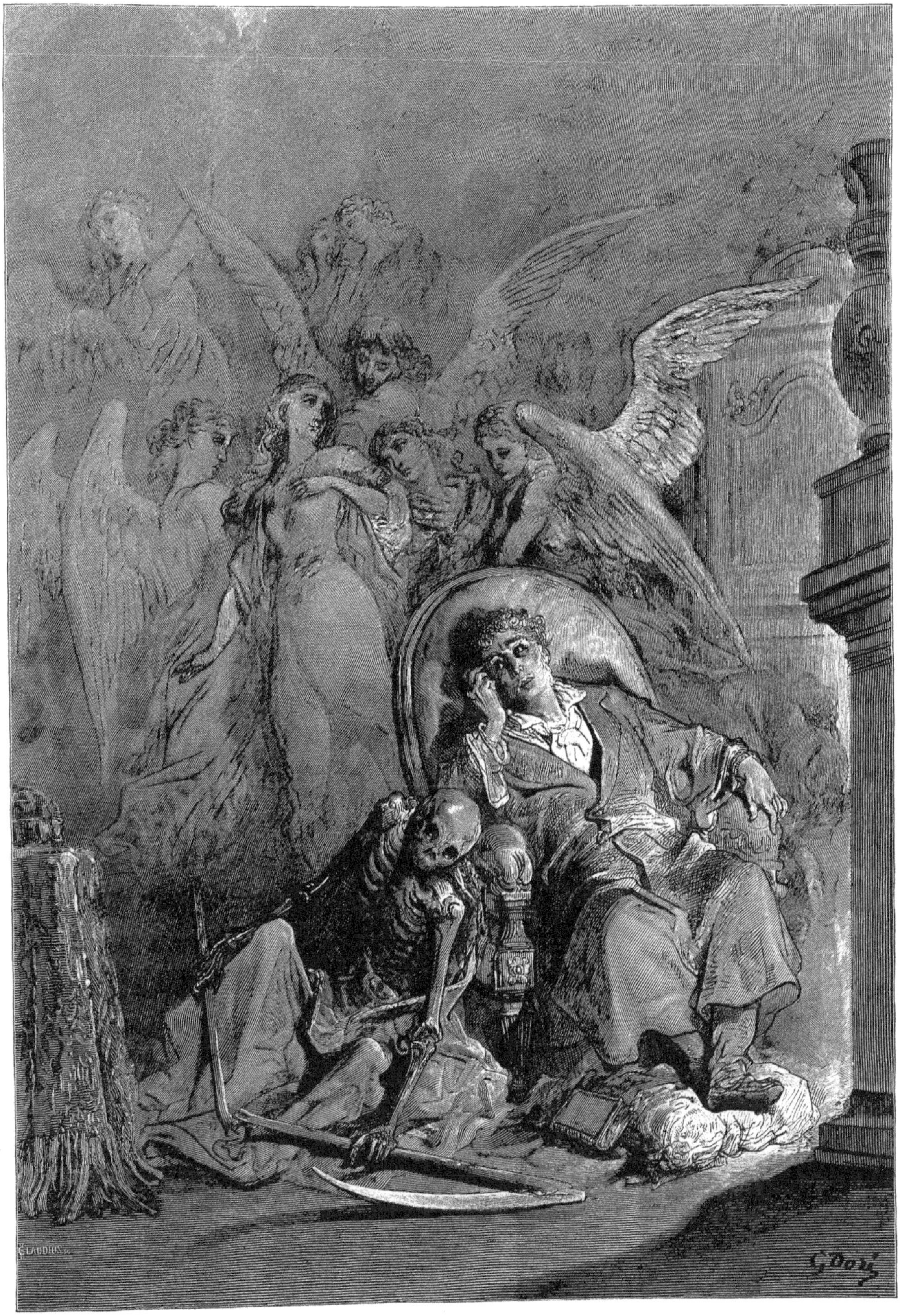

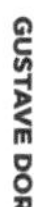

GUSTAVE DORÉ

107

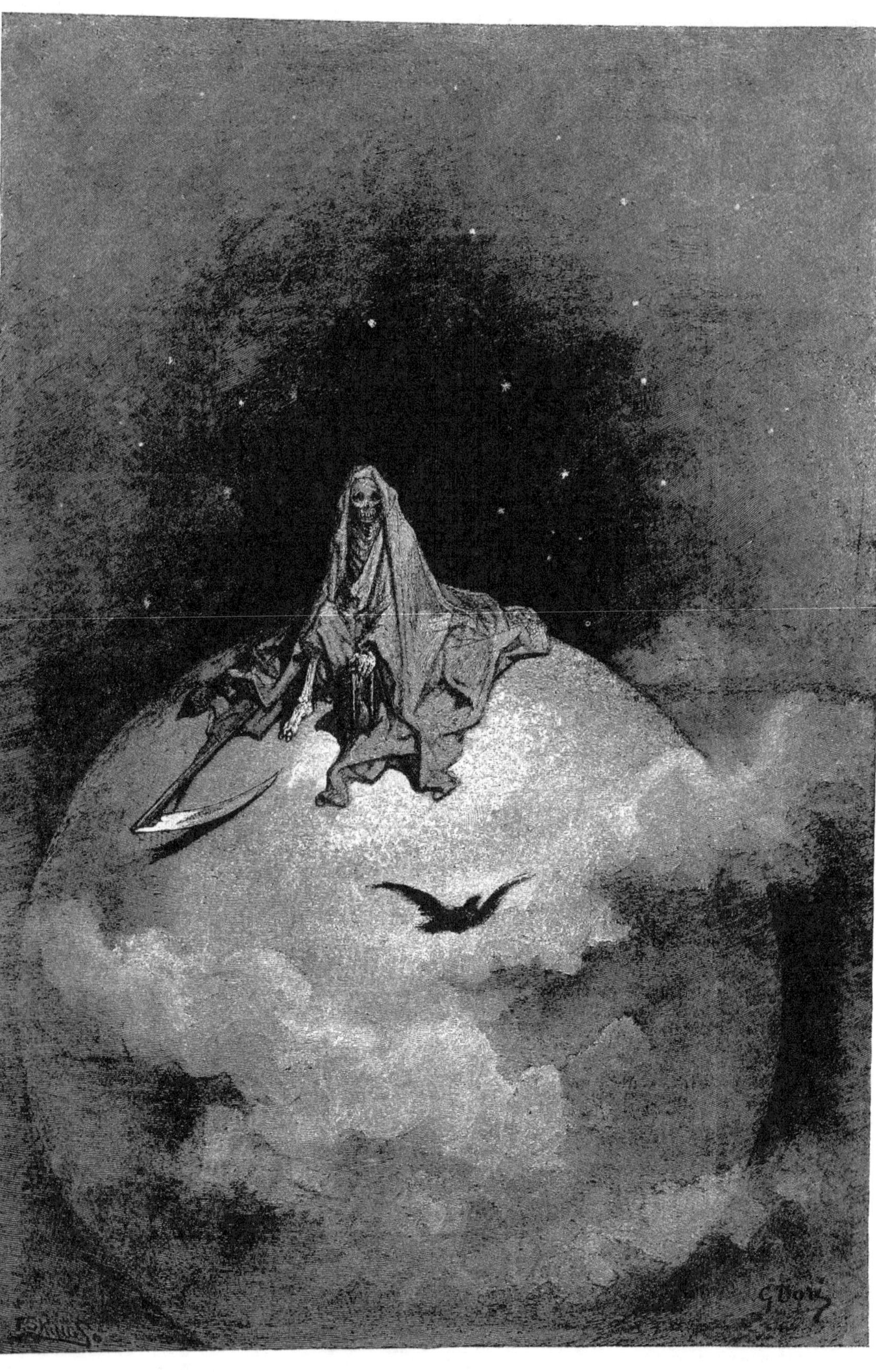

107. Doubting, dreaming dreams no mortal
ever dared to dream before. Gustave Doré.
1884

108

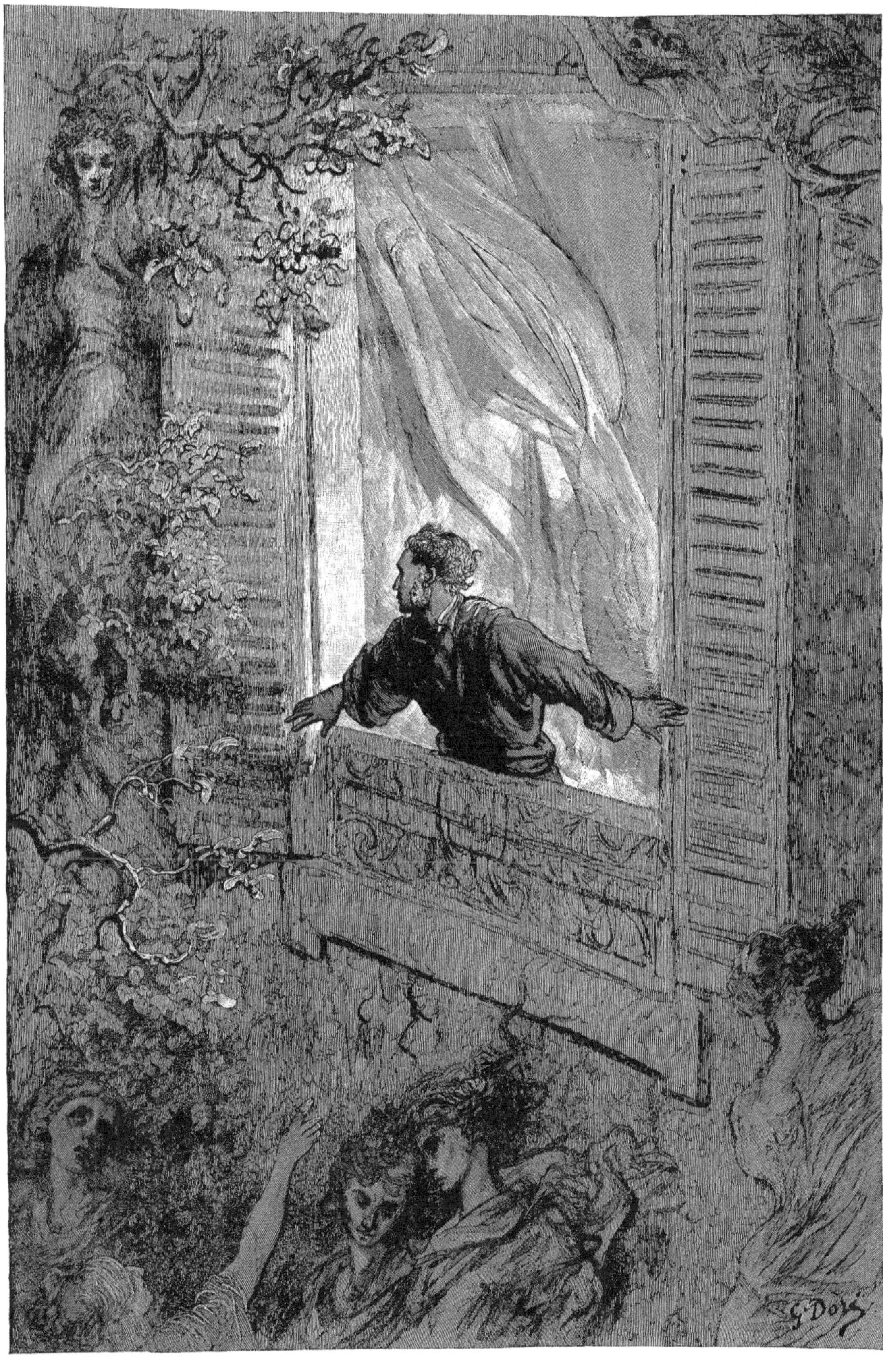

GUSTAVE DORÉ

108. Open here I flung the shutter. Gustave
Doré, 1884

109

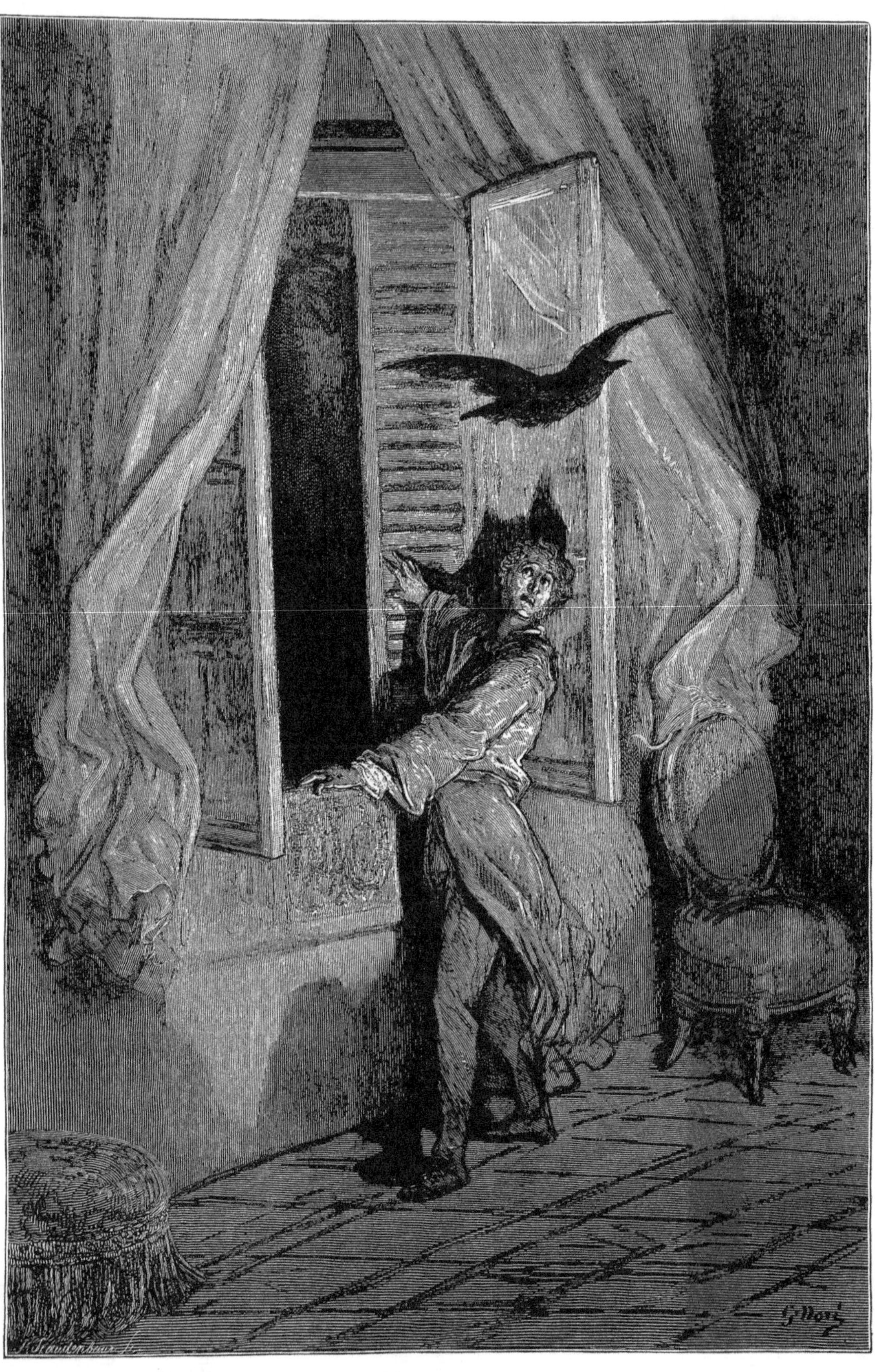

109. A stately Raven of the saintly days of yore.
Gustave Doré, 1884

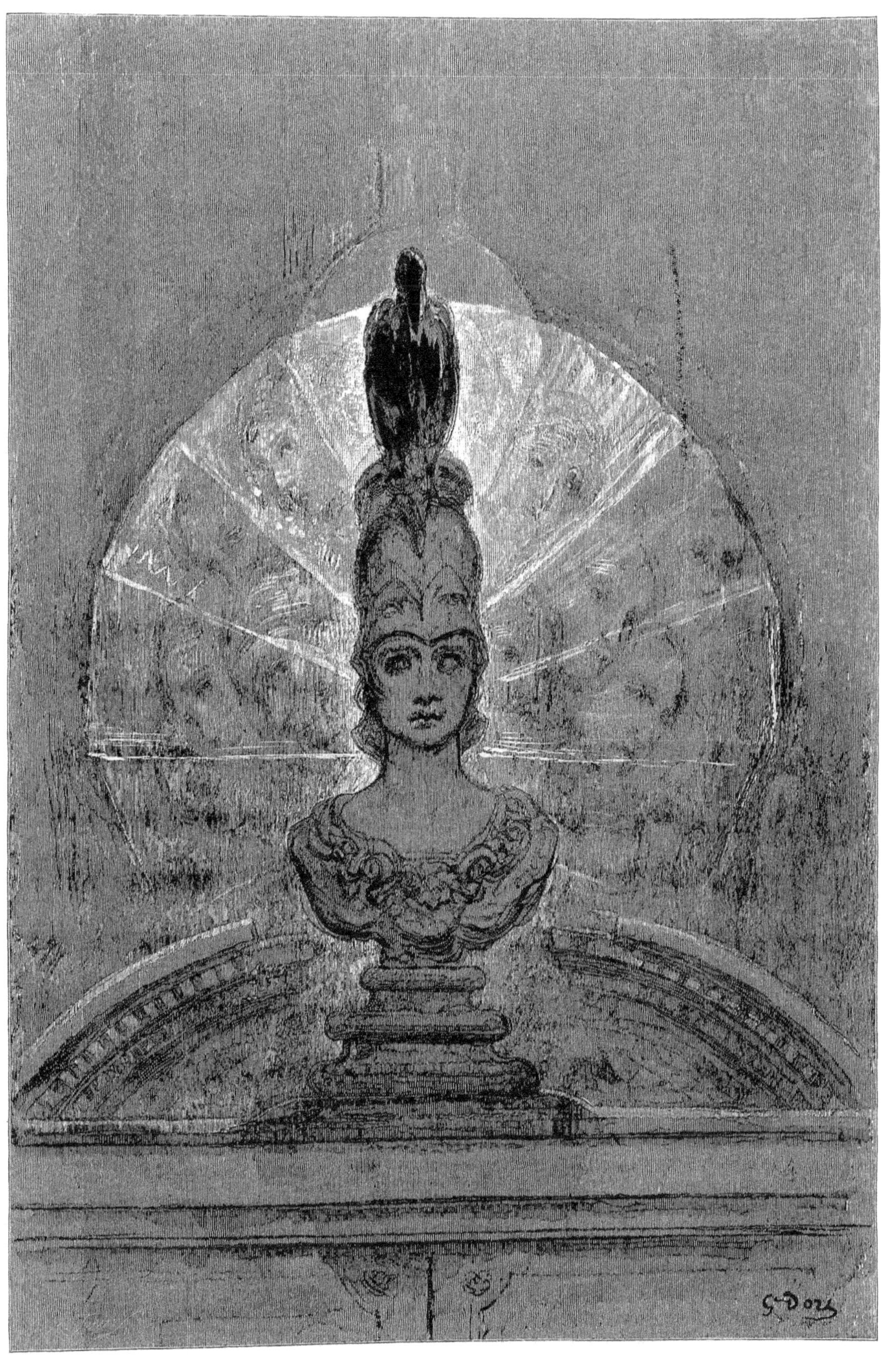

110. Perched upon a bust of Pallas just above
my chamber door—, Gustave Doré, 1884

111

GUSTAVE DORÉ

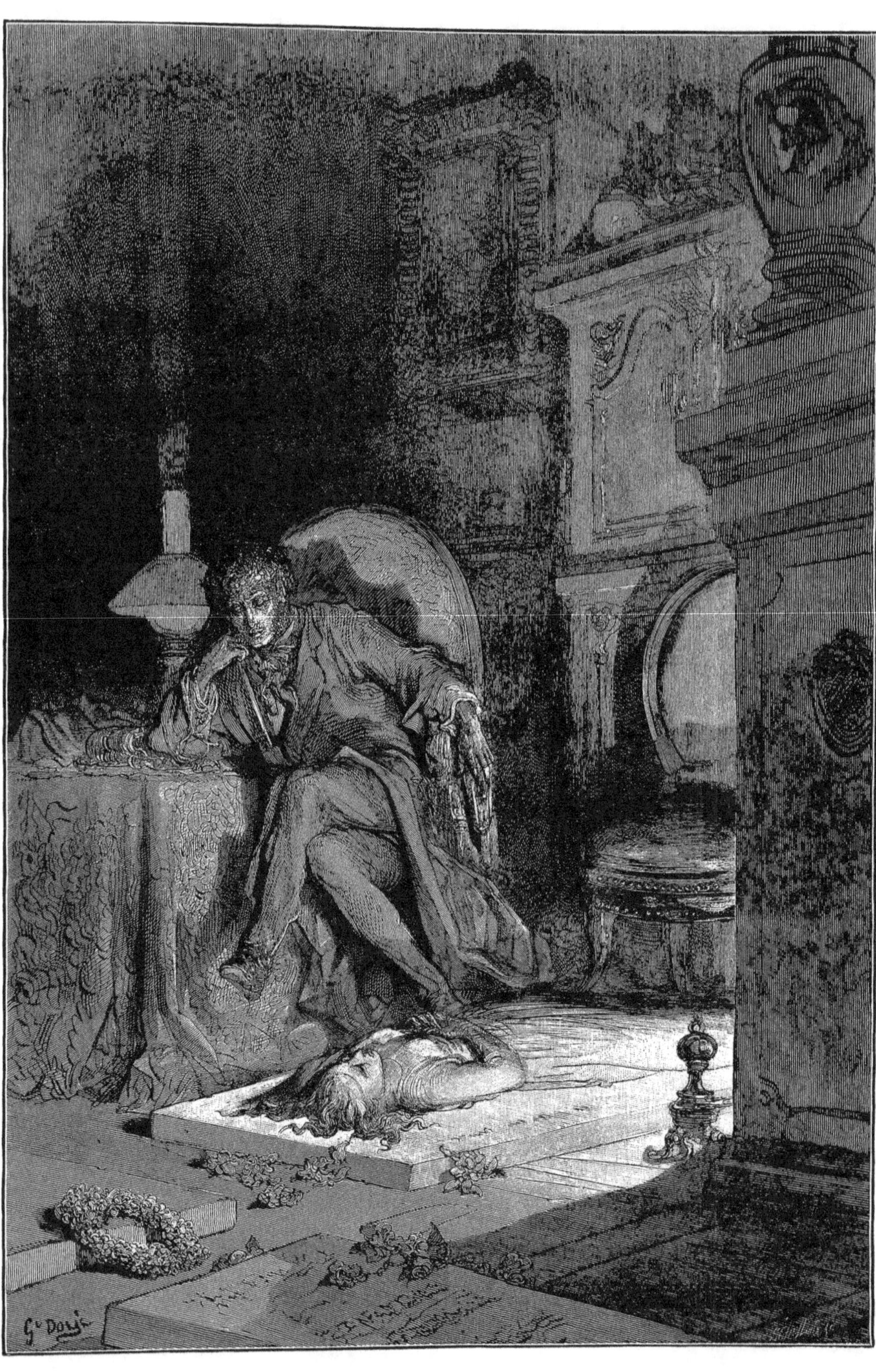

111. Then, upon the velvet sinking, I betook myself to linking. Gustave Doré, 1884.

112

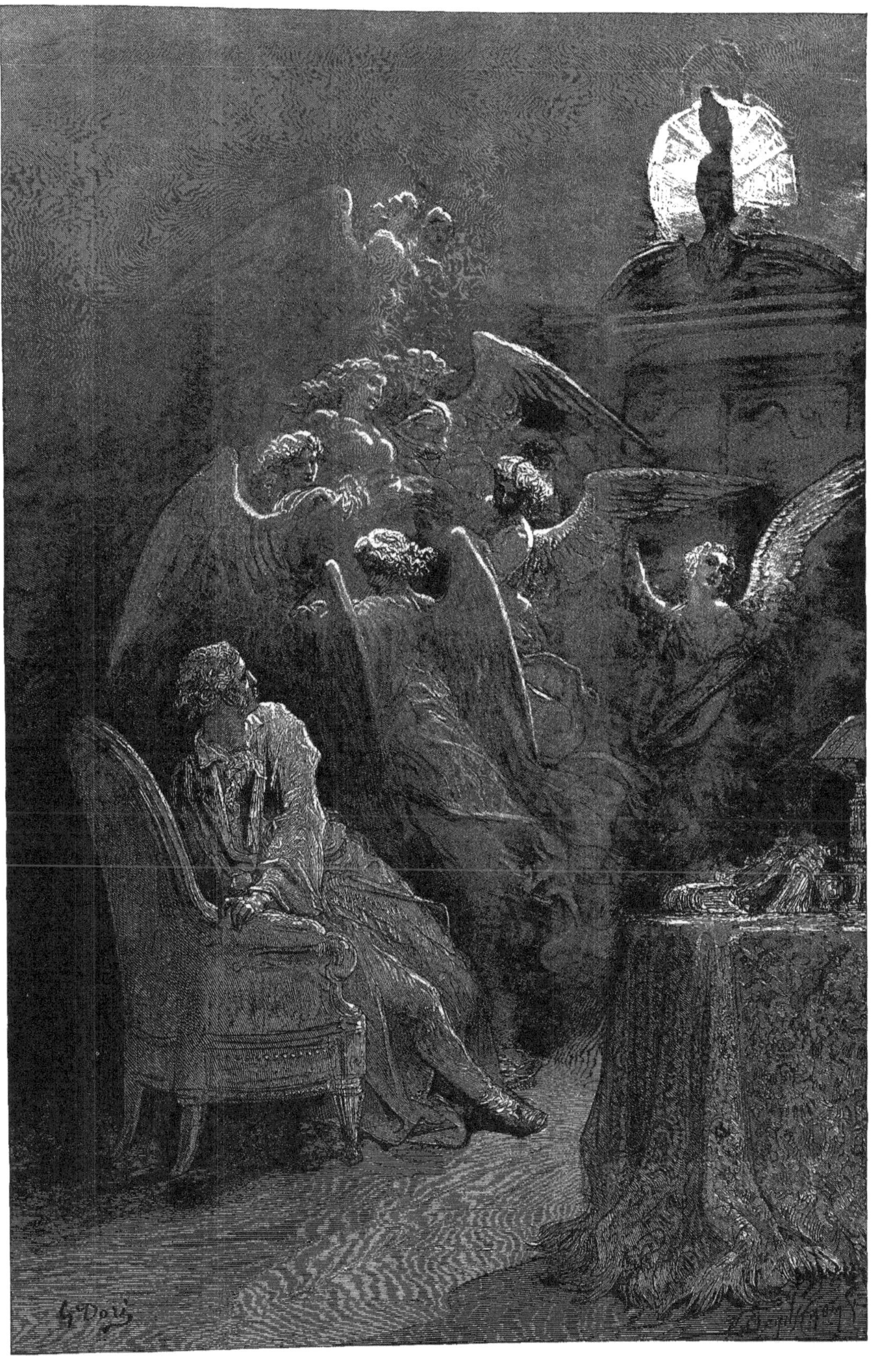

GUSTAVE DORÉ

08

PARADISE LOST

Paradise Lost, first published in 1667, is John Milton's epic masterpiece that recounts the biblical story of the Fall of Man. Written in blank verse, the poem explores Satan's rebellion, his expulsion from Heaven, and the temptation of Adam and Eve in the Garden of Eden. Through its grand scope and profound philosophical questions, *Paradise Lost* remains one of the most influential works in English literature, celebrated for its vivid imagery, theological depth, and masterful use of language.

Gustave Doré produced 50 illustrations to accompany *Paradise Lost*. His stunning images captured the grandeur and cosmic scale of Milton's epic. Through his dark, atmospheric style and masterful use of light and shadow, Doré brings to life the battle between Heaven and Hell and the tragic fall of Adam and Eve. His sweeping landscapes transport the viewer from Hell's shadowy depths to Eden's ethereal beauty.

These images, first published in 1866, are widely regarded as some of the most iconic interpretations of the poem and have continued to inspire and captivate readers for more than 150 years.

113

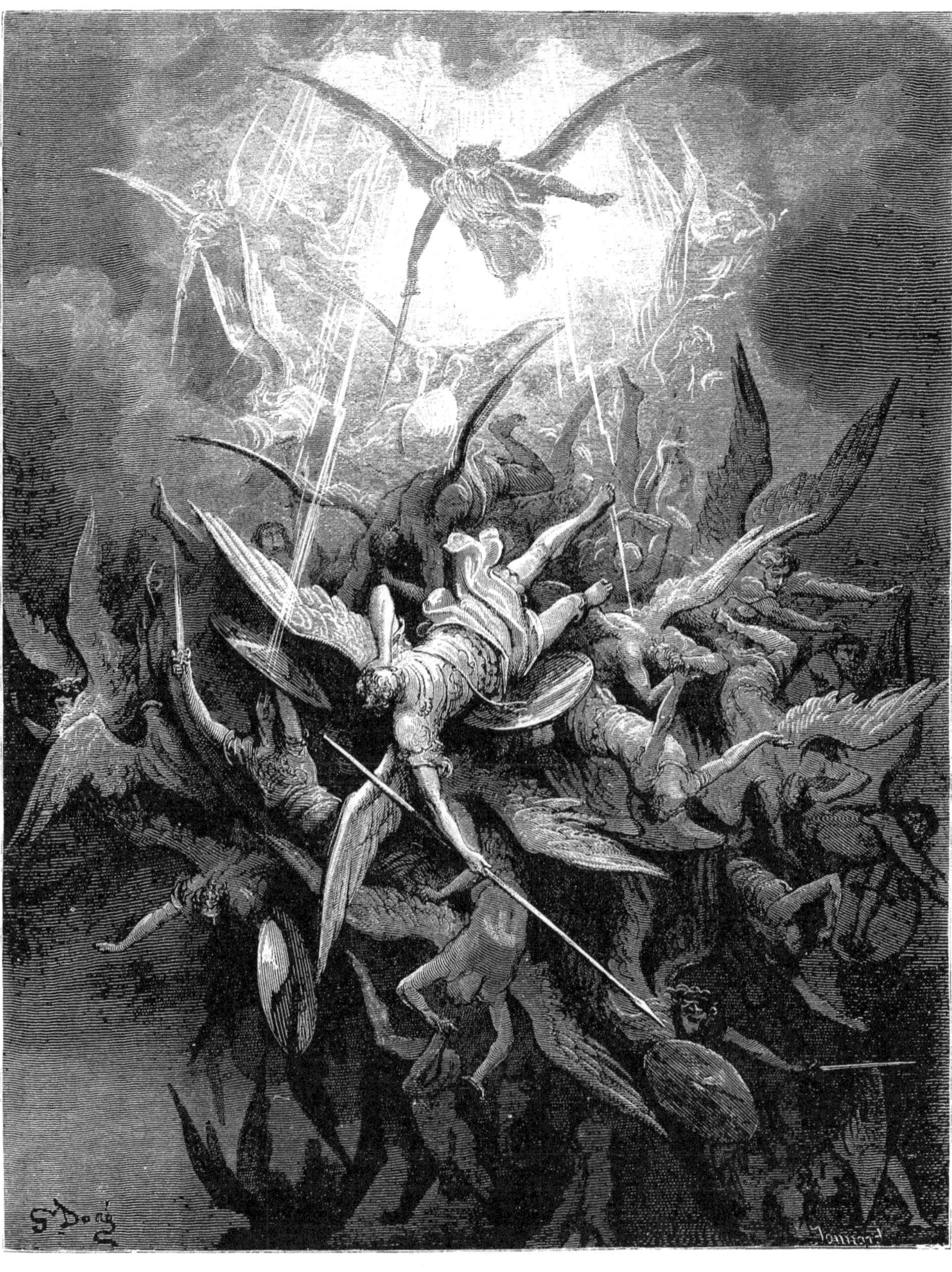

113. Him the Almighty Power, Hurled headlong flaming from the ethereal sky, Gustave Doré, 1866

114

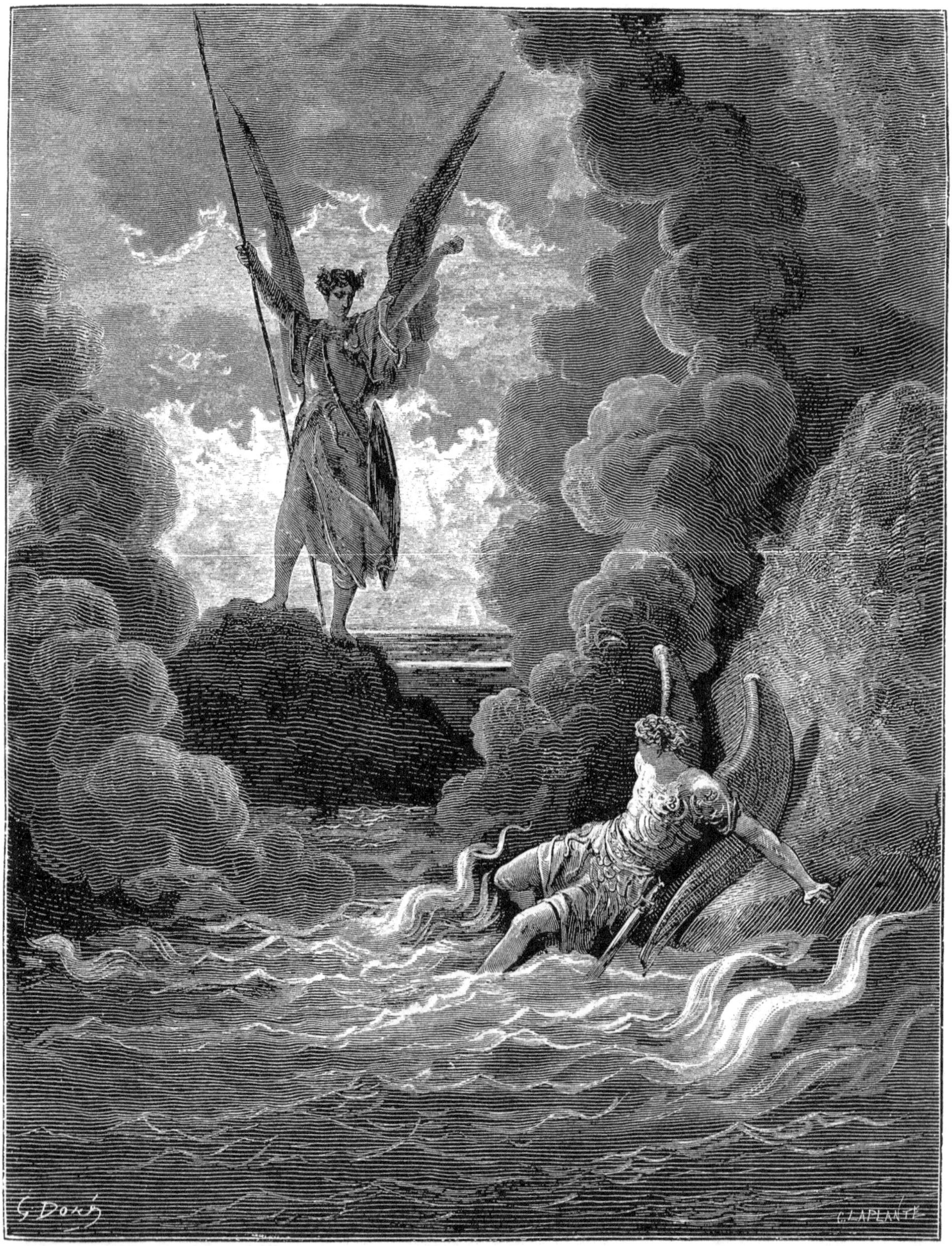

114. *Forthwith upright he rears from off the pool, His mighty stature, Gustave Doré, 1866*

115

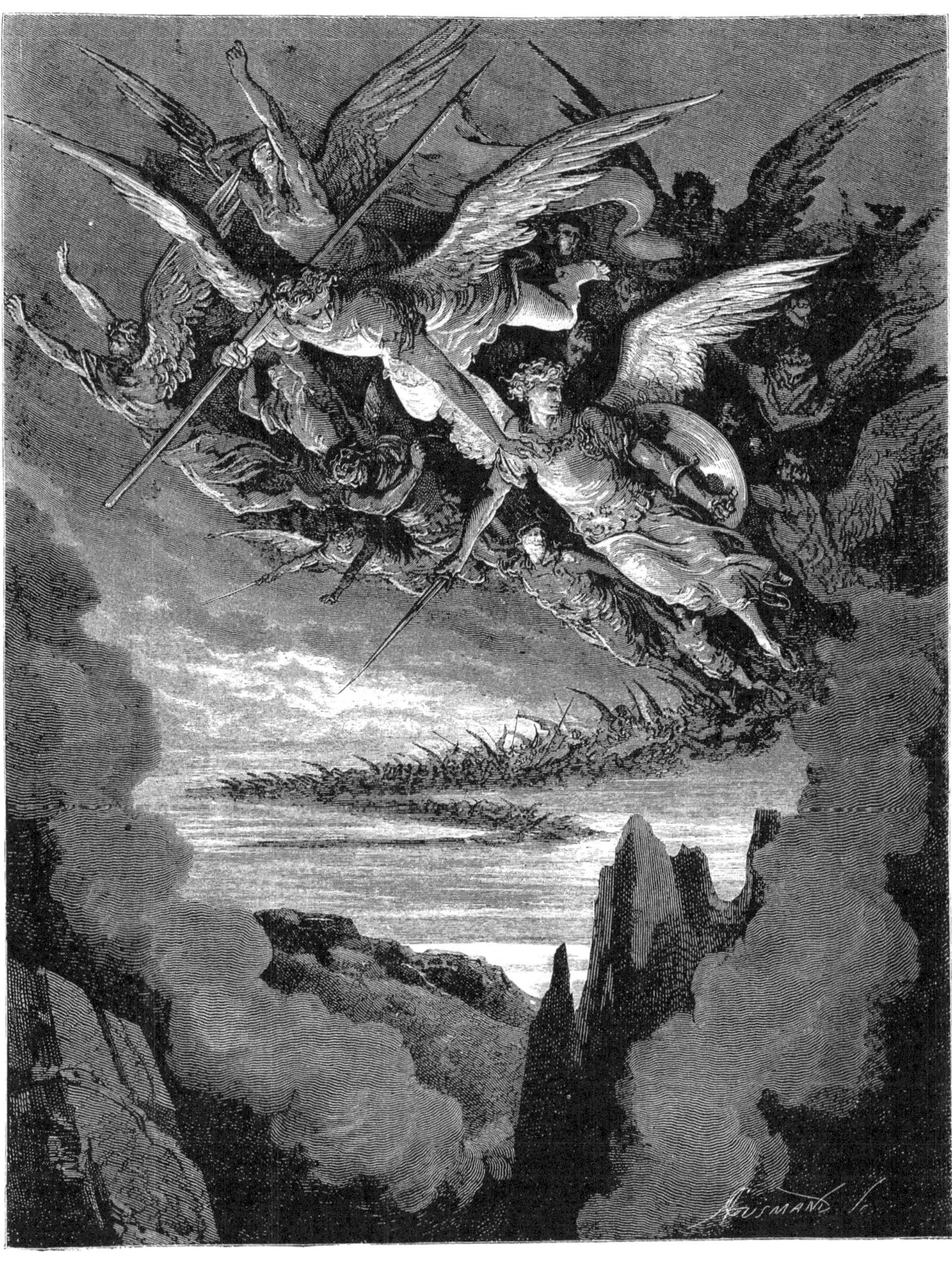

GUSTAVE DORÉ

115 So numberless were those bad Angels
seen, Hovering on wing, under the cope of Hell.
Gustave Doré, 1866

116

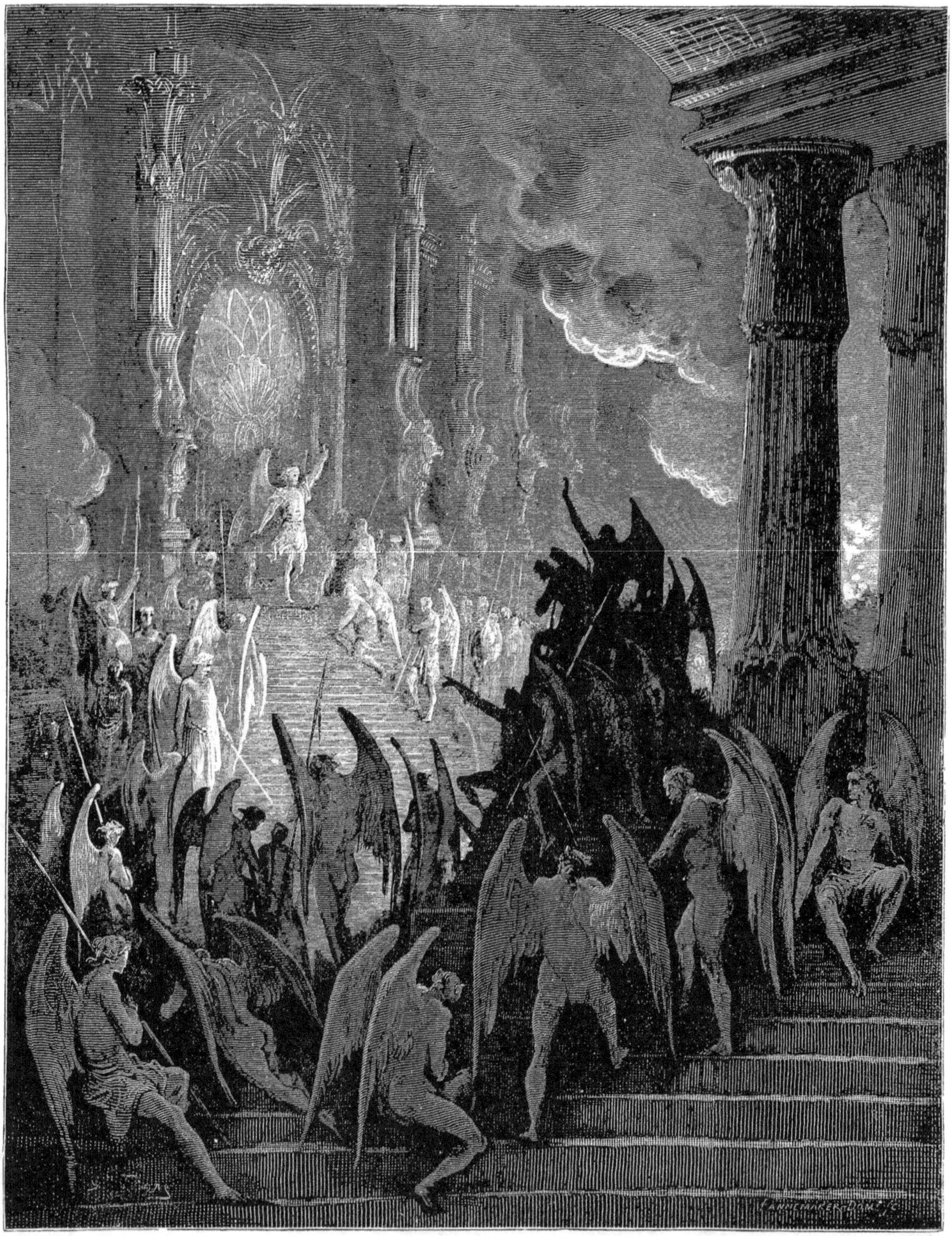

GUSTAVE DORÉ

116. *High on a throne of royal state, which far,*
Outshone the wealth of Ormus and of Ind.
Gustave Doré, 1866

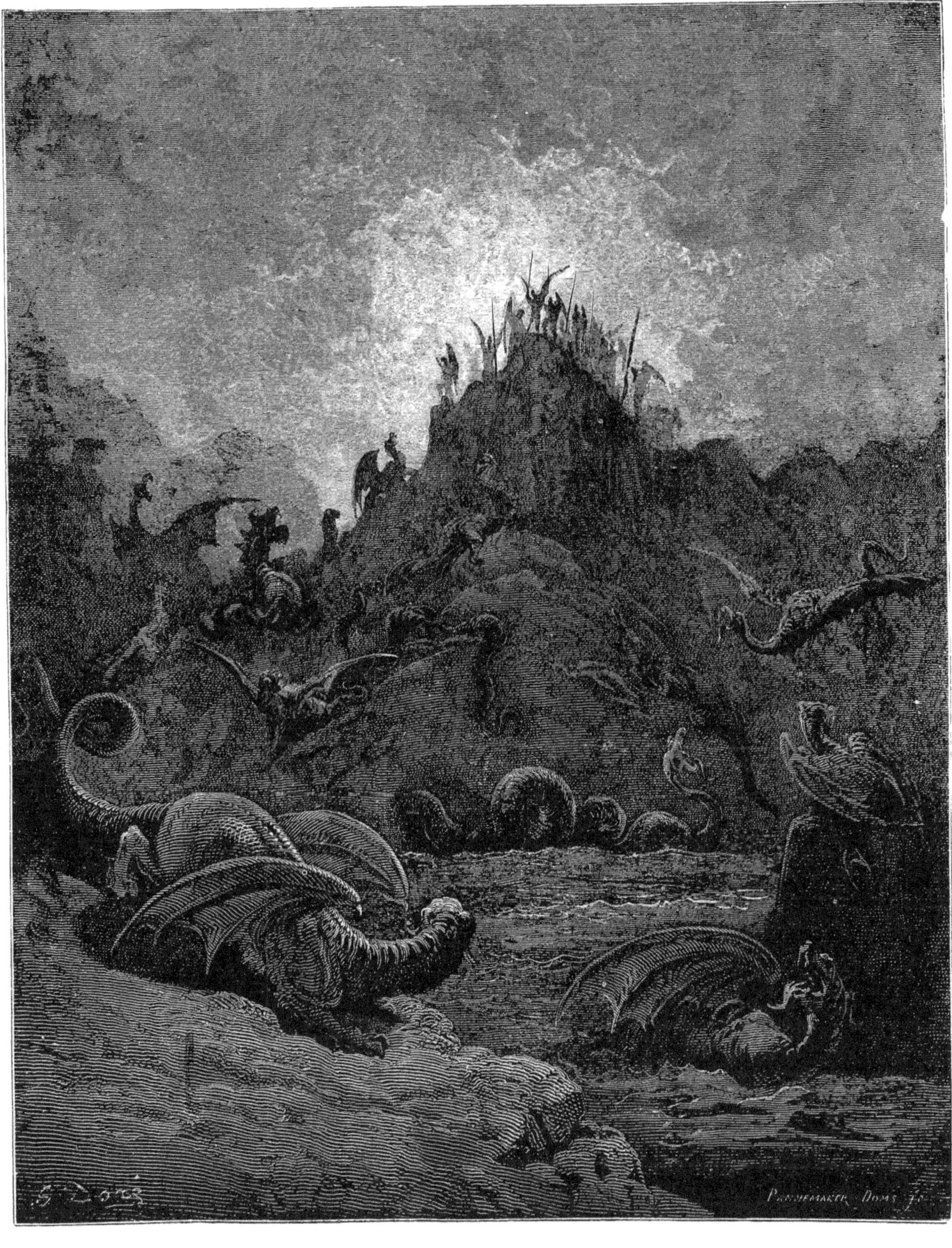

117. Gorgons, and Hydras, and Chimeras dire,
Gustave Doré, 1866

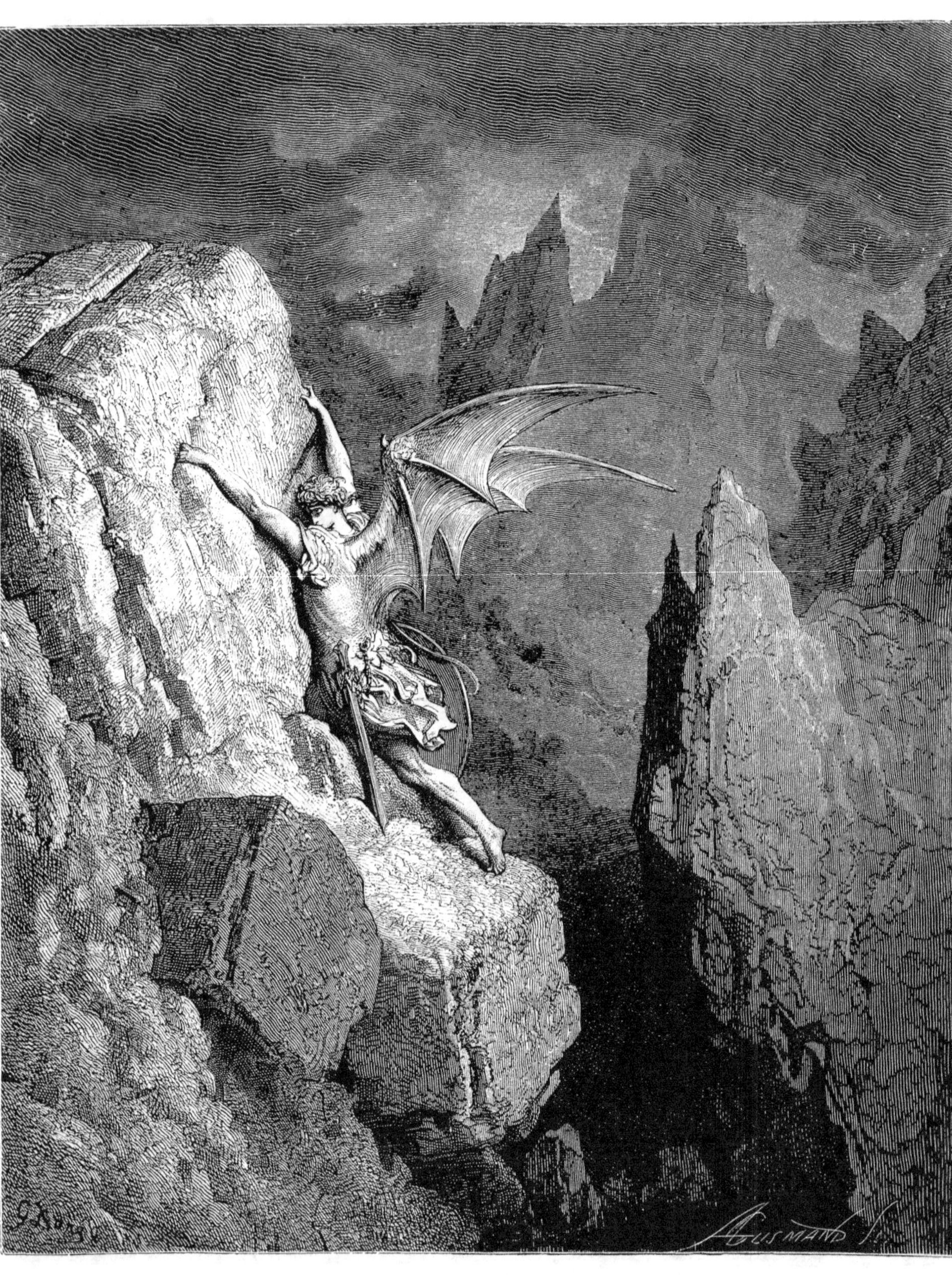

118. With head, hands, wings, or feet pursues his way, And swims or sinks, or wades, or creeps, or flies. Gustave Doré, 1866

119

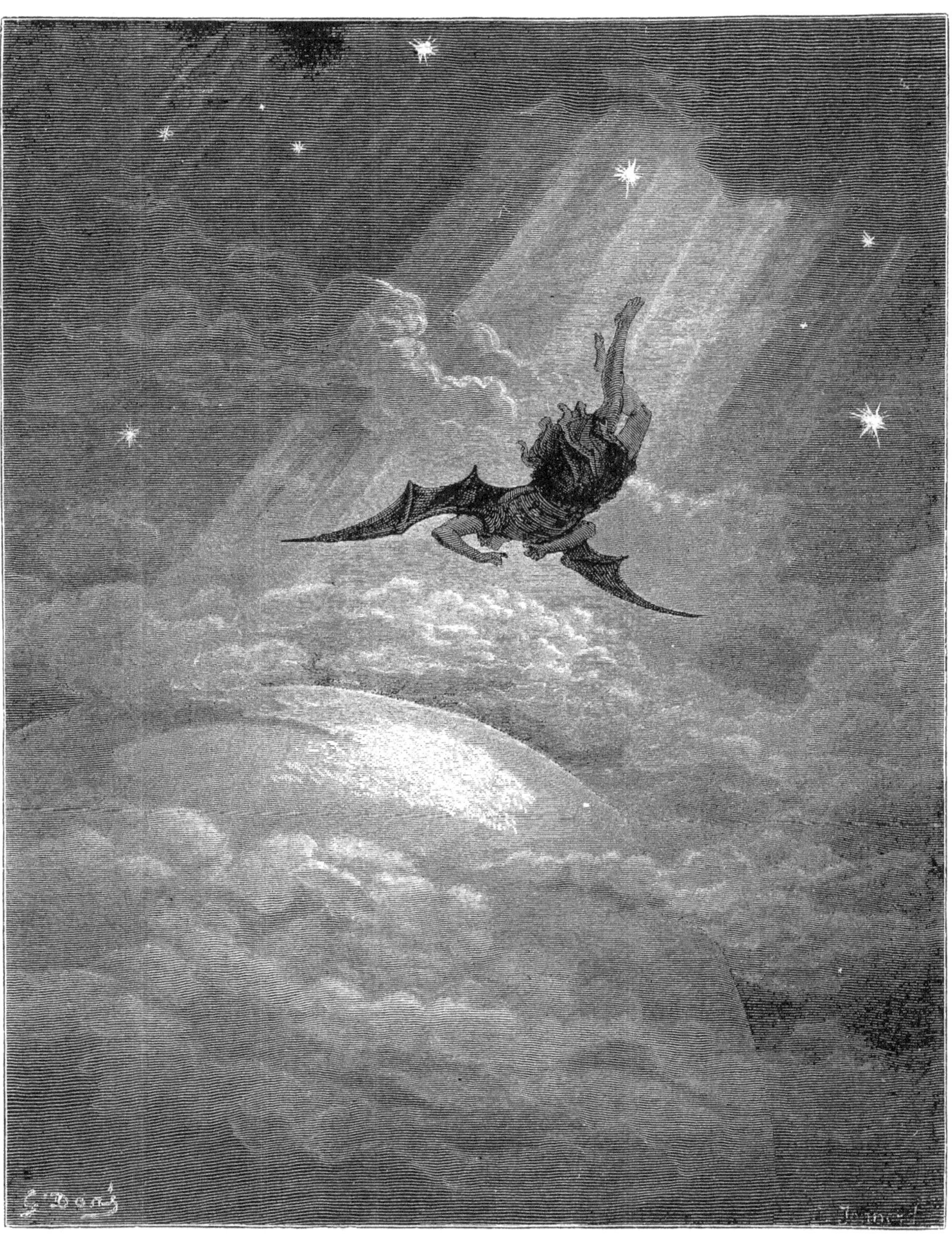

GUSTAVE DORÉ

119. Towards the coast of Earth beneath, Down from the
ecliptic, sped with hoped success. Throws his steep
flight in many an aëry wheel. Gustave Doré, 1866.

120

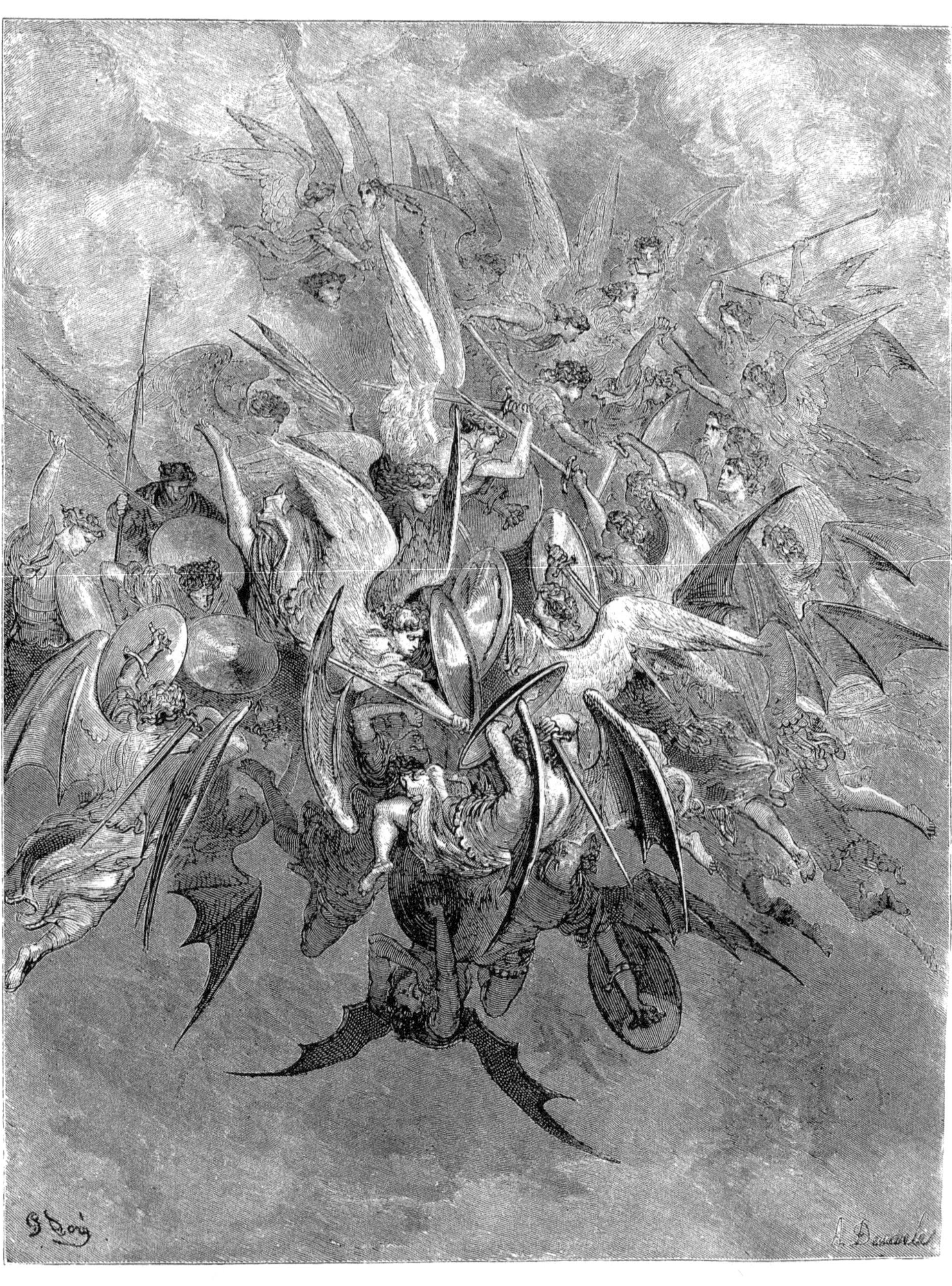

120. Now storming fury rose. And clamor, such
as heard in heaven till now. Gustave Doré, 1875

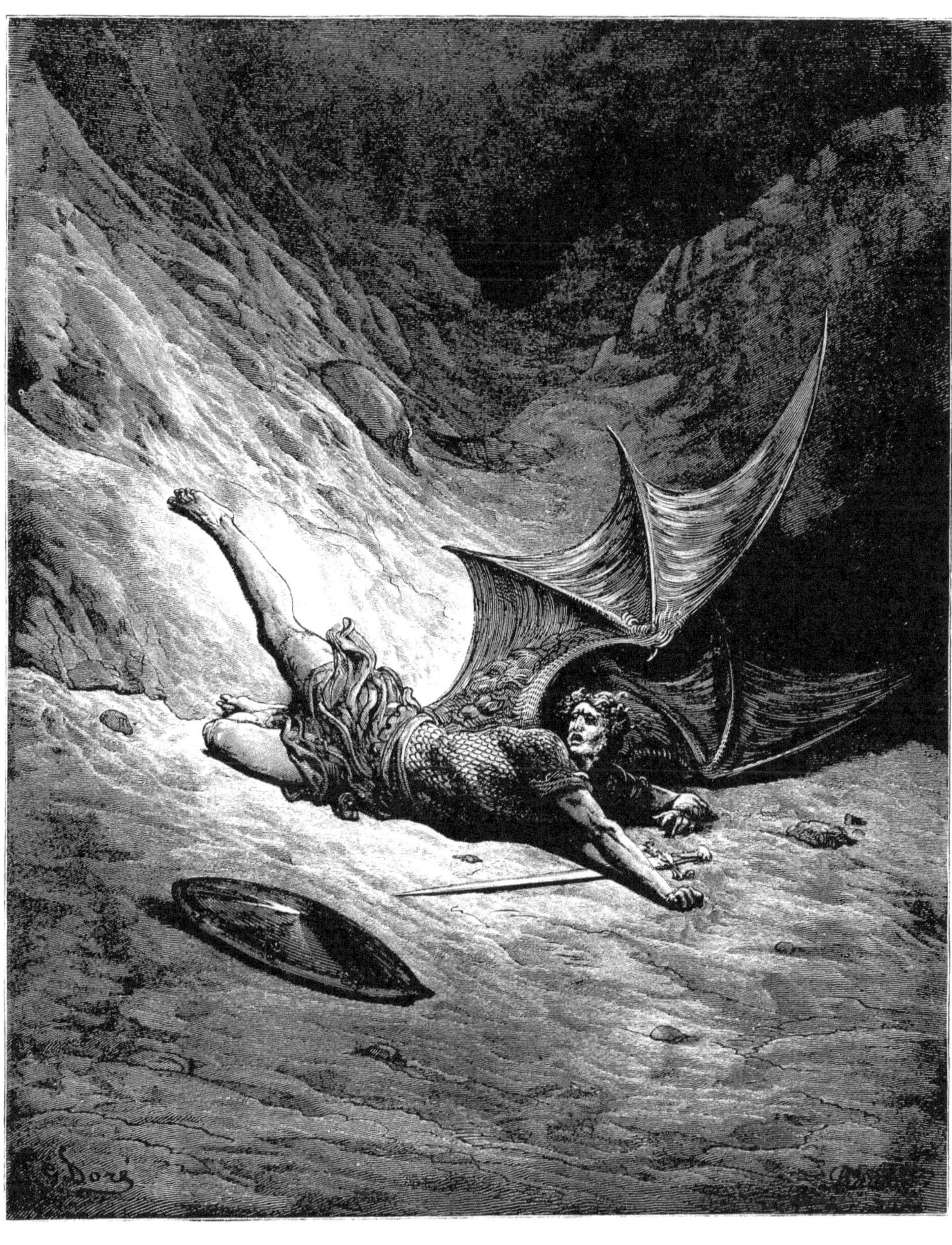

GUSTAVE DORÉ

121. Then Satan first knew pain, And writhed him to and
fro. Gustave Doré, 1866

122

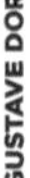

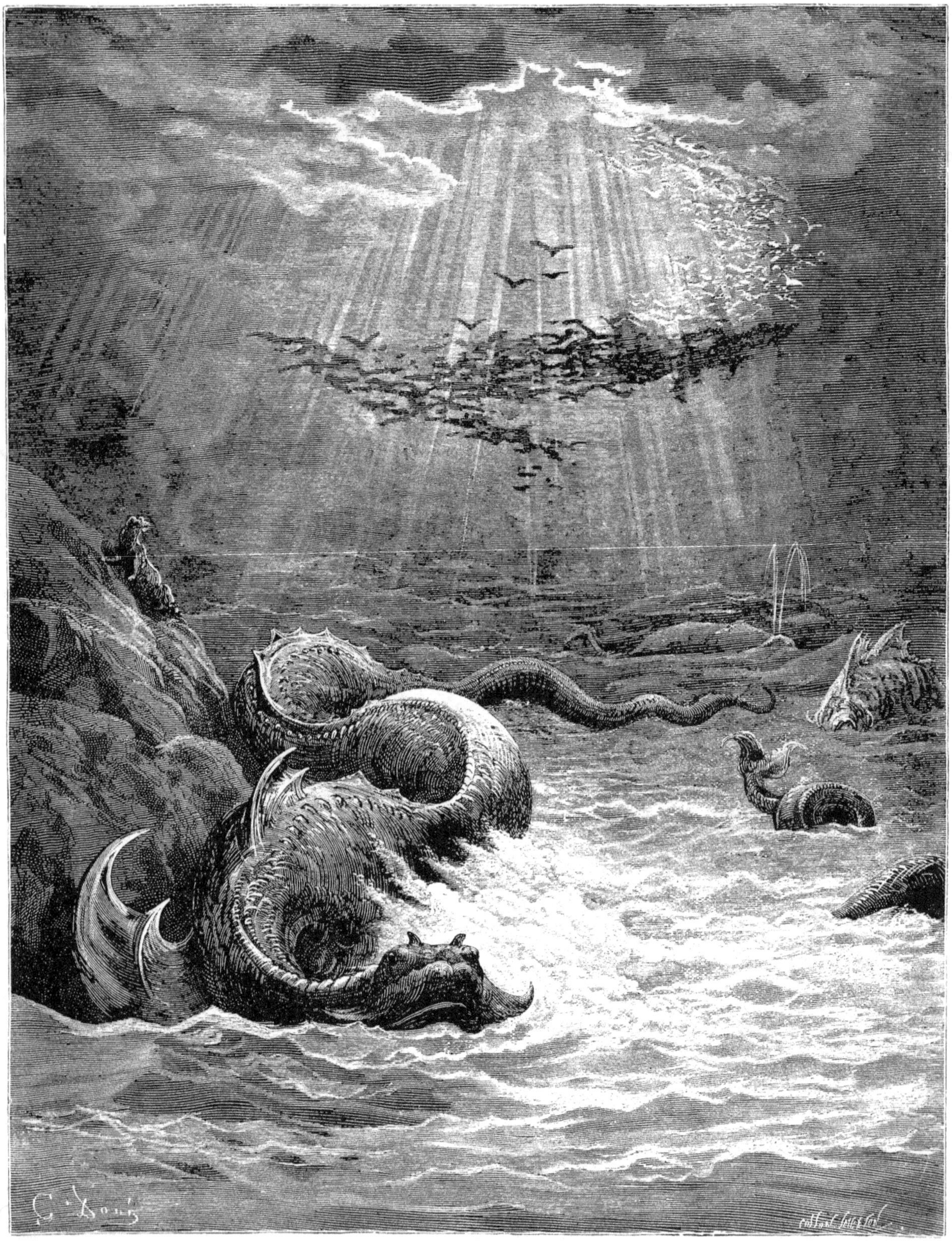

122. And God said - Let the waters generate
Reptile with spawn abundant, living soul: And
let fowl fly above the earth. Gustave Doré, 1866

123

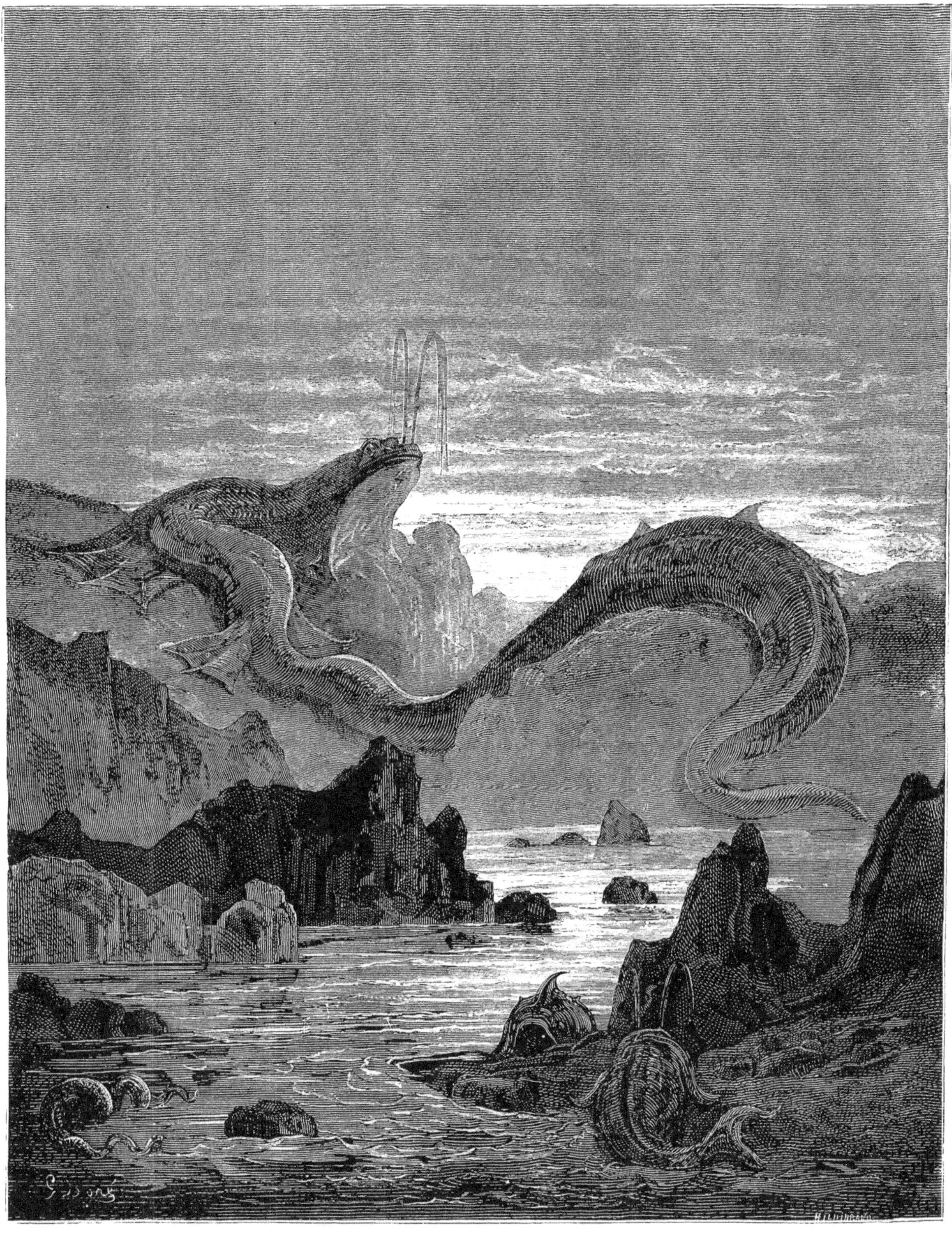

GUSTAVE DORÉ

123. And seems a moving land; and at his gills
Draws in, and at his trunk spouts out, a sea.
Gustave Doré, 1866

124

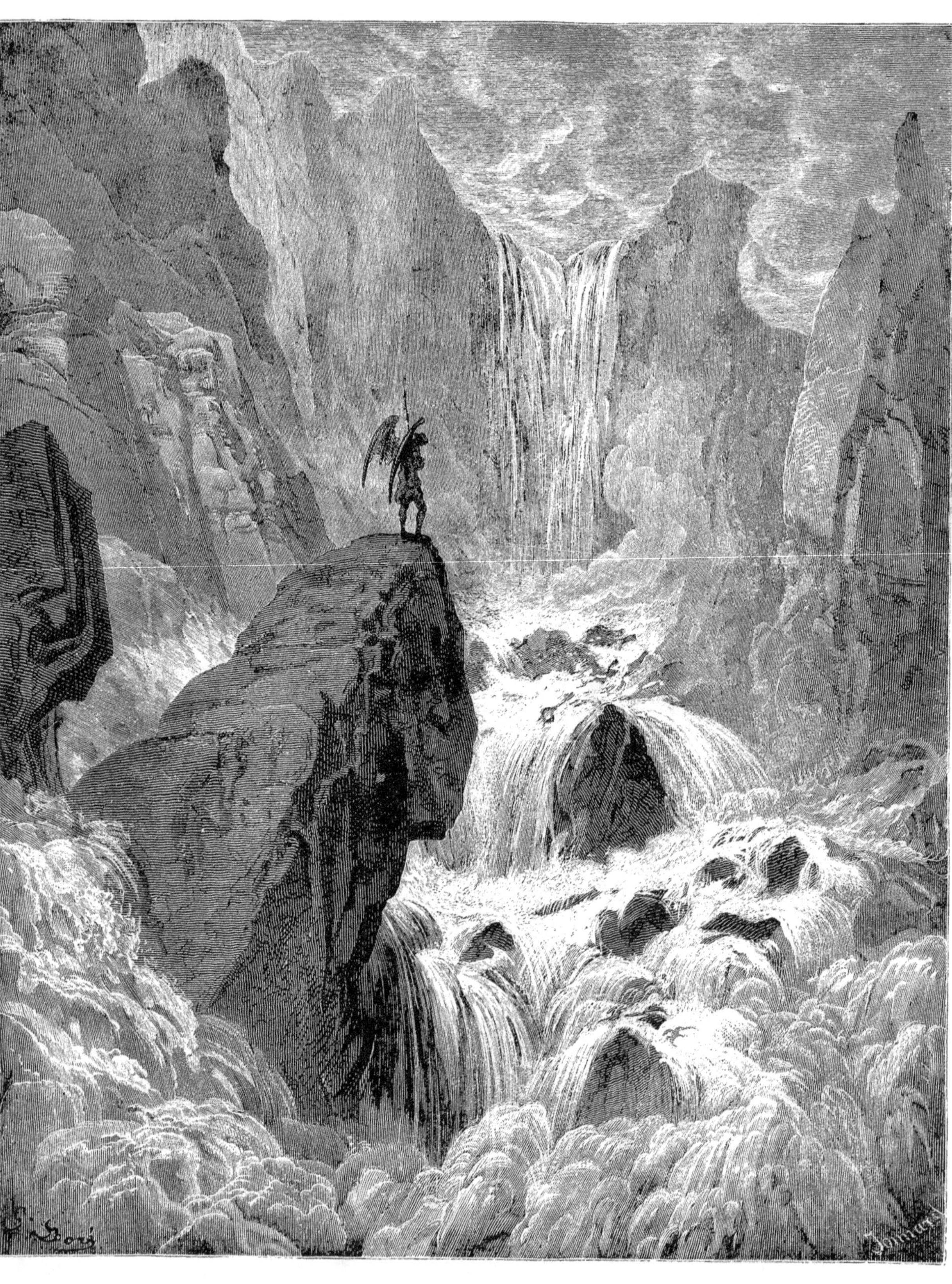

124. In with the river sunk, and with it rose.
Satan, Gustave Doré, 1866

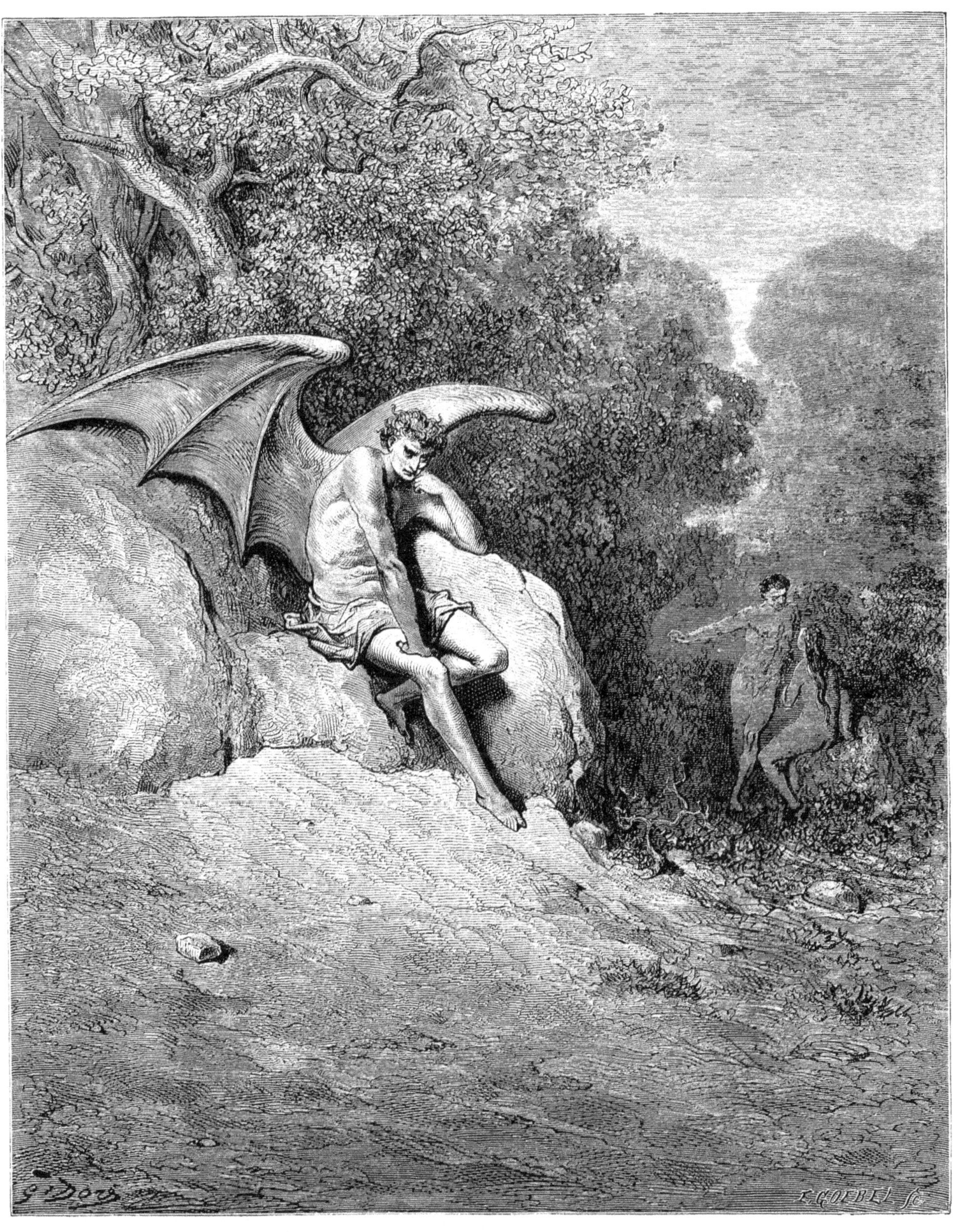

125. O Earth, how like to Heaven, if not preferred.
More justly. Gustave Doré. 1866

126

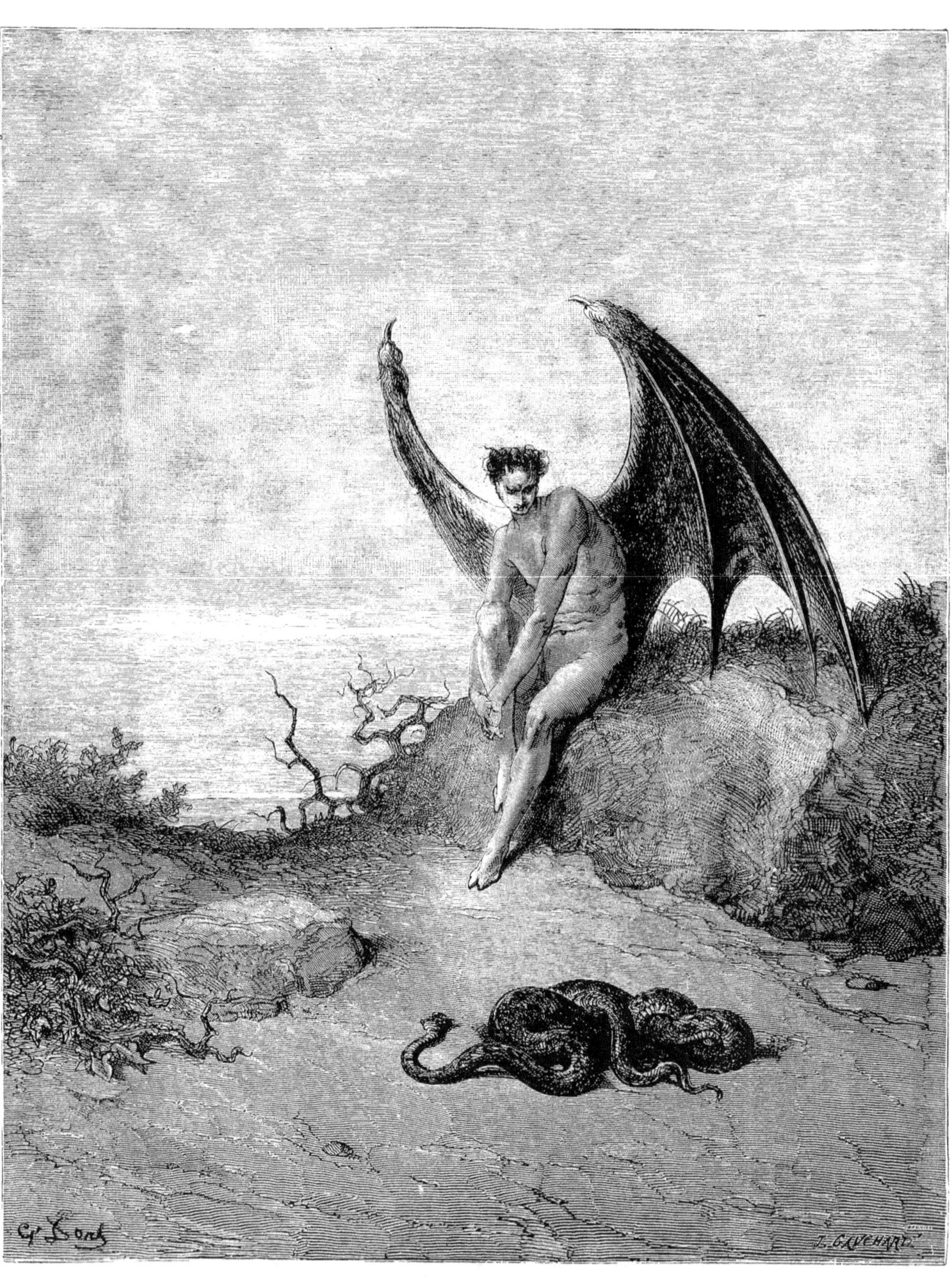

126. Him, fast sleeping, soon he found, In labyrinth of many a round, self-rolled. Gustave Doré, 1866

127

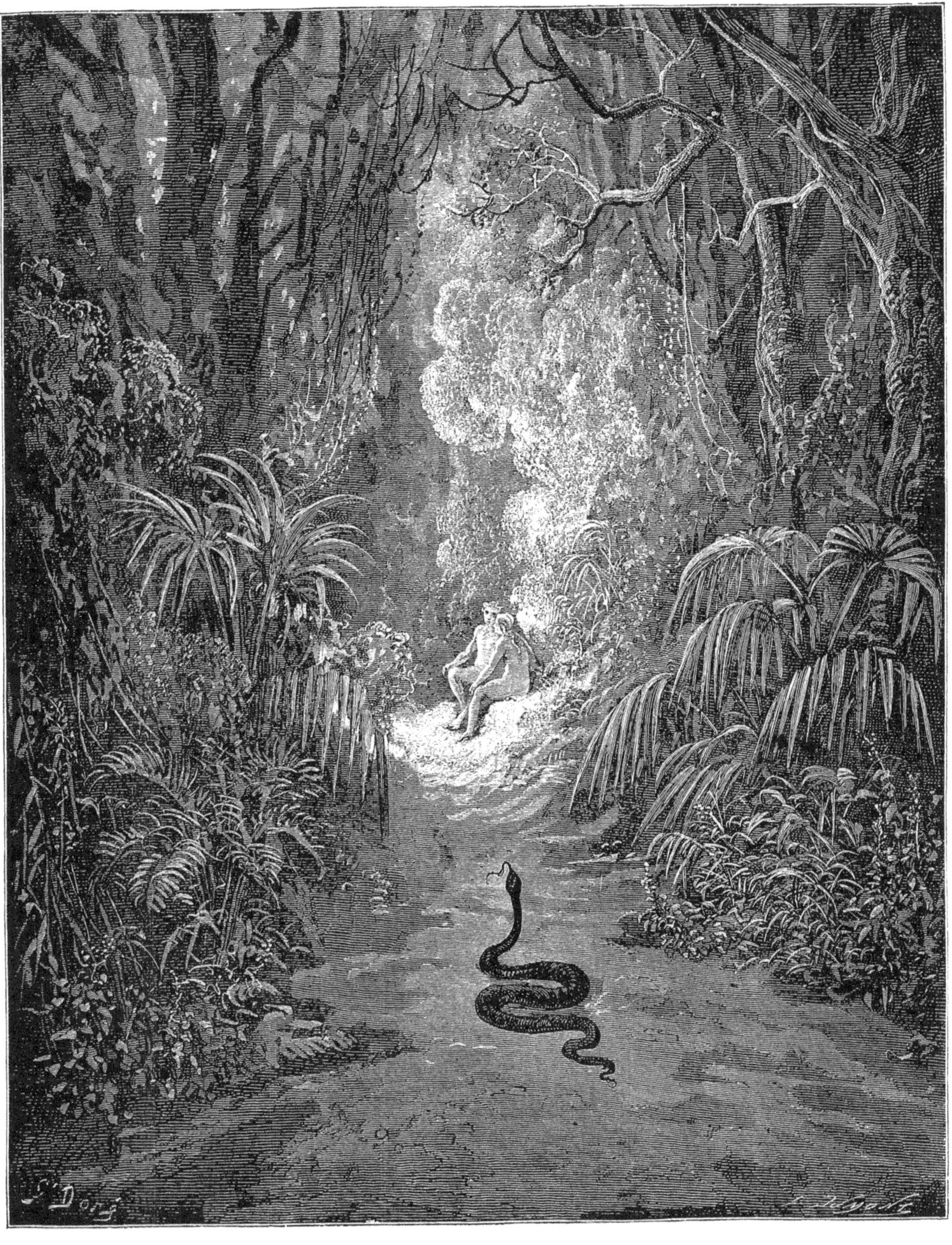

127. Nearer he drew, and many a walk traversed,
Of stateliest covert, cedar, pine or palm, Gustave
Doré, 1866

128

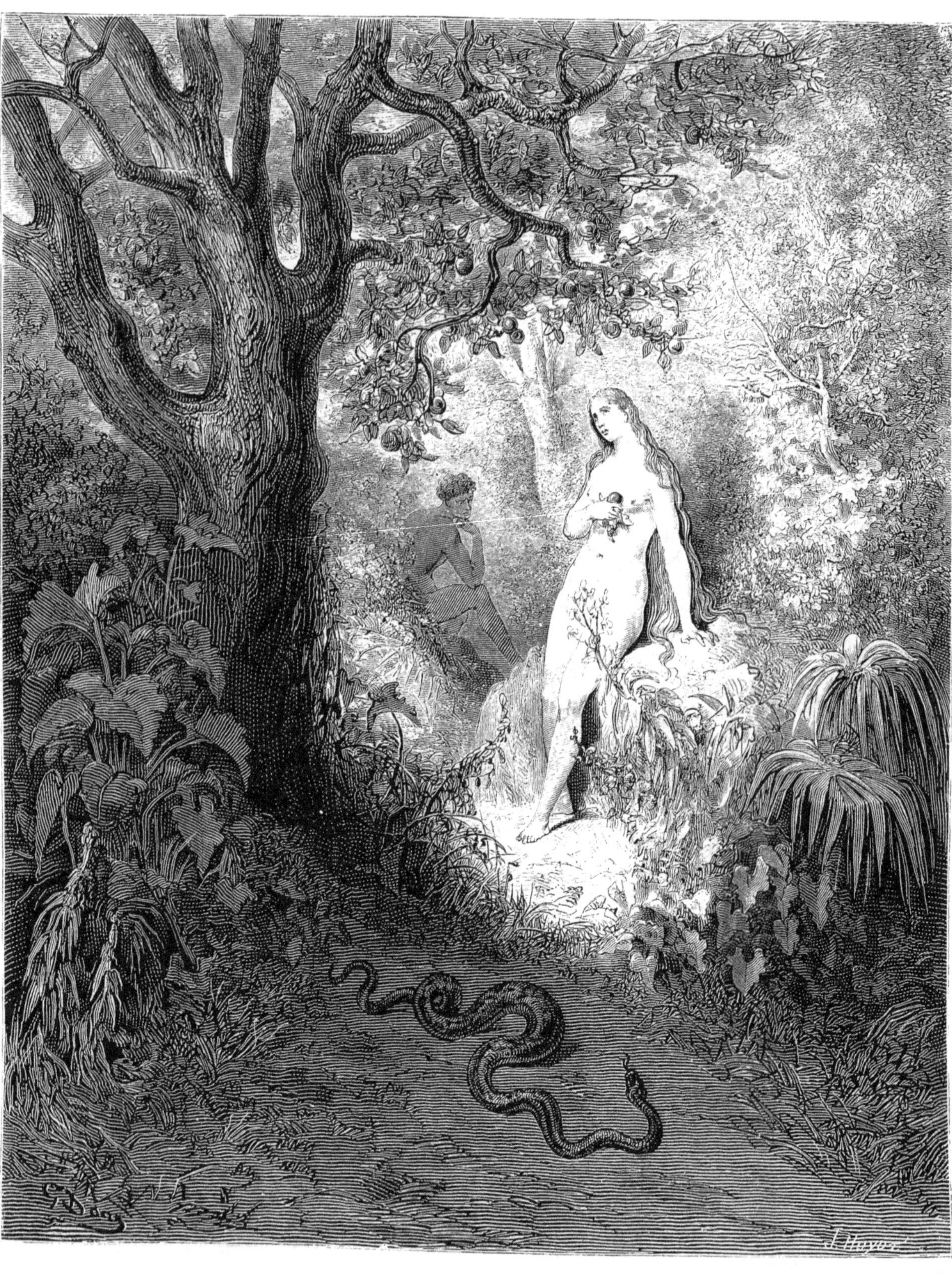

128. Back to the thicket slunk, The guilty
serpent. Gustave Doré, 1866

129

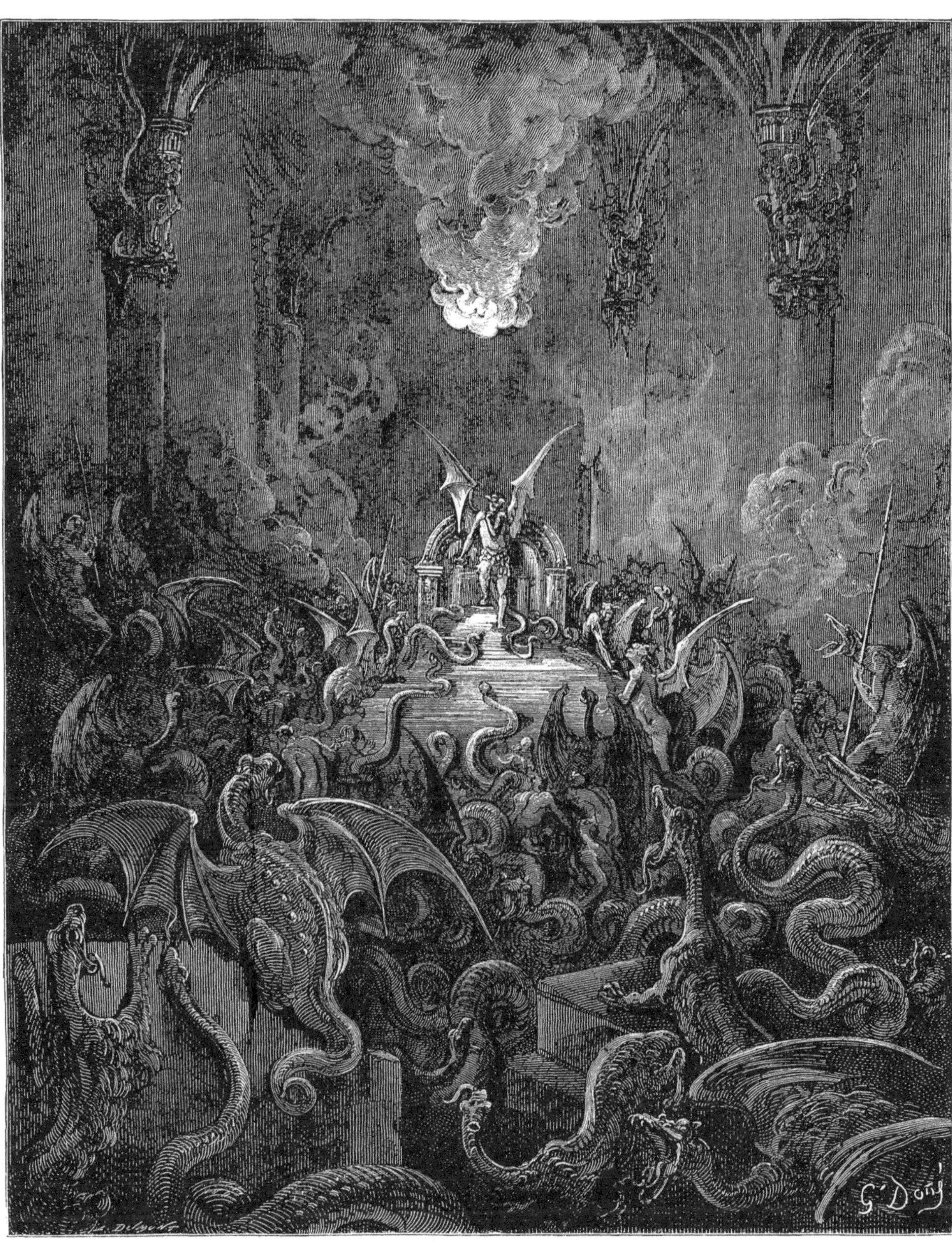

GUSTAVE DORÉ

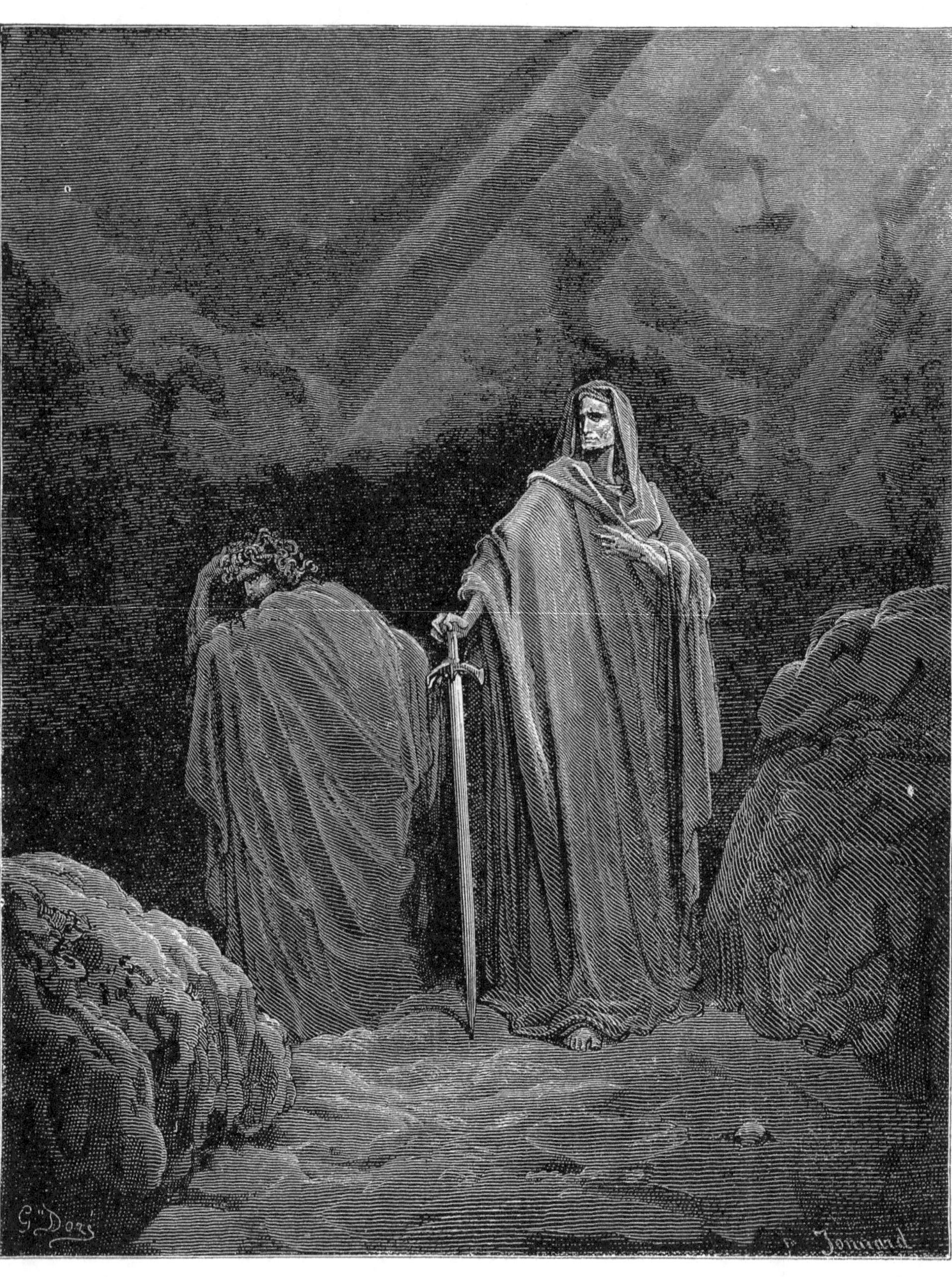

*130. This said, they both betook them several
ways. Gustave Doré, 1866*

131

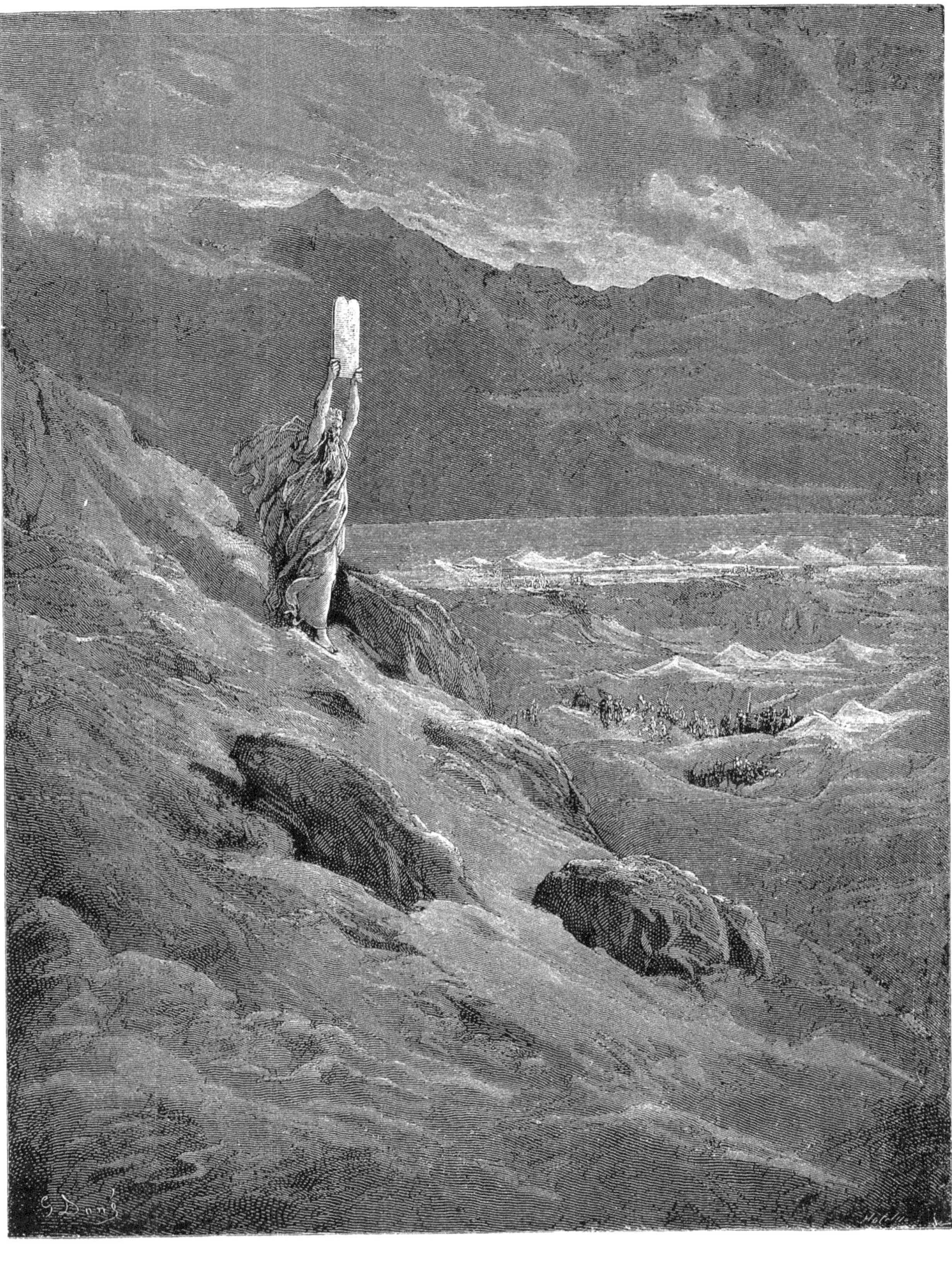

131 They beseech, that Moses might report
to them his will, And terror cease. Gustave
Doré, 1866

09

THE BIBLE

Gustave Doré's illustrations of *The Bible* are one of the most iconic artistic interpretations of biblical scenes ever created. This monumental series, comprising 241 wood engravings, was first published in 1866. Doré's intricate and dramatic engravings breathe new life into the stories of *The Bible*, offering readers a visual dimension that captures both the majesty and the mystery of these ancient texts. The illustrations, widely praised for their emotional depth and technical brilliance, became a cultural phenomenon, shaping how people visualise biblical scenes for generations. Doré's distinctive style—his ability to blend light and shadow, his mastery of movement and emotion, and his glorious vision—imbued *The Bible* with a sense of epic scale. His illustrations of biblical narratives, from the nativity to the apocalyptic visions of Revelation, remain a profound testament to his genius.

132

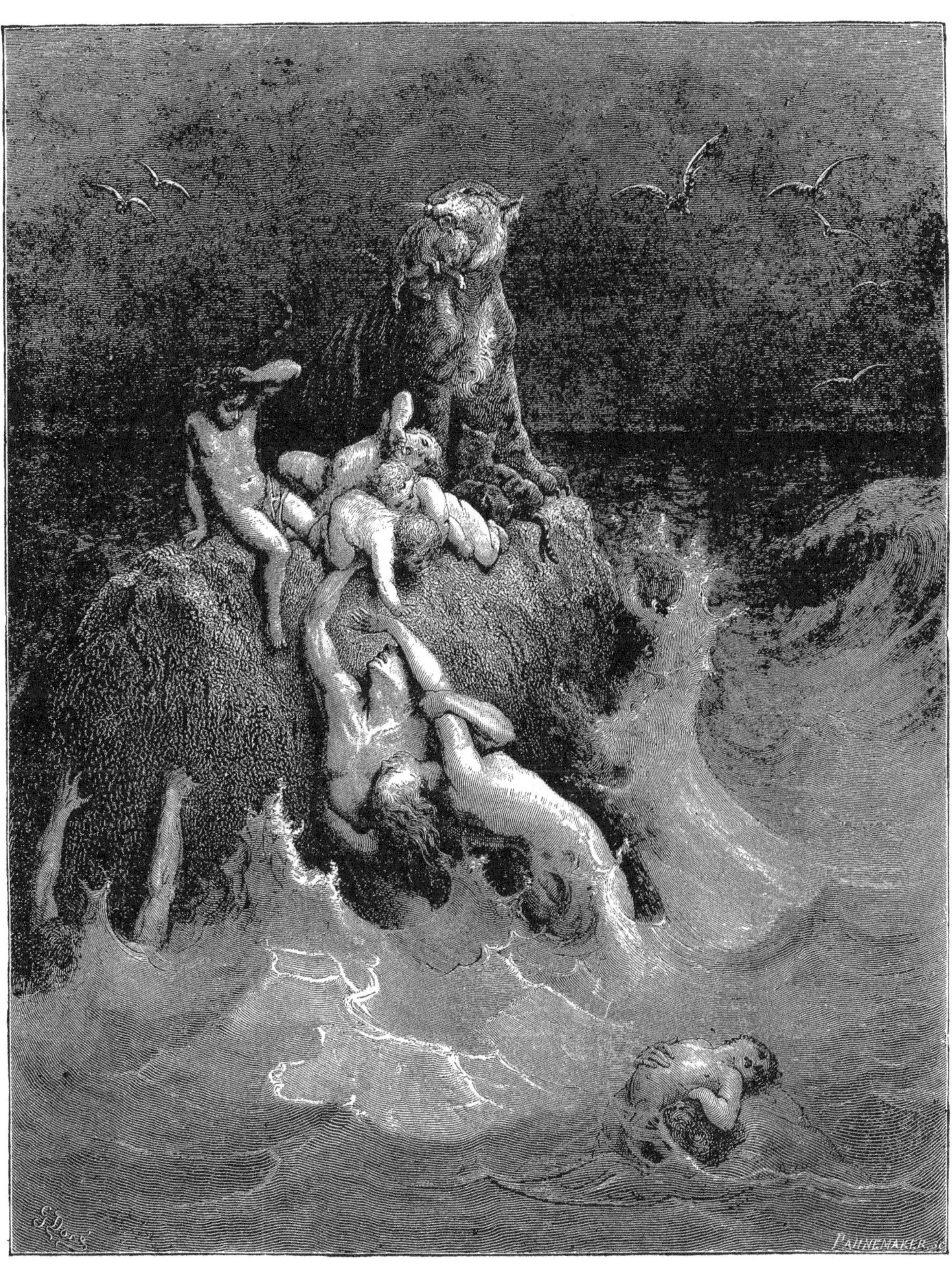

GUSTAVE DORÉ

133

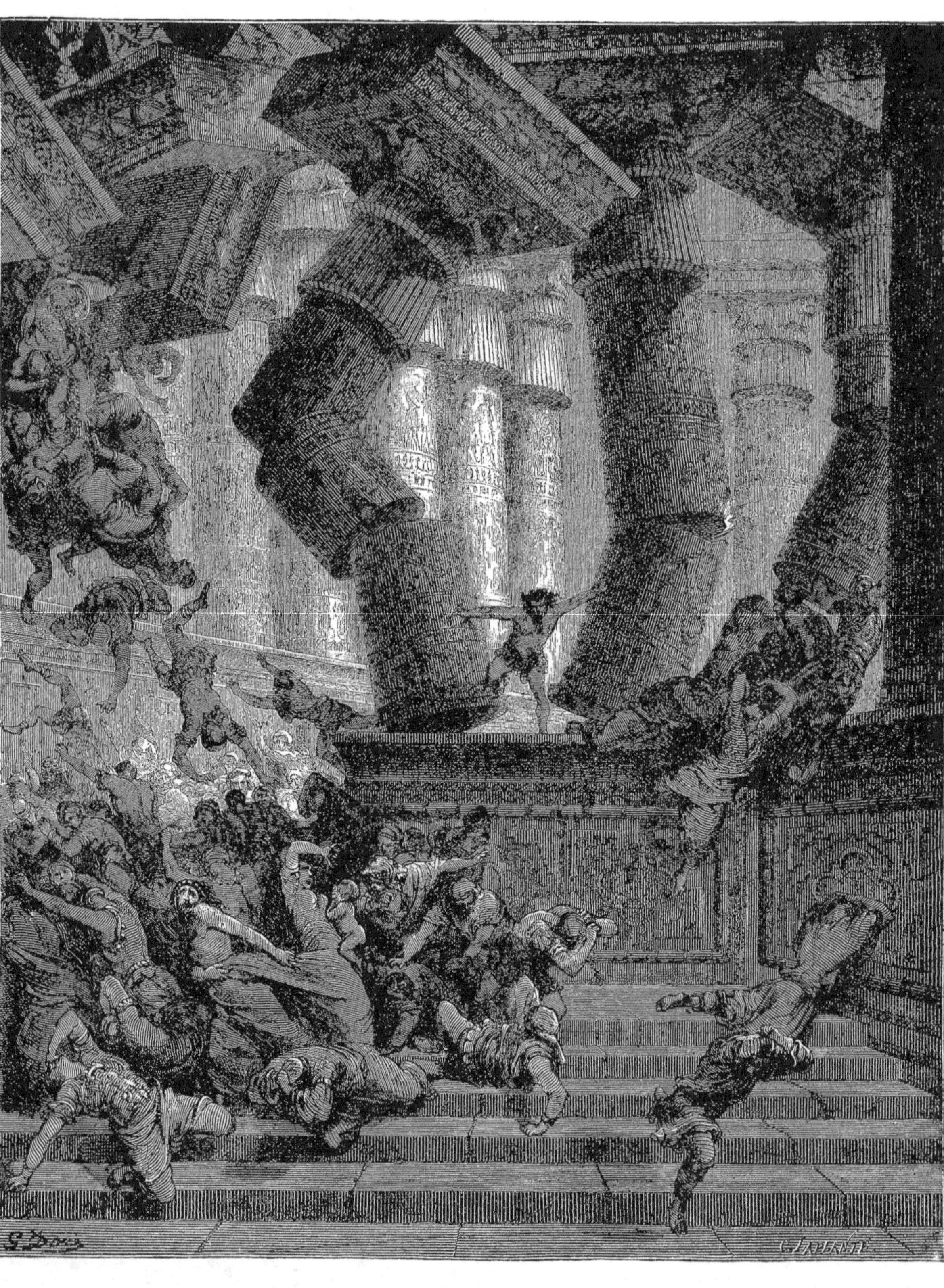

133. Death of Samson, Gustave Doré, 1890

134

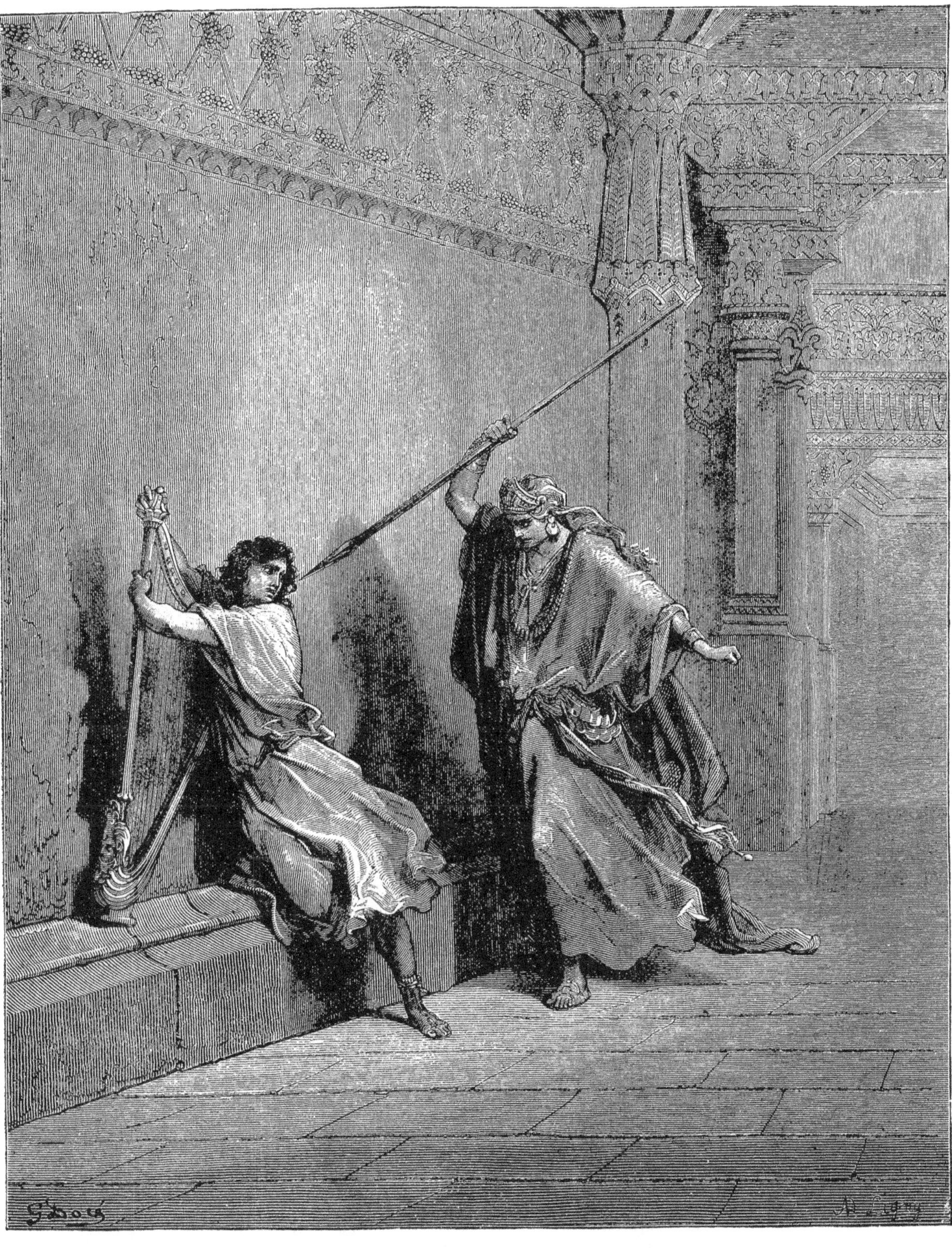

134. Saul and David, Gustave Doré, 1890

135

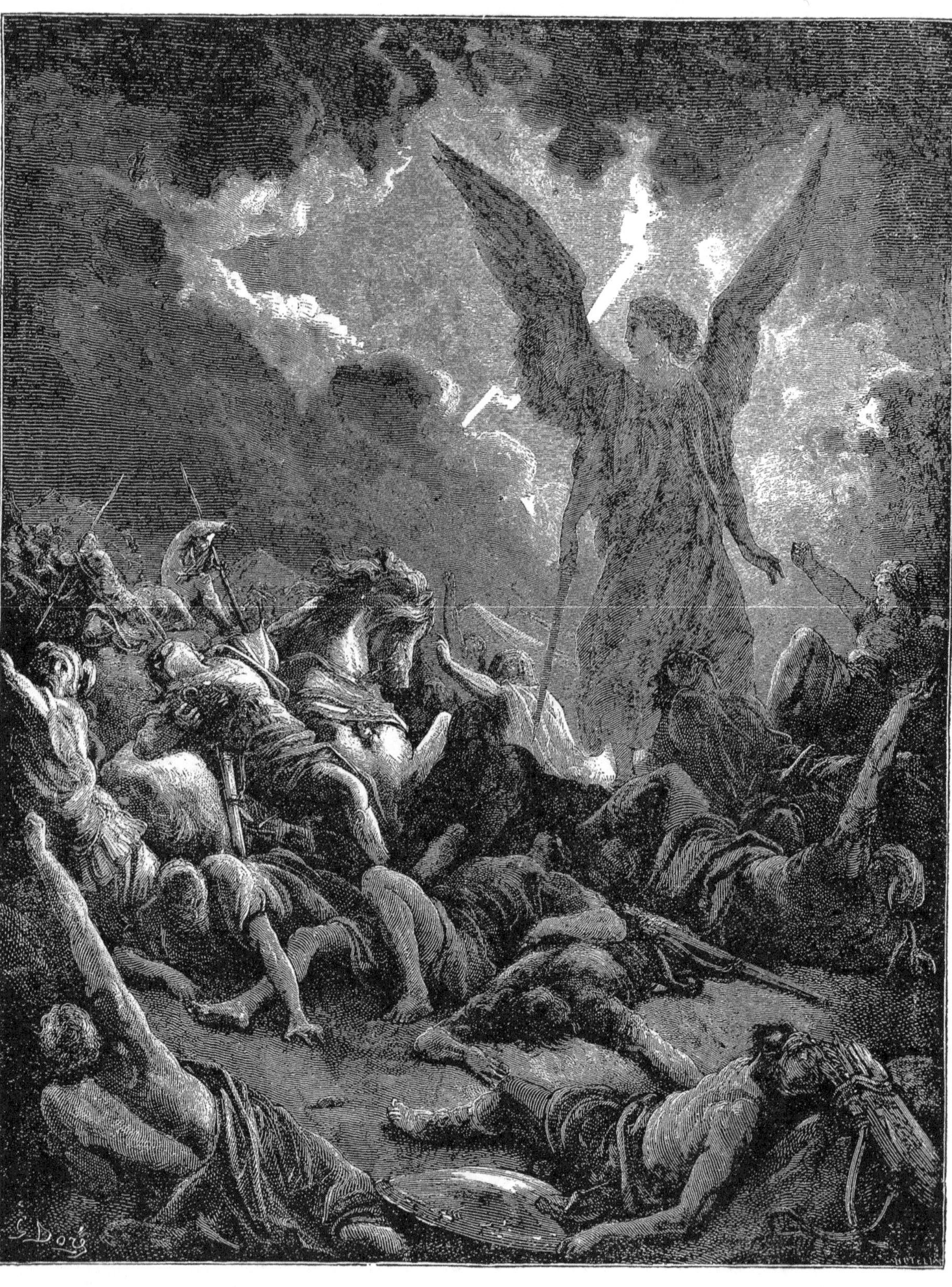

135. *The Destruction of Sennacherib's Host,*
Gustave Doré, 1890

136

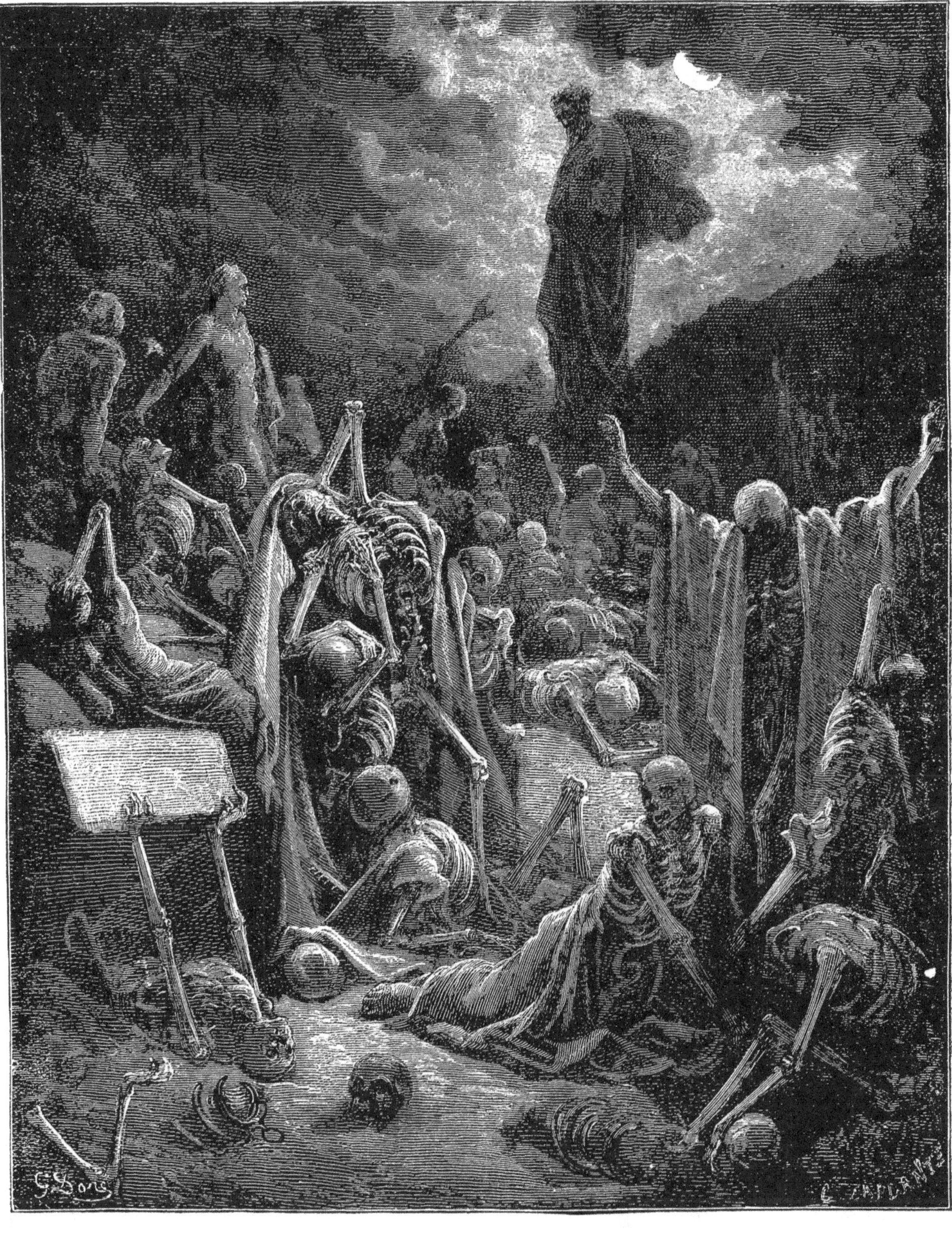

GUSTAVE DORÉ

136. *The Vision of Ezekiel, Gustave Doré, 1890*

137

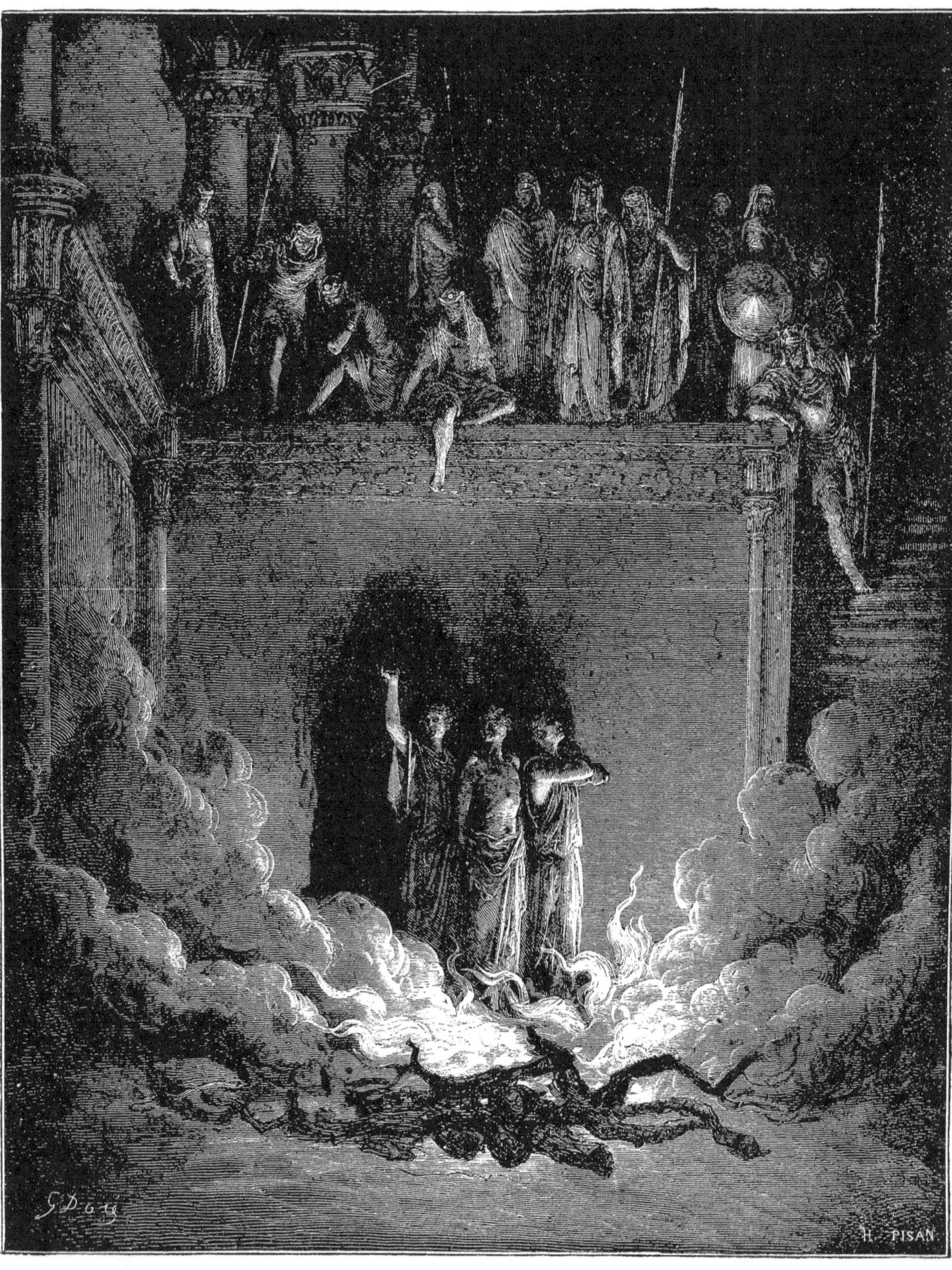

137. The Fiery Furnace, Gustave Doré, 1890

138

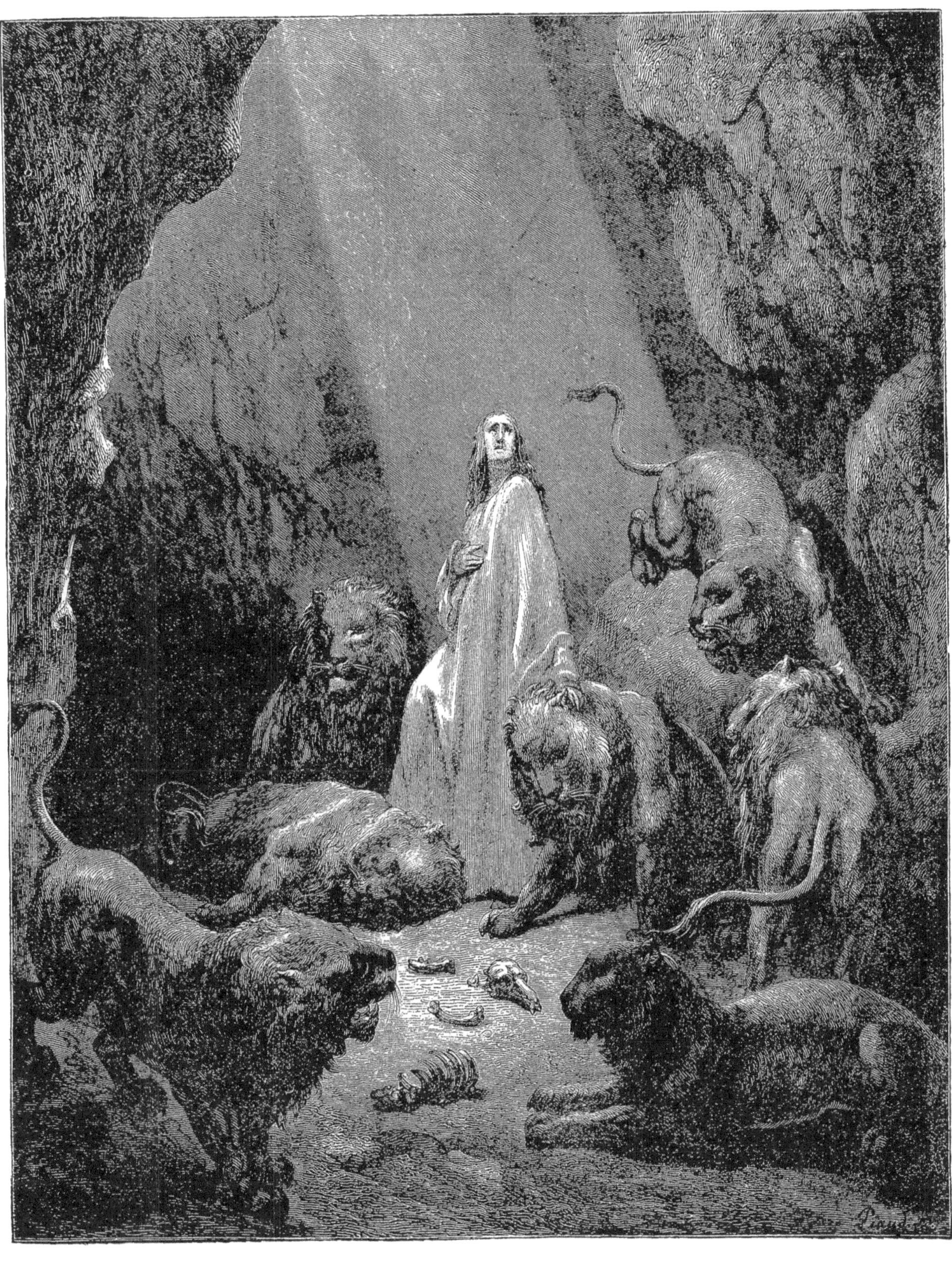

GUSTAVE DORÉ

139

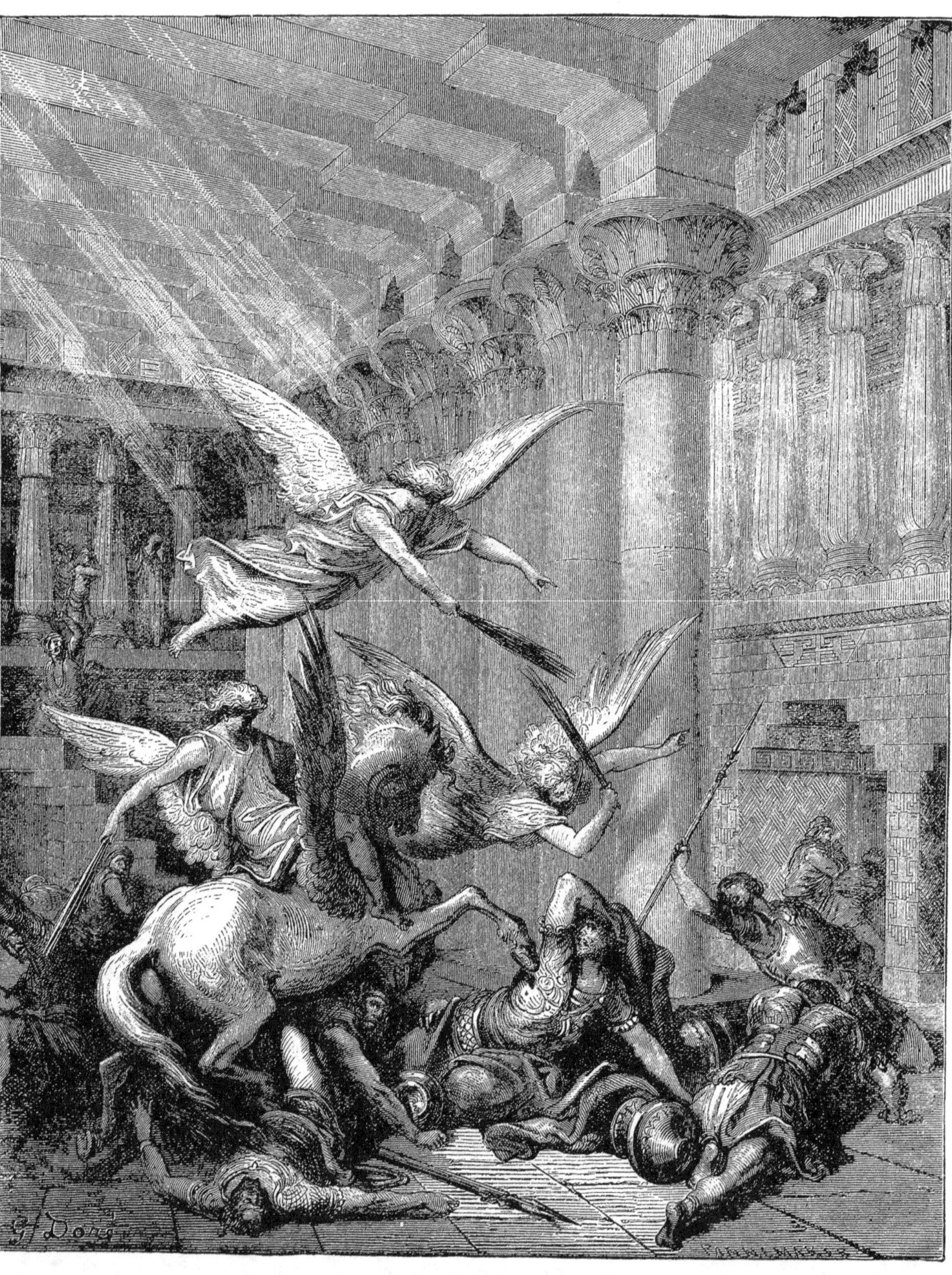

139. *Heliodorus Punished in the Temple.*
Gustave Doré, 1890.

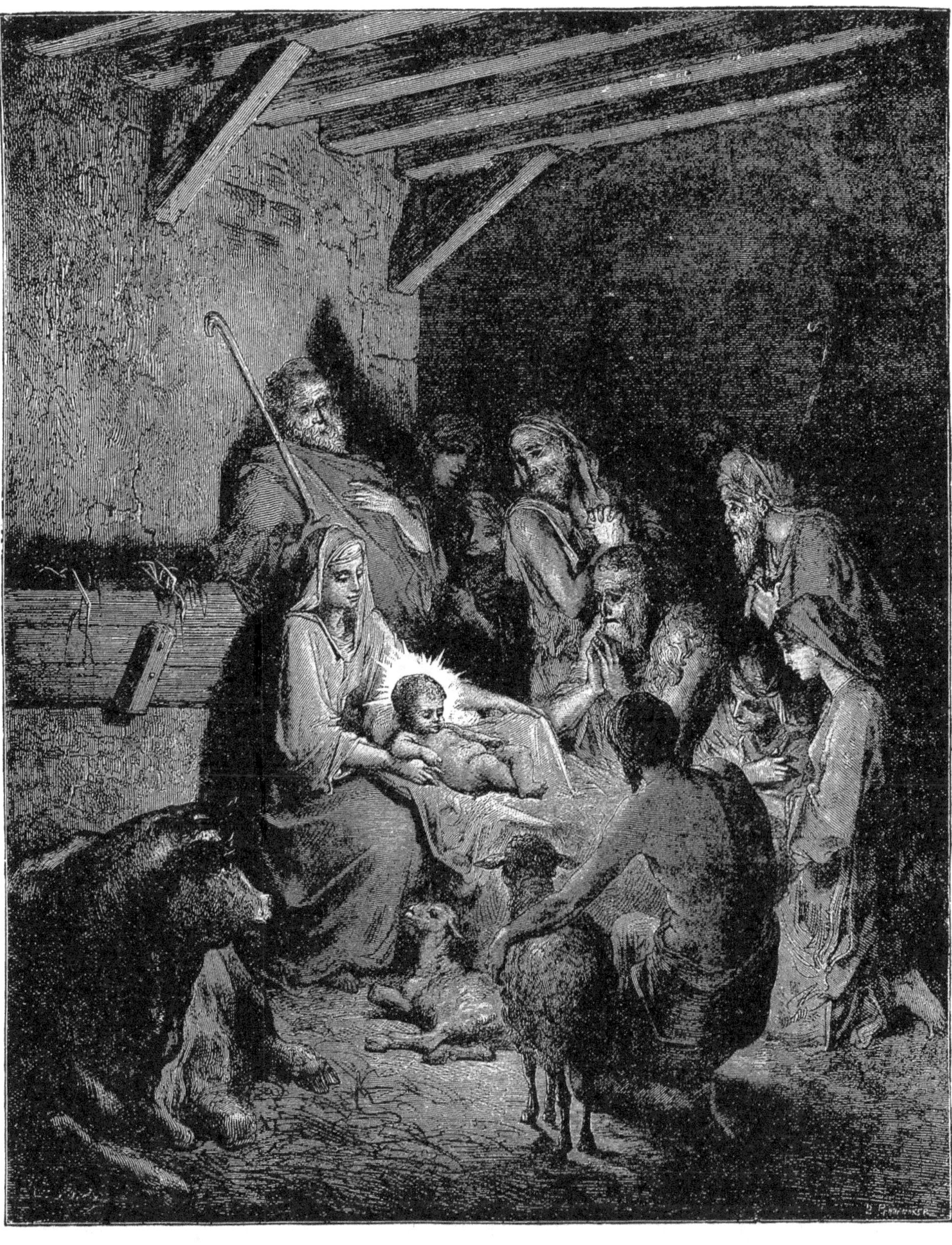

GUSTAVE DORÉ

141

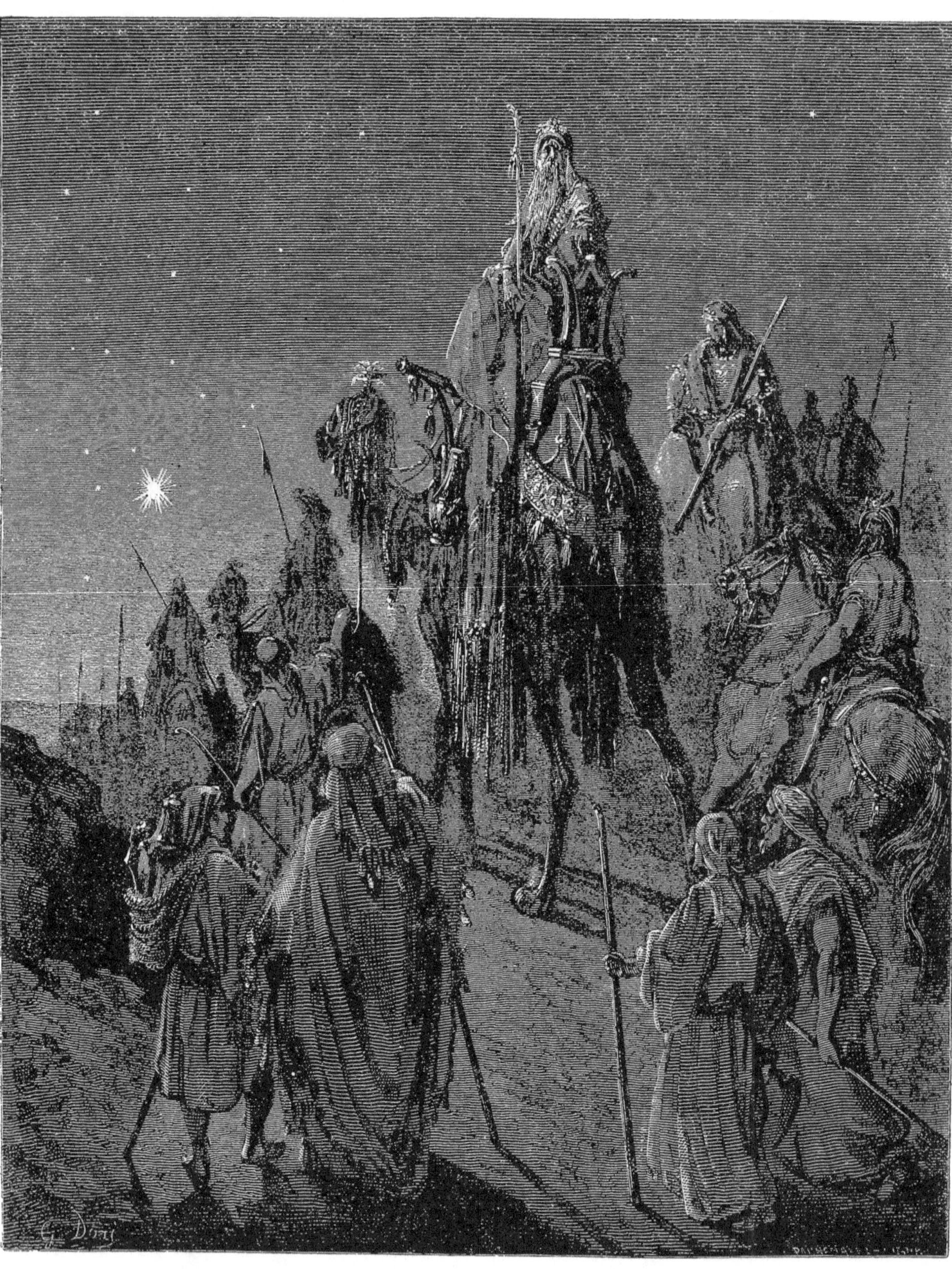

141. The Star in the East, Gustave Doré, 1890

142

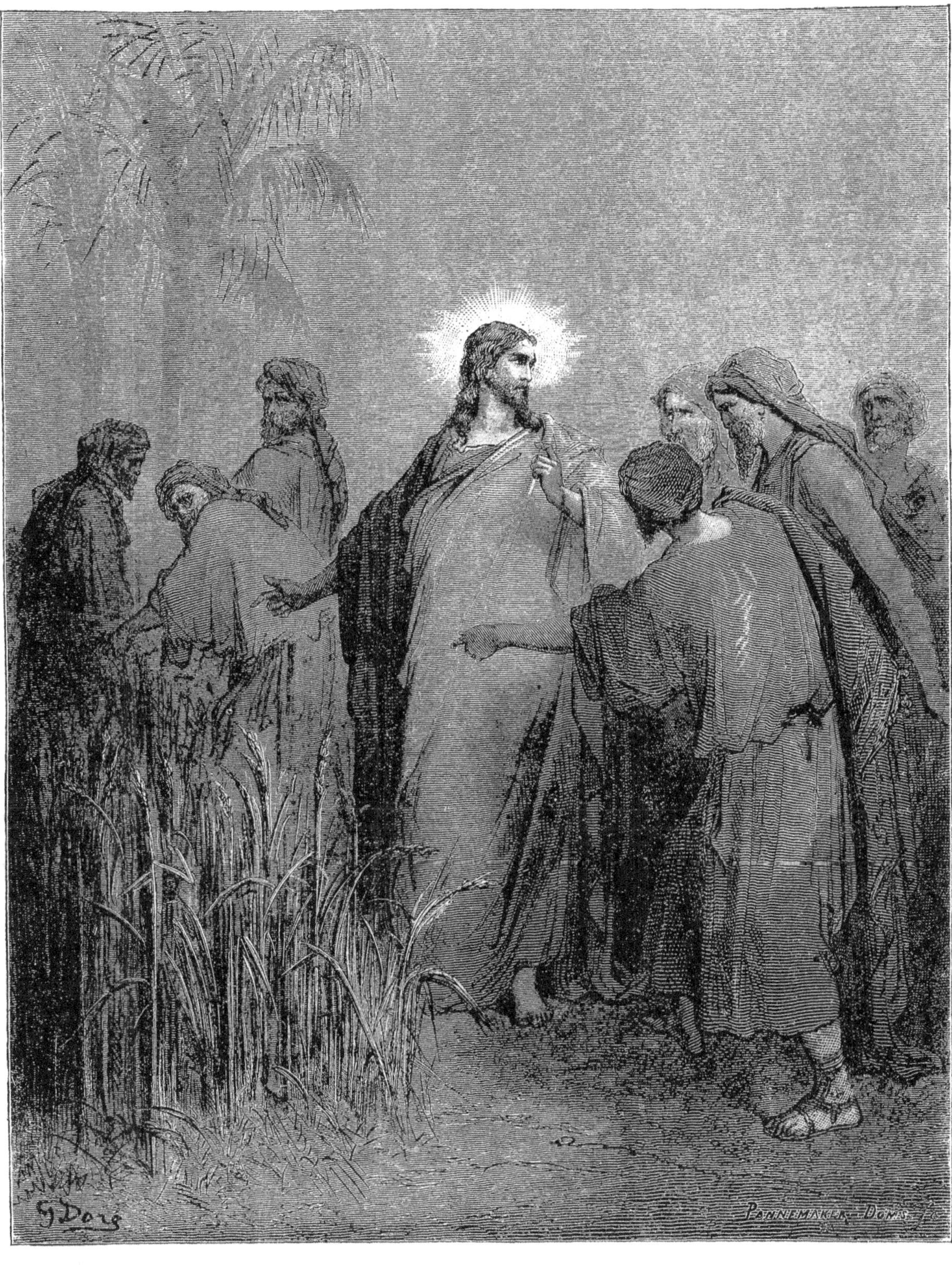

142. *The Disciples Plucking Corn on the Sabbath, Gustave Doré, 1890*

143

GUSTAVE DORÉ

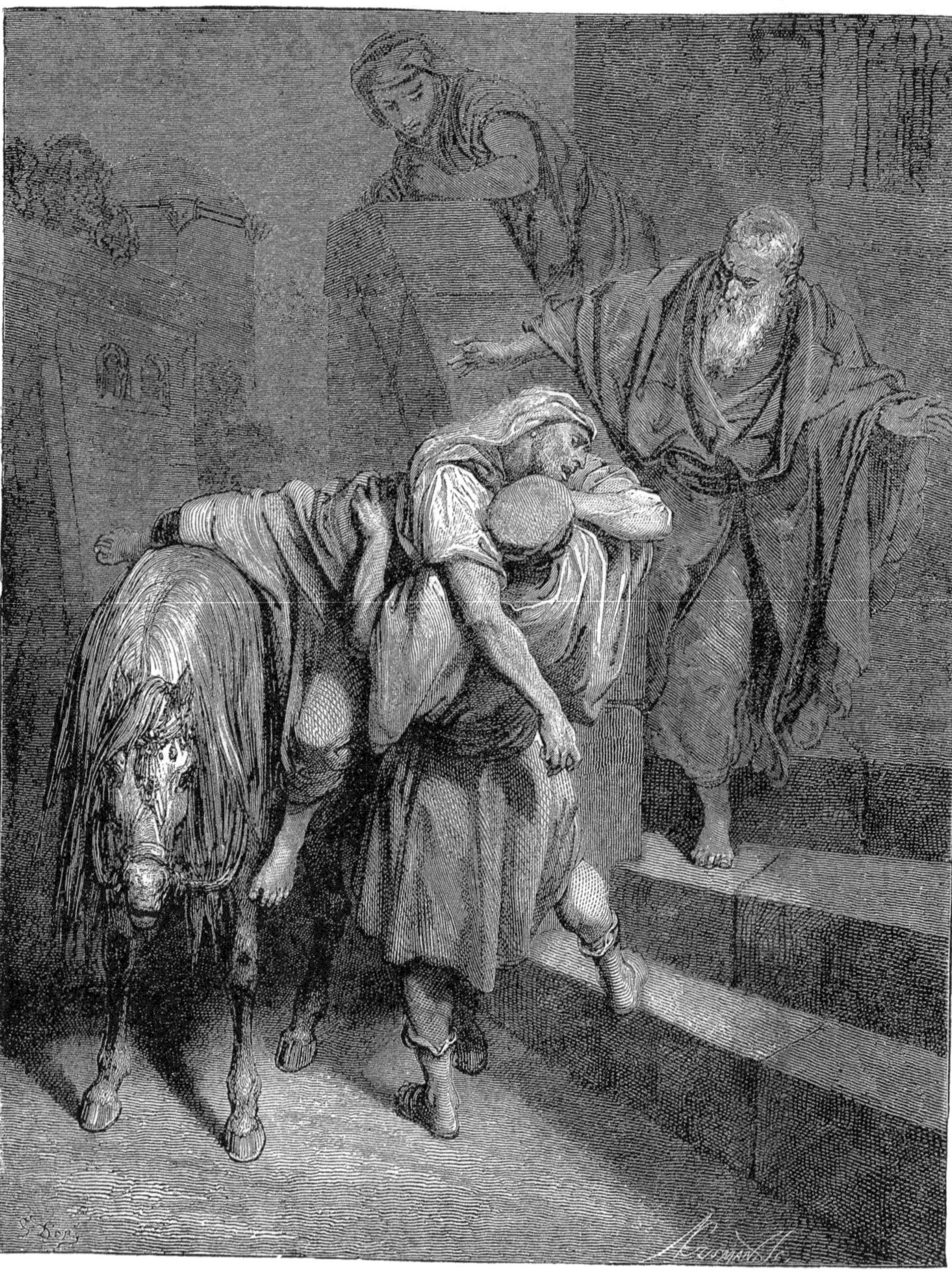

143. *Arrival of the Samaritan at the Inn*, Gustave
Doré, 1890

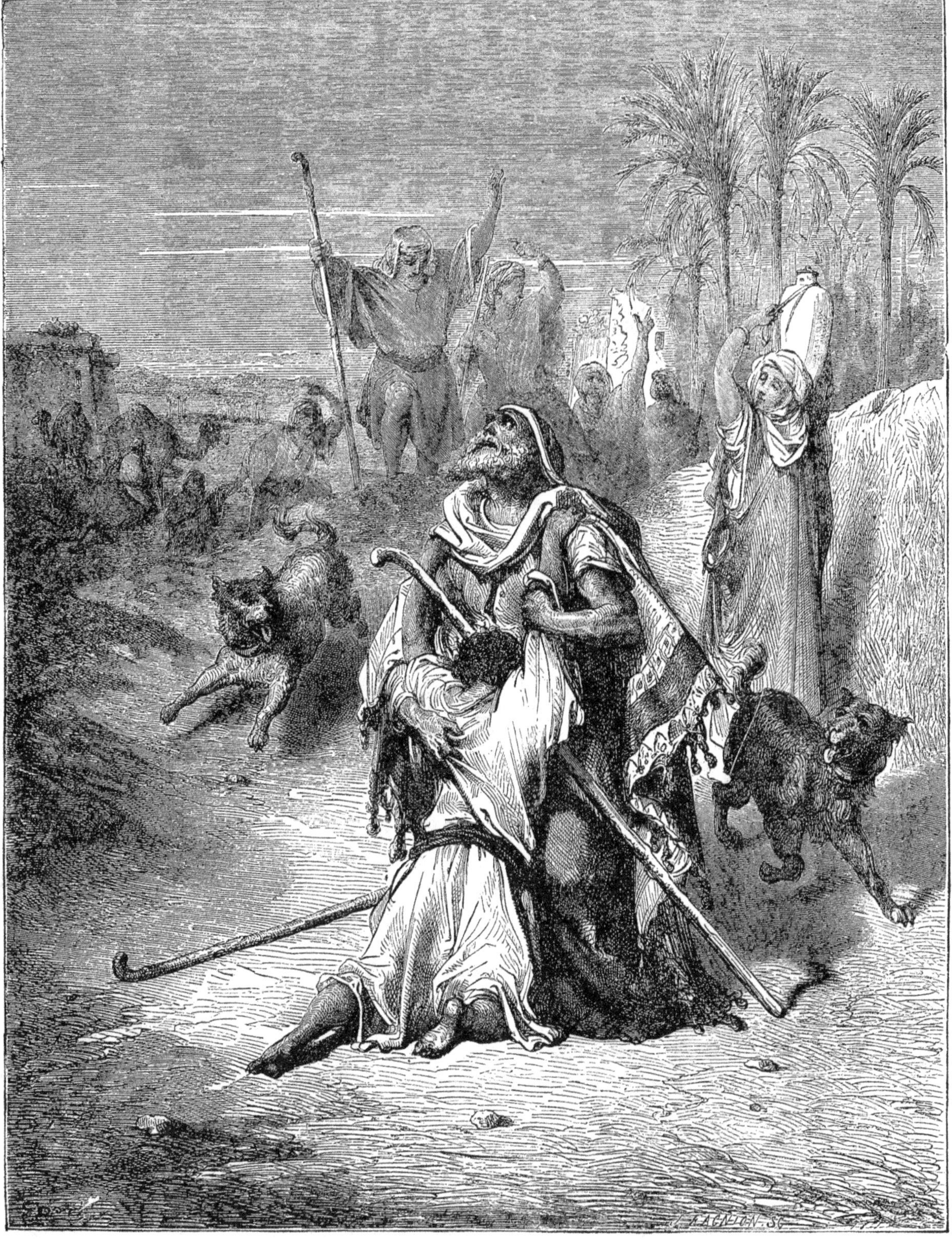

144. The Prodigal Son, Gustave Doré, 1890

145

GUSTAVE DORÉ

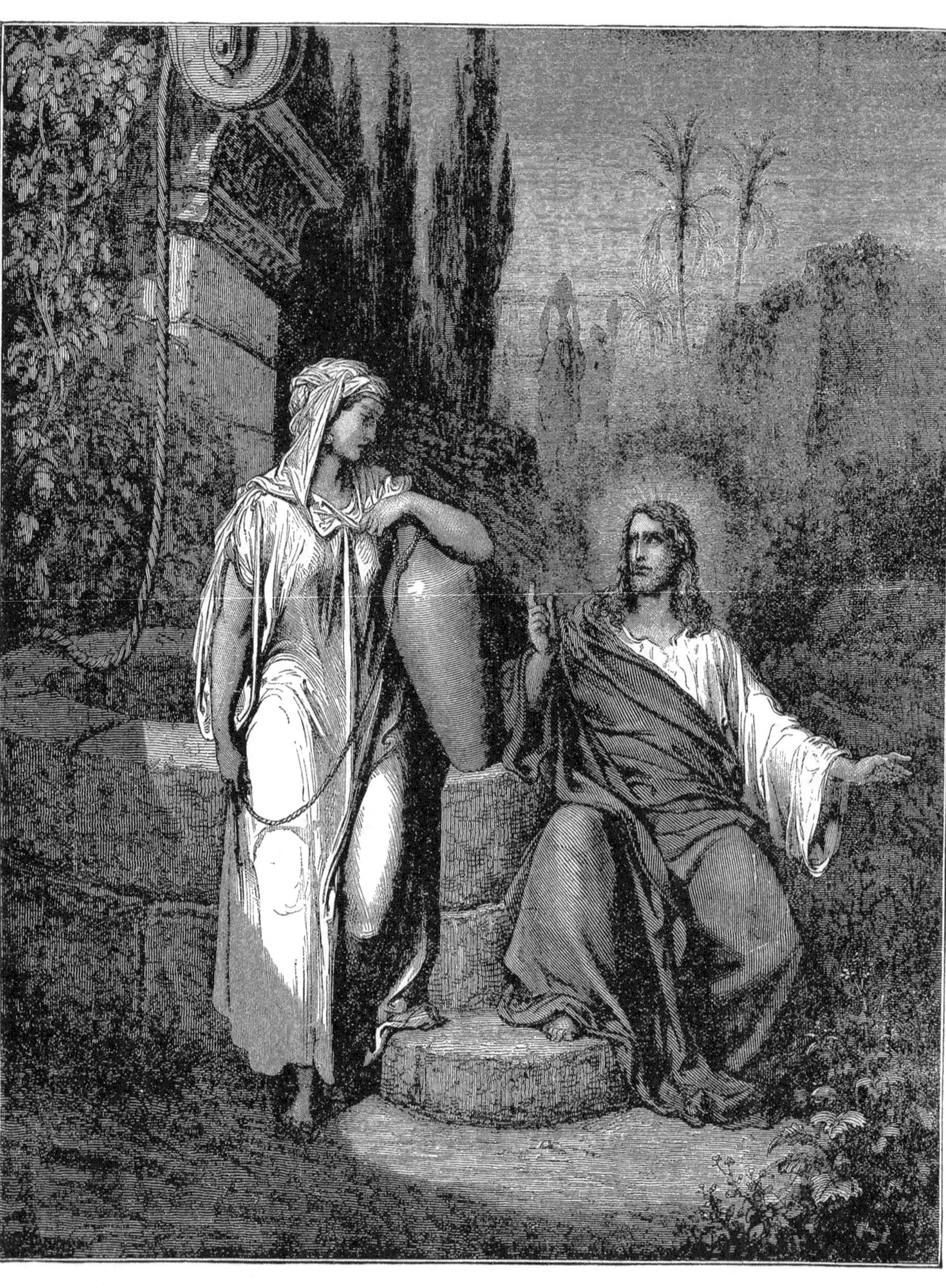

*145. Jesus and the Woman of Samaria, Gustave
Doré, 1890.*

146

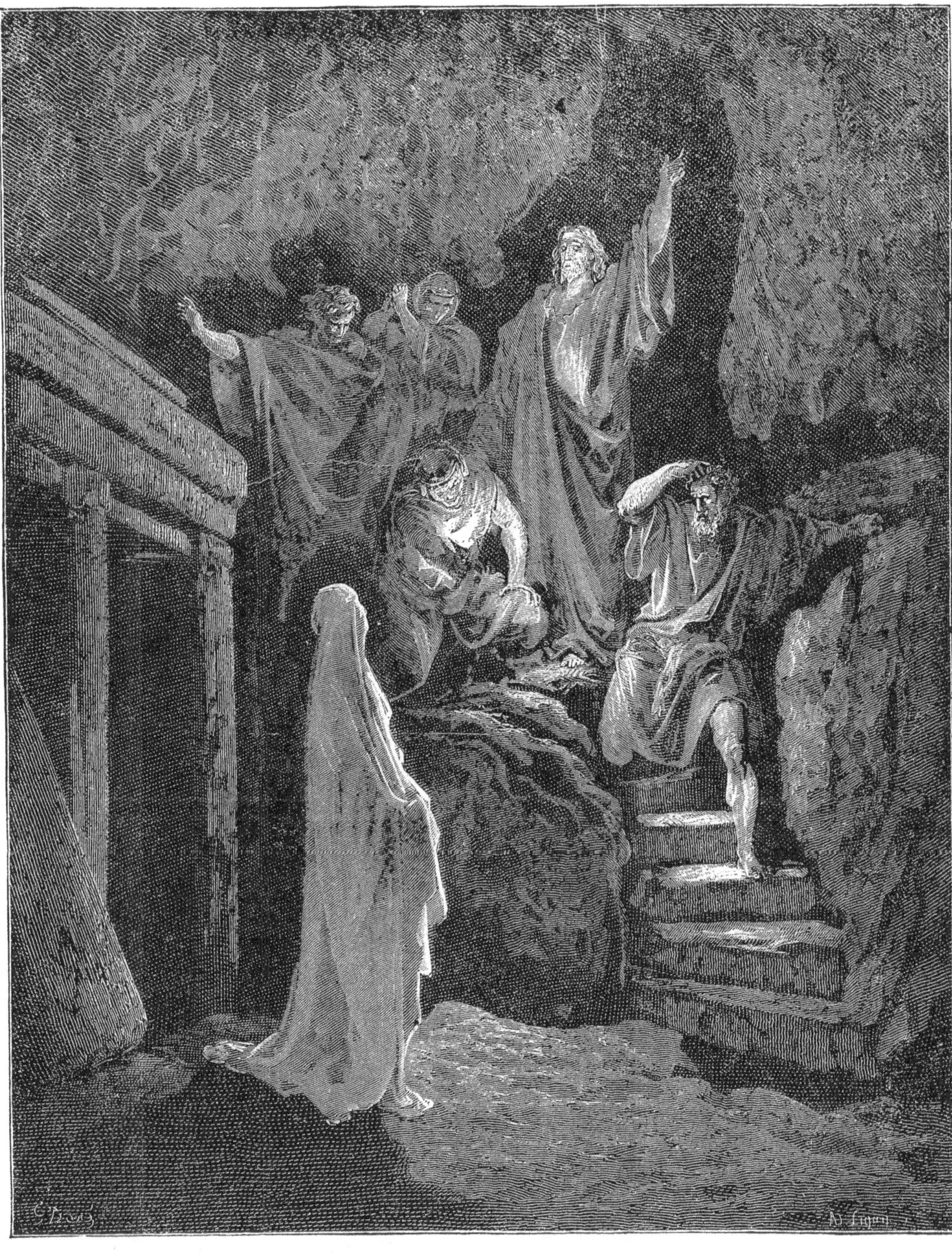

146. The Resurrection of Lazarus. Gustave
Doré, 1890

147

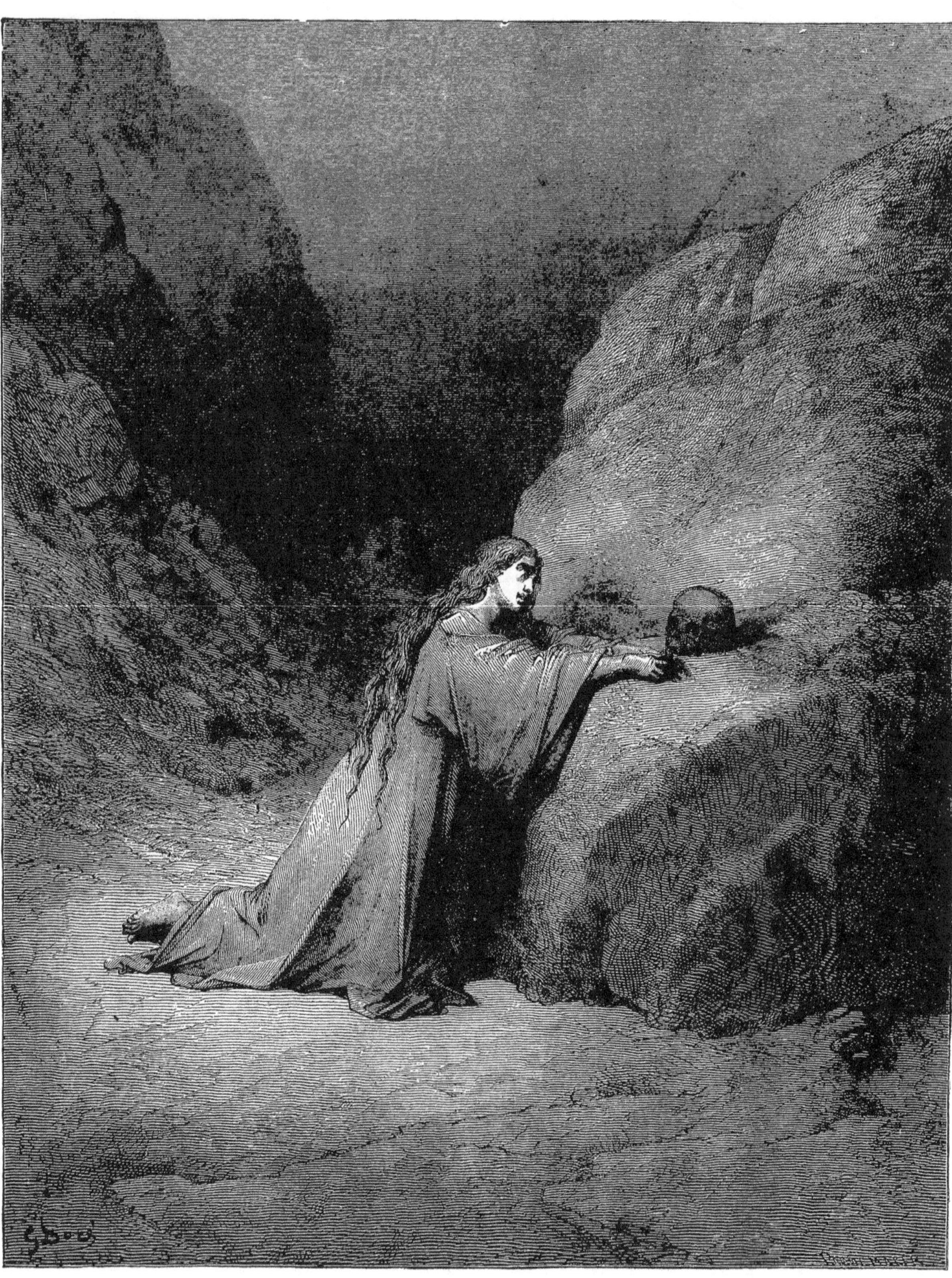

147. Mary Magdalene. Gustave Doré, 1890

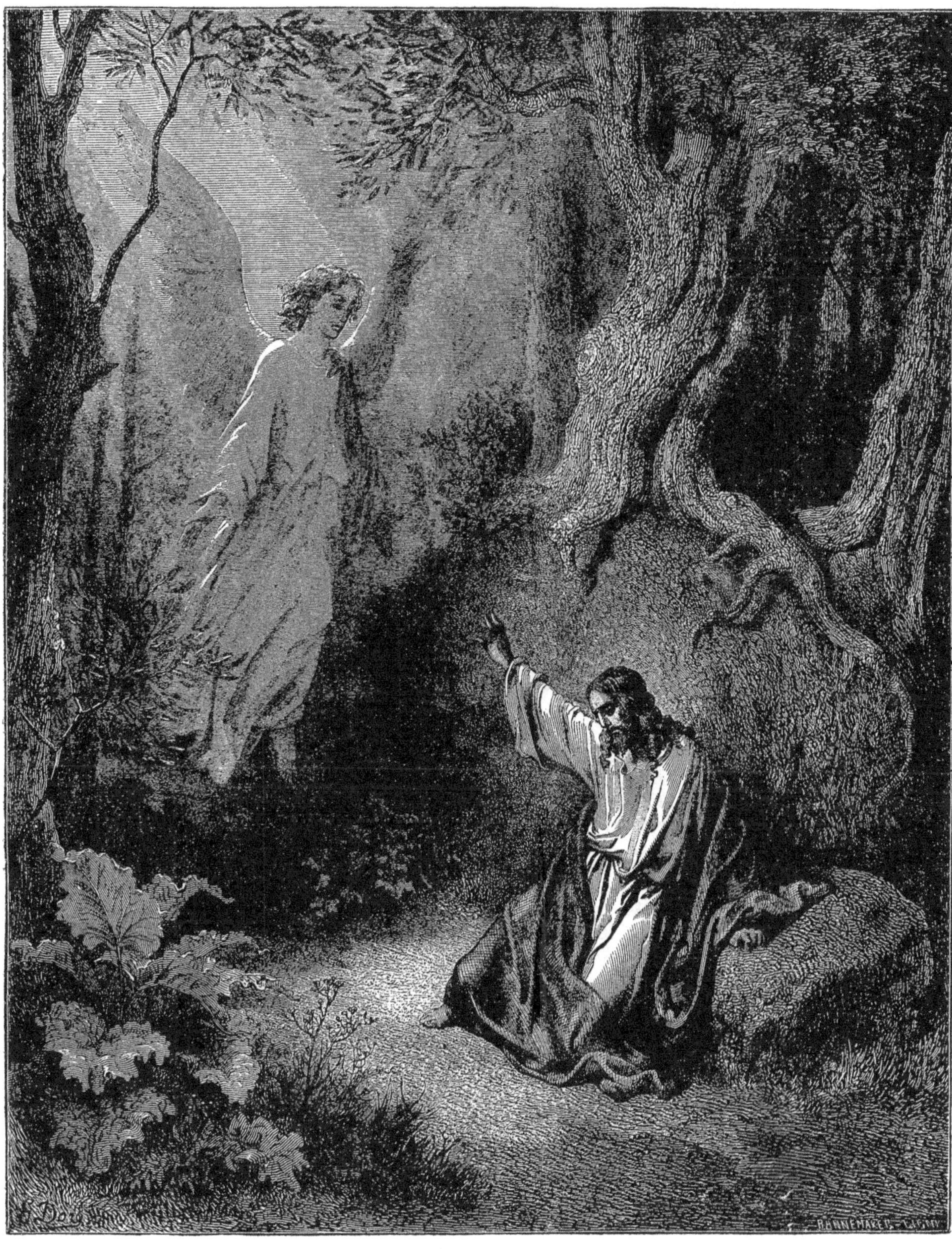

GUSTAVE DORÉ

148. The Agony in the Garden, Gustave Doré.
1890

149

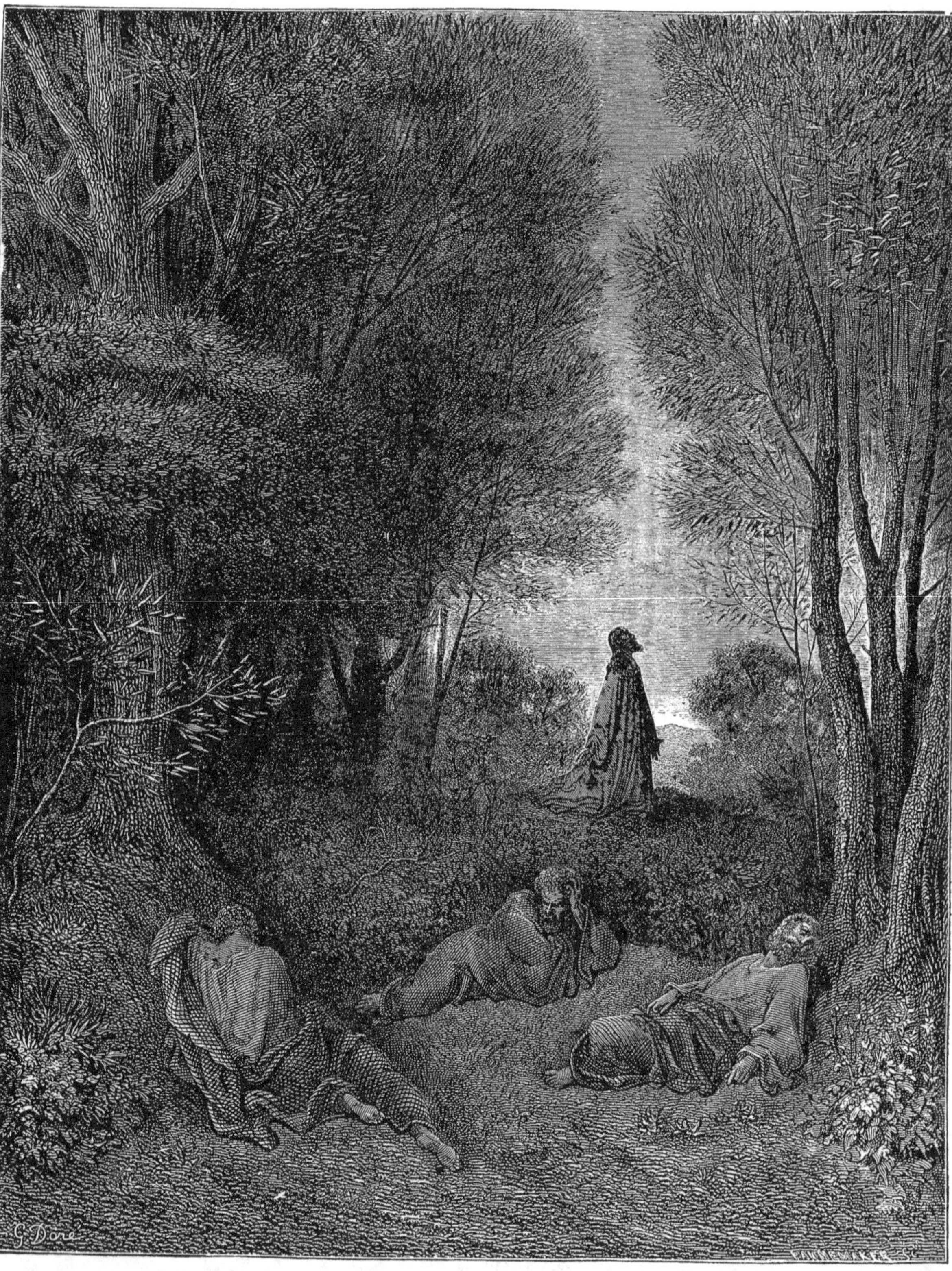

149. *Prayer of Jesus in the Garden of Olives.*
Gustave Doré, 1890

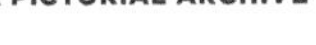

GUSTAVE DORÉ

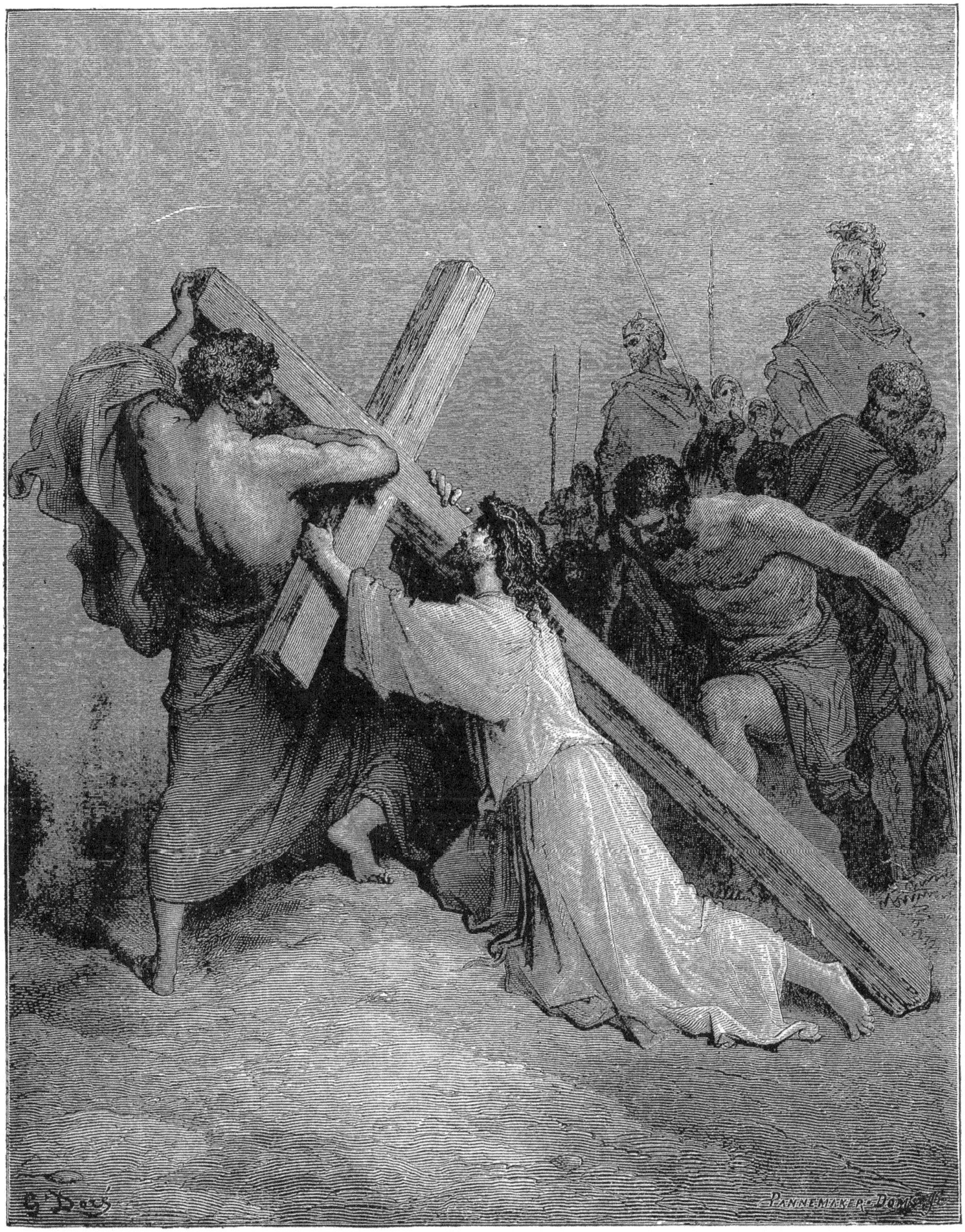

150. Christ Fainting Under the Cross, Gustave
Doré, 1890

151

GUSTAVE DORÉ

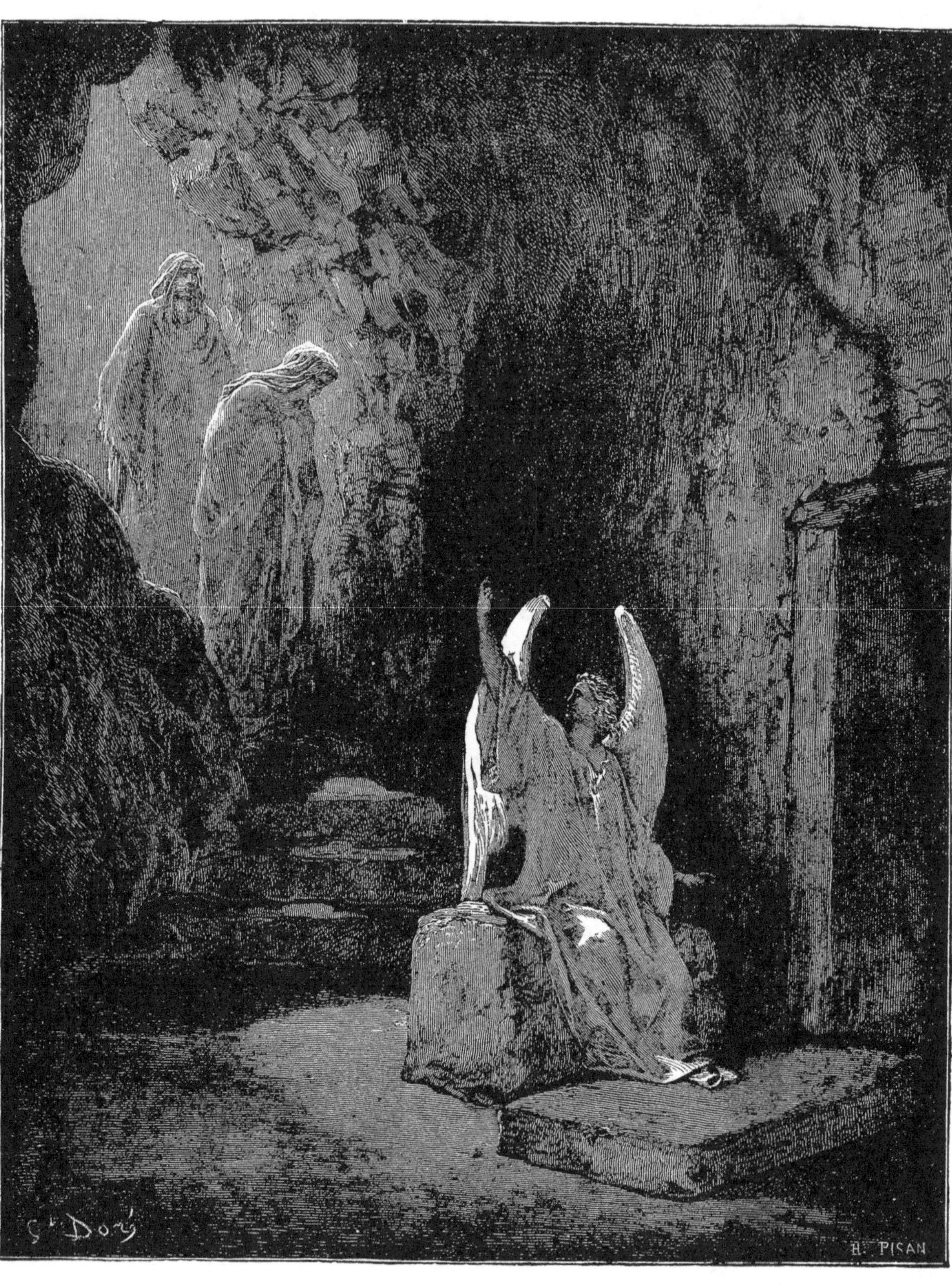

151. The Angel at the Sepulchre, Gustave
Doré, 1890

152

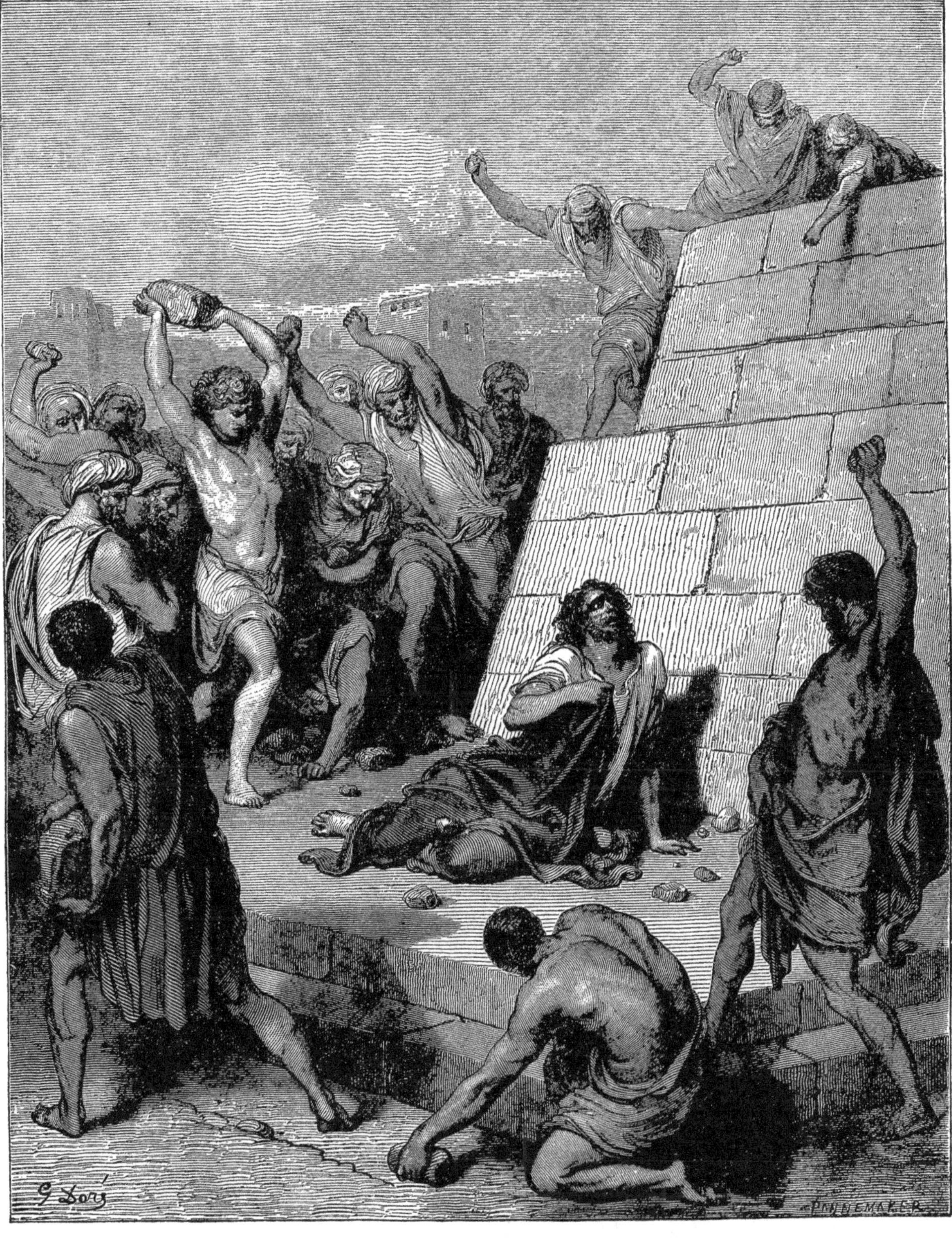

152 Martyrdom of St. Stephen, Gustave Doré,
1890

153

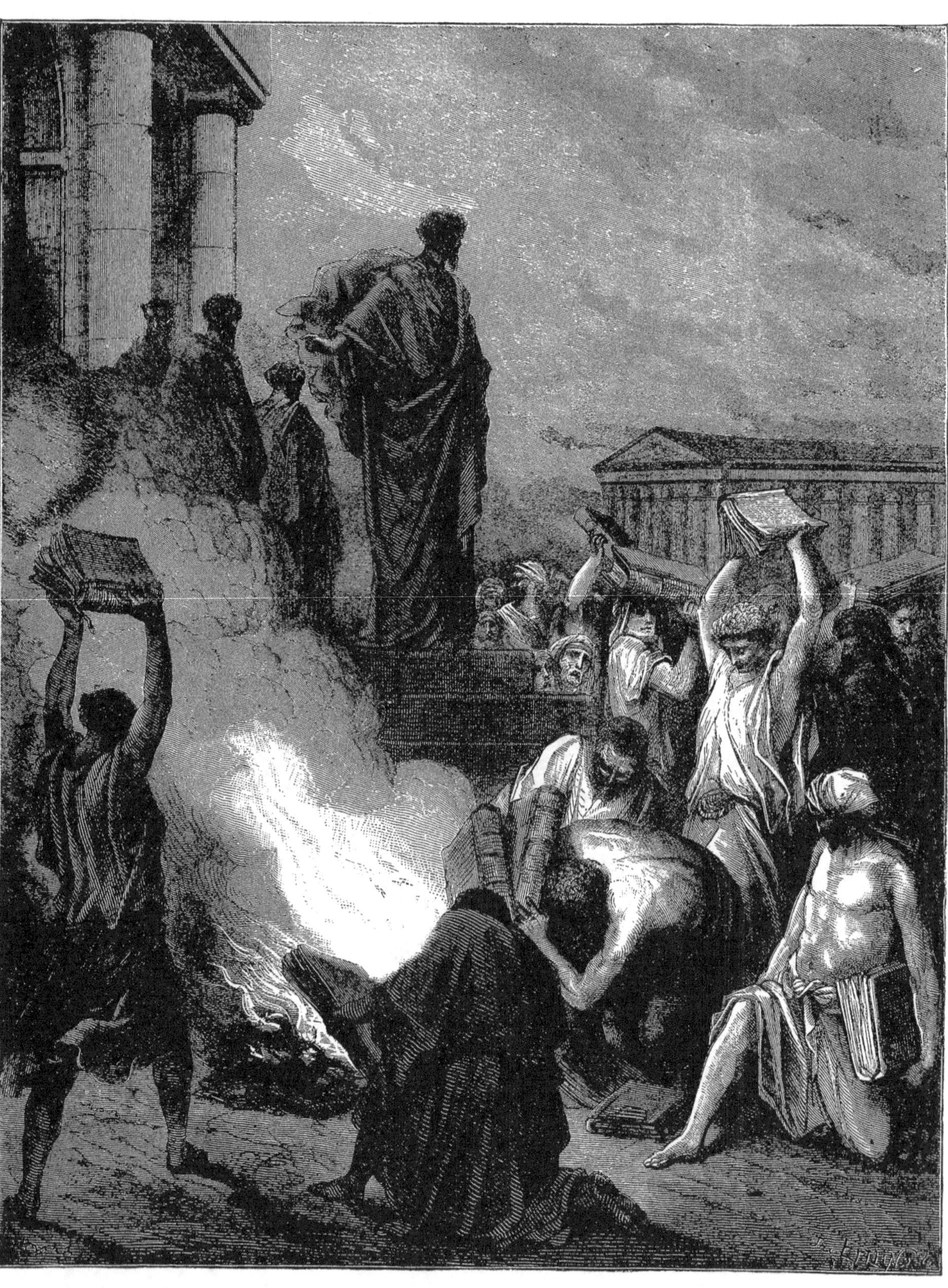

153. Paul at Ephesus. Gustave Doré. 1890

154

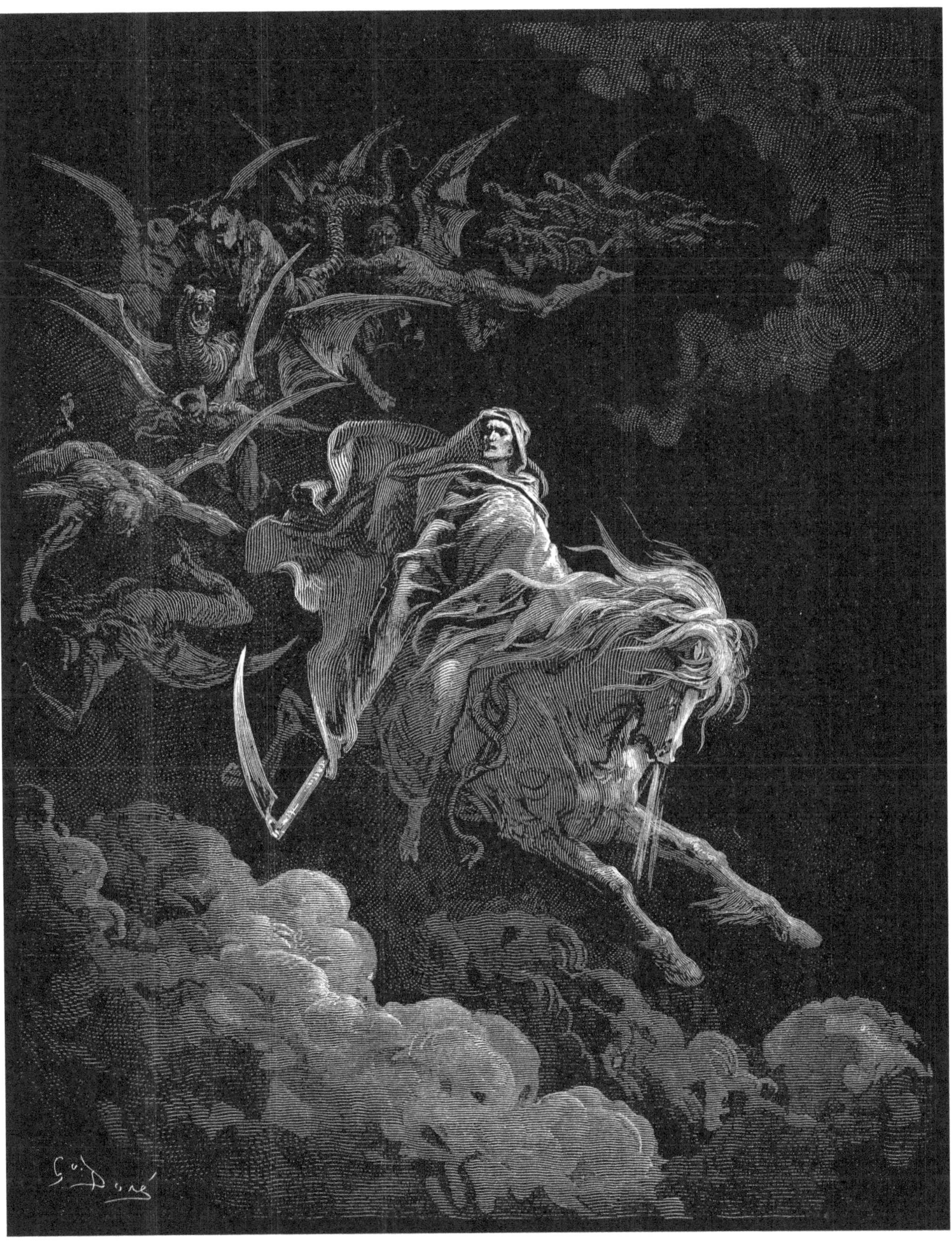

GUSTAVE DORÉ

LIST OF ILLUSTRATIONS

10

11

DOWNLOAD YOUR FILES

START HERE

Enter the following URL
in your web browser:
www.vaulteditions.com/pages/gdc

STEP 2

Enter the following password to
access the download page:

g d c 4 6 2 8 2 9 d i s a

STEP 3

Enter your email address
where requested and submit
your details. A download link
will be sent to your inbox.

TECHNICAL SUPPORT

Please email:
info@vaulteditions.com

DISCLAIMER:

Vault Editions Ltd. believes that
the images in this book are no
longer protected by copyright
and are in the public domain
after taking reasonable steps to
determine their copyright status.
However, please note that Vault
Editions Ltd. cannot guarantee
that your use of the images will not
infringe the rights of third parties.
It is your responsibility to conduct
your own analysis and satisfy any
copyright or other conditions for
your proposed use of the images.